RETURNED WITH A CREED

RETURNED WITH A CREED

RUTH JAMES

Allied Learning

CONTENTS

Photo Insert ix
Introduction xi

1	Cast Off	1
2	The Convoy	15
3	Fovant	25
4	To the Front	43
5	Battle of the Hindenburg Line	59
6	Warlus	79
7	War is Over	93
8	Christmas, 1918	107
9	New Year of Peace	121
10	Australian Corps School	131
11	Champneuf Farm	143
12	From April to Le Havre	159
13	Adieu to France	167
14	Last Weeks at Codford	175
15	H.M.A.T. Main	189

16	On Their Way	199
17	South African Shores	209
18	Into the Blue	225
19	Australia's Sons Come Home	237
20	The Homecoming	251

9/41st Battalion	263
Afterword	264
Illustration Reference Numbers	269
Acknowledgements	279
Glossary	281
References	283
About The Author	298
Photo Insert	299

First printed in 2022 by Allied Learning (alliedlearningonline@gmail.com)
Revised and reprinted in 2024
Cataloguing-in-Publication entry is available from the National Library of Australia. www.catalogue.nla.gov.au
ISBN 978 0 6454539 0 4
Copyright © Ruth James 2022
All rights reserved.

The moral rights of the author have been asserted. No part of this book may be reproduced, stored or transmitted by any person or entity in any form or by any means, electronic or mechanical, including photocopying, recording, scanning or by any information storage and retrieval system, without prior written permission of the copyright holder and publisher.

The author has made every effort to contact copyright holders for the use of material in this book and aboriginal entities in acknowledgement and appreciation of their custodial authority.

Anyone overlooked who requires acknowledgement should contact the author. Aboriginal and Torres Strait Islander people should be aware that this book contains references to names or images of people now deceased.

All paper product in this publication is provided by environmentally responsible certified mills.

The front cover image of Private James Henry Rainey was provided by joint contributors James H. Rainey Jnr, Clifford E. James and Russell V. James.

9th Reinforcements 41st Battalion group image courtesy of The Queenslander Pictorial and the State Library of Queensland.

Images from the dedication page, the beginning of each chapter and each chapter's concluding pages are identified as or by: the Queenslander Pictorial and State Library of Queensland, State Library of Victoria, Imperial War Museum, AWM P00369.012, AWM C03037, AWM P05382.001, AWM P02400.011, AWM J03224, National Australian Archives M1145 3B43, James Family, AWM C00598, Imperial War Memorial, Raymond Pepper, Chermside and District Historical Society, Bryan James, James Family, AWM C01288, State Library of Victoria H85.55/160/65, AWM H01171, AWM D00003, AWM H00043, AWM P01688.015.009, AWM E03392, AWM E03513, AWM E03418, AWM E04942C, AWM RCDIG1004546, AWM Appendix 582 of RCDIG1004547, AWM H12514, AWM E03591, AWM H15944, AWM A00948, AWM E03410, AWM E03630, AWM E03501, AWM E03788, AWM E02768, IWM Q9353, AWM E03412, Info Bretagne, AWM P10550.089, Rainey & Spry Families, AWM E01673, AWM H03965, AWM Art92129, Info Bretagne, AWM, H15943, AWM P04541.001, AWM P10700.001, AWM E05024, AWM E05036, AWM E05036, AWM E05037, AWM E05015, AWM E05028, AWM E05032, AWM E05022, AWM E05033, AWM E05075, AWM E05244, AWM P01861.005, James Family, AWM RELAWM00965, AWM

P00520.005, AWM C04797, AWM 05161, AWM E05159, AWM E03537, AWM A02044, James Family, unidentified donor, AWM C02574, AWM H01729, AWM P05845.046, AWM, AWM P11848.002, Rupert Williamson (Fovant History Interest Group) and Peter Harding, Network Rail, Imperial War Museum, AWM H01851, Hoboken Historical Museum, AWM H01840, AWM H01809, Lisk-Carew Bros., AWM H04170, AWM J02913, AWM P01425.015, AWM H02398, Royal Australian Navy, Cape Town History, unidentified donor, AWM P08129.002, AWM P08129.005, 432 Postcards, AWM P00562.158, Virtual War memorial (Pte A. Harris), AWM H16799, LH004708 Fremantle City Library History Centre and State Library of Western Australia, AWM D00935, AWM H11576, LH002058 Fremantle City Library History Centre, James Family, AWM H03422, AWM 11575, Queensland Places, Chermside Historical Society, Queenslander Pictorial and the State Library of Queensland.

July 1917. James Henry Rainey 3653.
Photograph courtesy of The Queenslander
Pictorial and State Library of Queensland.

This book is dedicated to our grandfather, his enduring will, and the boy within him caught in the crossfire between boyhood and brutal combat; to his little sister, Great Aunty Francie, for entrusting me as the keeper of Jim's treasured artefacts; and to my family who now knows his untold story.

"In whom during the war they had successfully implanted and encouraged a 'fighting morale', must now be instilled with a 'reconstruction morale'. They must be given a vision of the needs of Australia in the future days of peace so that each one would be keen to reinstall himself as a useful member of his nation."

Charles Edwin Woodrow Bean
The Official History of the 41st Battalion

INTRODUCTION

IN EVERY CORNER OF THE GLOBE, World War 1 portraits have hung on innumerable walls in memory of the soldiers they displayed, many having never returned. Grandchildren of veterans would gaze up in wonder at the handsome boyish faces of the youths their grandfathers once were, under the belief that the photograph's smoky background came from the grip of battle raging behind the young soldiers.

Some of those same grandchildren now proudly display that 1914-1918 portrait on their own lounge room walls in a dominating position especially chosen in their grandfather's honour. Similarly, a new generation of grandchildren looks up in question at the men who remain the crux of legends, mythical in the new world they fought to protect and finally rebuilt in the war's crippling aftermath.

These same young, adventurous Australian boys of World War 1 in their respective portraits have all received the bugler's haunting Last Post. They are remembered tenderly by those they once hugged or shook hands with, sharing the joy of weddings, Christmases, birthdays, and for the memorable visits to Grandma and Grandad's where 'the photo' drew the kids like a beacon.

But a silence shrouded these veteran grandfathers; a creed. Fated never to speak of their experiences from the war, the men would only share their innermost thoughts with those who were there, those who had endured the slaughter and barbarous days and nights in distant, putrid trenches.

No, no one needed to know the truth.

Instead, comments such as *The war was over by the time we arrived*, and more conveniently, as the veterans grew older, *Oh, that was a long time ago, and I don't remember much about it these days*, provided the perfect deflection to change the subject.

Many veterans re-enlisted in World War 2, haunted by images they could not unsee as Australia's sons and daughters stepped up to face it all again. The veterans, now 20 years older, were prepared to return overseas if necessary, but most would remain stationed on Australian bases where their logistical experience was crucial. No one could better comprehend what the threatening Japanese invasion meant for the soldiers fighting in the New Guinea Campaign to protect our shores, let alone the war consuming Europe.

When one veteran was asked by his granddaughter why he re-enlisted, his reply was succinct:

Well, someone had to help the poor bastards.

In the wake of the Allied-won Second World War, sights were yet again focused on rebuilding the ruins of a broken world, delivering the vibrant 60s and 70s to the veterans' eager grandchildren. Anzac Day Parades stopped the nation in admiration and gratitude for the ageing soldiers now joined by those of World War 2, and eventually the Vietnam veterans, the conscripted progeny, who also never returned the same. No one ever returned the same.

By now, the veterans could see the vision of their new world rising from the ashes of World War 1's global smoking wreckage. Through the years, they had held their pain close while time allowed them the flexibility of healing as they could. This same luxury enabled them to reflect on their legacy as the old troops became increasingly fewer and more frail. What was once a parade of tens of thousands of hearty young men had diminished to units of less than 50 fragile veterans, the remnants of their once glorious battalions represented by noticeably fewer with each passing year.

Now, as if in vigil, those grandchildren who once held their veteran grandfathers' hands, the aged hands belonging to those fresh-faced young soldiers in photos on countless walls, will be the last generation who will have known the warmth of their grandfathers' touch or the sound of their quiet laughter. They will be the last to have heard their voices telling their witty stories or their sharp reprimand when an errant grandchild fell into their freshly planted garden.

These grandfathers' hands were the same hands that had zeroed their Lee Enfield Rifles with their lethal bayonets to the tune of heavy artillery, had held these grandchildren as babies for the first time; their *own* children for the first time. They were the same hands that built their daughters' houses when they married, mended council roads, turned on the television to watch Man walk on the moon, 'threw a line in' at their favourite fishing hole, and raised a beer to mates lost on those bloodied battlefields half a world away each Anzac Day since.

This was the new world they had built with the 260,000 others who returned from those blood-soaked battlegrounds, a legacy less than half lived long enough to witness as new generations followed, all borne under a doctrine.

Now, when the last of these same grandchildren are gone, that final connection to the veteran grandfathers will be severed. No longer will there be anyone who would have heard that voice, been cradled in that warm hug or, more fairly, none old enough to remember.

Let their stories neither go untold nor their legacies forgotten, for both are what brought us here in the promise of our freedom and the future of coming generations.

They returned with a creed, a creed of unyielding silence, that their enduring legacy now demands is broken.

CHAPTER 1

Cast Off

If there was anywhere that may be suitable for their last memory of him, then this was as good a place as any beneath the smoky arches of the station.

Troopship R.M.S. Ormonde in dazzle camouflage. Photograph courtesy of the State Library of Victoria.

JAMES HENRY RAINEY, 18 YEARS old and keyed for patriotic duty, stood in awe at the sheer size of the imposing steamer in front of him. Nothing could have prepared him for the staggering sight she presented as the 9th Reinforcements of the 41st Battalion, Australian Imperial Force (A.I.F.), entered the wrought iron gates to see her docked before them in all her splendour, guns and all. None had seen anything like it until that day, 2 March 1918.

Some may not have noticed the wreaths laid at the entrance by grieving mothers who had come to visit this one last place they ever saw their soldier sons. Now, these gates to this dock were their last tangible connection to their boys' smiling faces, the last place on earth.

Standing vigil, the newly built steamer was immense, with her upper decks and clean lines strung with taut rigging from her two masts, one on each side of her twin pluming smokestacks. Her lifeboats hung in secure parallel rows along the upper deck's full length, and an empty designated storage zone awaited the gangway's return in the shadow of the forward funnel. She was clean, immaculate and painted in dramatic black and white camouflage of curves, triangles and quadrangles; the *R.M.S. Ormonde* was as breathtaking as she was magnificent.

Days before their arrival, the 41st and 42nd Battalions, numbering 1,000 strong, had left Rifle Range Training Camp at Bells Paddock, Enoggera, Queensland, for the last time. Their designated route followed Kelvin Grove Road, Countess, Roma, George and Ann Streets before the troops' spectacular arrival at Brisbane's Central Railway Station for 'entraining' on the two-day journey to Sydney, Australia.

Winding for hundreds of yards, the column was led by the 41st Battalion Band, followed immediately by the 41st and 42nd Infantries, their respective Motor Machine Gun Units, the 18-pounder guns of the field artillery, Service Corps, Army Medical Corps and, finally, the Red Cross wagon.

Shrouding them was a palpable atmosphere, not only electrifying but completely intoxicating as the 9th Reinforcements marched with bursting pride, knowing each step was yet another closer in their journey to fight for their country.

Thousands of cheers rose from the crowds hailing them along the route - family, friends and onlookers alike. It was not until they arrived at Central Station that Jim had seen his parents, brother and four sisters waiting in their anxious devotion to farewell their departing boy soldier. If there was anywhere that might be suitable for their last memory of him, then this was as good a place as any beneath the smoky arches of the station. Alternatively, this was precisely where he would stand on his return, should he be so blessed.

Now, onboard this magnificent troopship, Jim and his four mates, Harry Larsen, Bill Mitchell, Ted Marsh and Ernie Murr, had found their billets; newly painted four-berth cabins, each complete with hammocks, electric lights, fan and brand new cabinetry. She was positively splendid, and the five men could not believe they were sailing on her. As bonded friends, the five had known each other since boyhood and together shared a mateship that would see them through whatever lay ahead.

Along the upper timber deck, a group of 25 officers were poised in readiness for a photographer. One of the men Jim easily recognised as Lieut. Michael Joseph Flannery, the Attesting Officer, who had administered his sworn oath on enlistment. Momentarily distracted, Flannery had looked away briefly just as the official photographer's Box Brownie camera shutter captured the moment. For three of the men in the group, it would be one of the last photos ever taken of them in their homeland. They would not return.

A sudden reverberating blast of the *Ormonde*'s foghorn fuelled the cheering crowds below, energising the euphoria presently bathing the troops she carried. Poised dockside, the Embarkation Staff at the Wooloomooloo Wharf, Sydney, cast off the thick ropes holding the dazzle-camouflaged troopship as her exhilarated khaki cargo threw streamers and called out farewells from every available vantage point, rigging included.

Beneath them, the water churned in murky turbulence under the veil of falling streamers as the ship pulled slowly away from the wharf, aided by a lone tug out to starboard. The troops' destination would be withheld for some weeks, alleviating the risk of a letter or telegram slipping through the stringent censorship process and inadvertently alerting the enemy. Rumour had it they were bound for India, whereas Jim merely hoped they would get there in one piece amid the U-boat-infested waters. It was made abundantly clear that they were not to speak of their location in any correspondence wherever they found themselves.

The *Ormonde* was a part of Convoy 37, sailing with troopships *H.M.A.T. Wiltshire* and *H.M.A.T. Nestor*, although not in formation. The *Wiltshire* had sailed from Sydney six weeks earlier, followed by the *Nestor* over three weeks later, the three vessels sailing separately under strict naval regulations. No longer did troops sail from Australia in convoys spanning 15 miles long and 12 miles wide, as was the case of the original Australia and New Zealand Army Corps (A.N.Z.A.C.) fleet of October 1914 with its 30,000 men and 8,000 horses.

Today, the *Ormonde*'s course was set for Melbourne, the departure port for the Victorians and Tasmanians who had recently landed from Hobart. In five days, they would be hailed by throngs of lauding crowds from the great southern city eager to spur on Australia's sons, husbands, brothers and fathers leaving their homeland for cratered battlefields.

Many onboard endured unrelenting seasickness as the *Ormonde* fought her way arduously through the mile-wide swells between Port Melbourne and Fremantle. Her headlong thrust into the powerful winds of the Great Australian Bight's 'Roaring Forties' rendered almost all onboard insensible.

On calmer days, the miserable men had lain pitifully strewn across the deck with barely enough room for anyone to step between them in their haste for the nearest rail. Australians being Australians, of course, meant the more hardy took bets on the length of time between the pathetic pukes of those afflicted, with trifectas bringing the loudest howls of triumph.

While the coalers remained onboard to fill the *Ormonde*'s bunkers, the men were granted a few brief hours of Shore Leave to explore Fremantle and send any final farewell telegrams or letters home. The town's warm hospitality provided home-cooked treats to be enjoyed, and plentiful stationery was available from the Y.M.C.A. Tent, generosities welcomed by the departing soldiers.

A troopship lay at anchor approximately 150 yards out to starboard from the *Ormonde*. She was the *S.S. Tofua*. Fitted out in traditional navy blue and white fashion with her single funnel wafting dark grey smoke, the *Tofua's* New Zealand flag fluttered sporadically in the afternoon breeze of the 'Fremantle Doctor', the light onshore wind that typically blew in around mid-afternoon. Tomorrow, she would sail out independently through Gage Roads, the outer reaches of Fremantle Harbour, ahead of the *Ormonde*, the New Zealanders equally as ready for what lay ahead as the Australians with the A.N.Z.A.C. spirit burning indelibly within them.

In the early dawn of the following morning, approximately 2,000 troops lined the *Ormonde's* rails to watch the orange sunrise bursting over Australian soil for the last time. For many, it would be almost another two years before they would enjoy this splendour again. Others would take this final vision of 'home' to their graves.

Beyond this western edge of Australia, a brutal unwritten chapter awaited as the *Ormonde* drew further from the timbers of Fremantle's Victoria Quay to the crowd's buzzing cheers and farewells. The myriad of streamers flung from the exhilarated soldiers took up their slack until the prevailing tension set them free, hanging on the updraft until finally spiralling down towards the *Ormonde*'s stippled reflection in the water below. The circling gulls overhead sought refuge on pylons and channel markers, their objecting squawks drowned out by the regaling Fremantle Band in all its finery.

Out from starboard, the *Tofua* raised her anchor, blowing her foghorn in response to those waving wildly to farewell the troops gathered along her rails. The accompanying armoured battle cruisers, one Australian and one Japanese, took up their escort positions in readiness.

In time, the *Ormonde* would be attacked by U-boats three times in a series of Mediterranean convoys, narrowly evading disaster to safely deliver her final tally of 30,000 troops throughout the war. But there would be no U-boats today on her second voyage to a far-away war zone, just the brandished sunset on the vast Indian Ocean ahead of the two troopships at day's end.

Now, the men would begin to see changes in their daily routines between Australia's west coast here and Africa's east, four weeks away. Those fit for duty were assigned Guard or Dining Room Duties, the latter having unexpected benefits - generous extra helpings of food and conveniently being relieved of Guard Duty. As expected, these luxuries came at a price; laying and clearing the well-secured tables in the troops' dining room, along with endless washing up.

Each of the long, ten-seat mahogany-trimmed dining room tables had its matching varnished chairs in position, all of them topped with thin beige cushions. Serving tureens of fruit were temporarily placed at each end of the numerous well-laid tables, gleaming in readiness for the next three-course sitting of jostling, rowdy troops. Remaining in awe of their Third Class Dining Room on 'F' Deck, the men's imaginations aggrandised the officers' fancy indulgences.

Breakfast was a standard menu consisting of generous portions of mutton chops, vegetable stew, grilled or stewed steak and onions with bread and butter, jam or marmalade and porridge...always porridge.

Dinner at noon ranged from stewed rabbit, roast beef, mutton or corned beef on their allotted days, all accompanied by potatoes and vegetables unless the meal was curry and rice. Pudding was invariably met with great enthusiasm and as simple as stewed prunes, rice pudding, or the more elaborate golden or plum puddings served with sauce.

Varying significantly at night, the menu began with either corned beef or ham sandwiches with pickles. Otherwise, their raging appetites were quelled by a generous helping of hot pot or cold meat and potatoes with the occasional scone, washed down with every meal's fundamental tea or coffee. No one was about to starve.

Above them on 'E' Deck was the Third Class Lounge, one of the many lounges where the men would congregate to play cards or write when it was not converted into classrooms for lectures during the day. The endless rows of panels in the ceiling housed the white glass electric light fittings nestled lavishly in their brass fixtures on either side of several well-spaced ceiling fans, which, in themselves, were a novel experience for the men.

Rifle practice was scheduled intermittently on the rear deck, weather permitting, in spite of the mishaps known to result in the occasional gunshot wound to a random leg here or there. On calmer days, their lunges and follow-through tactics without fixed bayonets would put the troops through their paces in the interest of fluency and speed under unpredictable conditions. With the weather expected to be dominated by blustery Southwesterlies swinging up from the Antarctic, the men would attend their assigned lectures in lounges and other protected areas of the ship. And so, the reinforcements, or 'reos' as they were more casually known, began their first days abroad.

As the weeks progressed, so too did drills, Picquet Duties, Submarine Watch, lectures and sports, all ideal for breaking the monotony of these long sea days, until arriving at the Equator. Here, no one was sacred. In true tradition, 'Neptune' committed all those who were virgins to the equatorial divide to be summarily baptised by dunking, with rank having no bearing under 'Neptune's Law'. Absconders of any denomination, rank or creed were sought out and prised from their hideaways for their customary dousing. There was nowhere to hide.

'Neptune's Court' onboard a troopship guaranteed immeasurable entertainment with one of the many 'sentences' involving two very willing participants knocking the stuffing out of each other with pillows as the two perched precariously on a horizontal pole above a canvas pool.

Rowdy, enthusiastic Aussies would be standing, lounging, hanging or leaning where any suitable free space allowed, watching mates or brothers smashing their best aims into their hapless opponents. As 'Neptune's' defeated victim cannoned into the water below, enthusiastic cheers rang out, followed by the gleeful victor diving in straight after.

Depending on the 'ceremony' awaiting the uninitiated, they could find themselves sitting on a stool to plunge backwards into the makeshift pool, chair and all, to be later presented with a certificate by 'Neptune' in the formality of this jubilant occasion.

The maritime antics didn't stop there, though. With seasickness finally dissipated, popular onboard games such as Tug-of-War and various sports resumed for fitness and wagers, Two-Up being a typical favourite pastime for almost all onboard, and all bets were on. Hobbies were wholeheartedly encouraged, with photography catching Jim's attention as a popular pastime, although more critically, Submarine Watch introduced the men to this crucial duty as sentries, stationed daily in the lifeboats where they were outfitted with 75 rounds of ammunition.

After weeks of speculation and false rumours surrounding their secret destination, the craggy east coast of Africa's horn gradually rose above the distant haze. The atmosphere on deck left the troops buzzing in anticipation as they grew nearer to their first polarising glimpses of a foreign shore.

The unforgettable sight of the *Ormonde* approaching under the escort of an additional destroyer, cruiser and torpedo boat electrified the eager troops. They had been sailing through enemy waters without lights for three weeks with their portholes entirely blacked out under a warning of maximum punishment should anyone so much as emit the meagre glow of a fleeting cigarette.

Gradually, hour by hour, they entered the Gulf of Aden until finally passing through Hells Gate, the entrance to the Red Sea, where the convoy regrouped before proceeding cautiously towards the Gulf of Suez 2,000 kilometres ahead.

As Suez finally rose from the horizon, so too did the heralding spires of the domed Suez Canal Office glowing distantly in the morning rays. Many had not so much as heard of Suez, but their introduction was about to start. Even those on Guard Duty risked 'Dereliction of Duty' to snatch that first irresistible look at the long-awaited view where they would set foot for the first time on foreign soil.

Also known as Port Tewfik, Suez came more clearly into view, with the single spire of the Suez Canal Administration Office easily visible high above its dome. Adjacent was the covered train station where a troop train presently waited at the end of the concrete walkway, only it would not be for them today.

Among many things, Suez was the landing point for the famous Mena Camp, where the A.N.Z.A.C.s had trained for Gallipoli on their arrival in December 1914, training in the shadows of the Great Pyramids of Giza, 10 miles from Cairo, in their full spectacular view.

Training for the 9th Reinforcements, however, would see them posted at Australia Camp, Wabour-el-Maya, 2 miles from Suez. Here, they would undertake skirmishing, elementary bayonet fighting, close order drills and tactical training, including artillery formation and platoon attack drills. In addition, not only did the camp offer all the usual amenities, including the Y.M.C.A. Canteen, hospital, mess huts, motor garage and cemetery but provided a modern cinema where the men would indulge in recreation and news.

Disembarking, the troops formed into columns under the cover of night, their 2-mile route march delivering them through the parched Sahara sands before marching up the main road into camp in the infinitely cooler breaking dawn. Their introduction to Australia Camp that day, 4 April, then saw them Taken on Strength and, as such, their initial training in a foreign camp had begun.

Adjusting to camp life in the desert, the men briefly remained haunted by the pulsing in their legs and a lack of coordination from four weeks of incessant rolling sustained during the *Ormonde*'s voyage. Their training was an endurance run of intense 8-hour days, six days a week, fully packed with the desert wind blowing mercilessly against the battalion of heaving drenched bodies.

Barely a few days in camp, Jim, Harry, Ed Barnett, a 20-year-old plumber from Darwin and Tommy Edwards, an 18-year-old labourer from Maryborough, were just a few among the many reinforcements who were struck down with measles. The contagious illness was endemic, resulting in the four disgruntled men being Taken Off Strength from the battalion for isolation at the Segregation Camp.

Lying irritably in the immense canvas hospital ward, Jim and the others were covered inside and out with the tell-tale red spots the size of a pinhead, remaining in isolation and under treatment for at least a further week. Typically, the men were hardy and up for any lark, but not today. Today, they were not simply lacking wit and feeling all-round lousy but mourning the loss of one of their own, Cyril Ansbacher. The 25-year-old chemist from New Jersey, USA, succumbed to complications from his illness only three days earlier and now lay interred here at Suez, the telegram bearing the crushing news already on its way to his unsuspecting mother.

Another of Jim's best mates, Emmel Bray, who would eventually become his brother-in-law, was believed to be camped at Moascar nearby with the 2nd Light Horse Regiment. Emmel had enlisted in 1916 and was one of the inspirations for Jim putting his age up in an earlier attempt to enlist, so Jim was keen to catch up with him before the reos embarked for their next unnamed destination.

One of the finest horsemen Jim knew, Emmel sat astride a horse like he belonged with it rather than the horse belonged to him. Born for droving out in the open country, his life revolved around cattle and horses; give him a good cattle dog, and the man was complete. According to the latest accounts shared between their mothers, the two women being close friends passing on all manner of news between their families, Emmel had been in and out of hospital suffering from wounds and continuing illness.

Eight days after their hospitalisation, Jim, Harry and Tommie were released and assigned to their bell tents among the others of the 9th Reinforcements, leaving a dejected Ed to remain behind with complications. Their drills took them on 12-mile route marches out into the desert sands, and although Jim hadn't been diagnosed yet, he had a foot condition that caused his feet to ache mercilessly to the ankles.

Pushing the pain aside, he strove to keep step on the route marches under the glaring Egyptian sun, successfully managing to avoid heatstroke while others were hospitalised. Fortunately, the coarse sands were surprisingly firm, making training far more manageable.

The drills continued, as did the searing desert sun while the men struggled against the sandblasting from incessant winds, a typical induction at Australia Camp and a tenacious effort that caught attention. Major J.R.O. Harris, Australia Camp Commander, would report their April training in the War Diary of 27 April 1918 with satisfaction:

> *Troops Ex "Ormonde" and "Tofua" were in camp over three weeks and were able to carry out a valuable amount of training.*

Sundays brought leave to visit Cairo or sightseeing around the pyramids and the unique opportunity for Jim to finally catch up with Emmel before they left. By day's end, Jim's notebook sported Emmel's regimental address in the quiet drover's eloquently penned cursive:

No. 1233
Cpl E Bray
2nd Light Horse Regiment
1st Light Horse Brigade, Egypt

By then, Emmel had been promoted to Corporal but had not been destined to participate in the famous Light Horse charge at Beersheba six months earlier. Instead, he had found himself assigned 50 miles away in the Field at Moascar on the historic day the 4th Australian Light Horse Brigade stormed the ancient city, halting the advancing Turks. The euphoric atmosphere sparked through the camp like an electric current when the news of the staggering triumph reached them, filling each man's heart with burning pride.

In the ensuing days, Jim and the 41st Battalion would leave Ed behind in his recovery while they boarded the train at Wabour-el-Maya for Suez 2 miles away, embarking on their journey across the U-boat-infested waters of the Mediterranean. Their route would carry them westward through the Strait of Gibraltar, continuing along the Portuguese and Spanish coasts up to Le Havre, France. Many of the convoy would not survive.

41st Battalion marching through Brisbane, 1916. Photograph courtesy of the Imperial War Museum.

Australia Camp, Suez. AWM P00369.012.

RETURNED WITH A CREED − 13

An Australian battalion marching out past the tent lines of a camp in
Egypt to the training ground. AWM C03037.

An Australian battalion marching out past the tent lines of a camp in
Egypt to the training ground. AWM C03037.

S.S. Ellenga 1918. AWM P02400.011.

Kantara Camp, Suez Canal from H.M.A.S. Australia. AWM J03224

CHAPTER 2

The Convoy

"Extra guard arrived after sinking submarine and also we sunk one ourselves within three hundred yards."

Australian troopships leaving Port Said Harbour. Photograph courtesy of the National Australian Archives M1145 3B43.

ON 30 APRIL, THE 9th Reos assembled for the return route march from camp to Suez Port, where they found the *S.S. Ellenga* docked and ready for embarkation.

They would not be on the *Ormonde* this time, nor would the *Ellenga* be so striking as their previous dazzling transport. Only when they reached Port Said would they finally feel the power of their convoy comprising 11 ships, namely destroyers, heavy cruisers, torpedo boats, the British Arabis Class Sloop *H.M.S. Wallflower* among the minesweepers, Troopships *Ellenga, Ormonde, Tofua, Sant Anna*, the cargo ship, *Ingleside,* and a scattering of armed trawlers.

Entering the neck of the Suez Canal, the adjacent banks were comparatively bare as opposed to the camp structures and swing bridges ahead. Irrigation canals branched like tentacles issuing along the Suez Canal as the ships passed the massive Kantara Army Camp. Serving as an army storage depot for the Palestine forces, the camp housed masses of timber stores, countless crates of materials, numerous adjoining buildings linked by telegraph wires and its vast community of bell tents spread ethereally into the haze beyond the heaving dockyards. Closer to the ship, the pontoon bridge connecting the two sides of the canal had been disengaged for repositioning against the banks, enabling the flotilla to wend its way past.

Snaking carefully through the Suez Canal bottlenecks, the *Ellenga*, *Ormonde* and *Tofua* finally reached the Port Said Suez Canal Office with its ornate domes three days later. Navigating the narrow waterway involved masterfully pulling aside for the assembled troops to salute the dominant battleships and cruisers as they passed.

Ahead of them were the two torpedo boats, while bringing up the rear was the powerful presence of a destroyer; the rest waited for them in Port Said. This would be the ideal opportunity to replenish their coal supplies before heading into the cauldron of the Mediterranean's hostile waters, a graveyard for torpedoed vessels.

Vast lines of troopships, destroyers, battleships, cruisers, torpedo boats, and armed trawlers lay before them as an immense smoking factory of shipping on either side, a vision of magnificence as the convoy slowly came to anchor midstream, just three amongst over a hundred others. Everywhere the troops looked bristled with endless lines of masts above innumerable smoking funnels. The dark hulks of ships varying in sizes and variegated colours of camouflage lay peacefully at anchor like sleeping giants, casting their vast shadows onto the slick, shimmering water below.

Around the expectant troops, the bustling safe harbour of Port Said was lined with crowded rows of stone and timber buildings where soldiers and locals worked the timber docks while surrounding lighters loaded or unloaded their endless stream of khaki cargoes and supplies.

Lighters would usually be lowered into the water as the gangway dropped into place alongside the ship for the troops to descend into the smaller craft for transfer to the docks. Today, though, disembarkation would have to wait. From here on, the convoy would travel under blackness in zigzag formation; again, there would be no smoking on deck.

Instead, smoking was only permitted in the lowest regions of the ship, deep out of sight.

Opening his new issue black notebook, fresh from production, Jim loosened the pages by letting them flutter tightly against his thumb like a pack of cards. His pencil rested purposely between his two callused fingers as he flicked over a few pages before jotting his brief, humble notes of the journey since this morning:

Left Suez Tuesday 30th April 1918.

They left Port Said uneventfully on Friday, 3 May, entering the calm, open waters of the Mediterranean, where the flotilla formed up into an impressive convoy. Its sheer sight was extraordinary.

Ahead of them steamed a destroyer and *H.M.S. Wallflower*, one of the minesweepers armed with canon and depth chargers that would endeavour to eliminate any menacing submarines.

Behind them, a span of heavy cruisers, the *Ingleside*, British and Japanese destroyers, and torpedo boats flanked the *Tofua*. Alongside was another Japanese destroyer, and the remaining cruisers, torpedo boats, and armed trawlers also utilised for minesweeping but just as ready to evacuate any men from stricken vessels.

Destroyers cruised in rotation as they swung back and forth between the troopships, checking their positioning. The *Ellenga*, a smaller vessel than the *Ormonde*, was marginally slower at full speed, so the destroyers steamed in intermittently to check on them. Zigzagging in unison reduced the risk of enfilade or being broadsided by the marauding U-boats, an ever-present threat at any given moment that filled the men with utter horror.

No sooner had they settled into this day's routine with Abandon Ship Drills and familiarised themselves with their posts when a resounding boom unleashed ahead of them. One of the cruisers was burning and sinking rapidly, torpedoed before their eyes. Her surviving gun crew remained stoically at their posts. If there was an opportunity to sink the concealed predator, they would gladly oblige before all was lost.

Depth charges were being dropped nearby as a destroyer cruised in from behind to save the crew, naval performance at its operational best. Two armed trawlers scanned the waves, searching for survivors, while the padre presiding on deck committed those already lost to the sea.

While at breakfast the next day, the side of a destroyer tore open to the all too familiar boom of another explosion, accompanied by an intermittent series of eruptions sending water skywards as the *Wallflower* dropped her depth charges on the lurking U-boat. A cruiser pulled in alongside to safely transfer the surviving men from the sinking ship amid the clearing smoke from the heavy artillery as depth chargers continued to explode in the depths.

Jim, Harry, Bill, Ted and Ernie had hurriedly finished their breakfasts to head up on deck to assist with Submarine Watch, aware that just a glimpse of a periscope might save a ship, perhaps even their own. From the rails of the *Ellenga*, they watched the destroyer disappearing lower into the stunning blue waters, her rails now sunk beneath the waves, leaving only her ghostly smoking funnel, hoists and masts to disappear from view forever.

It was unclear if the submarine was damaged as there was no detectable oil slick, so briefly turning their attention to the destroyer, they watched the last of the orderly crew transferring onboard before the doomed vessel sank out of sight in a surge of heaving turbulence.

Later that night, in the quiet of his bunk, Jim added six simple words to the previous two lines, stating simply:

Port Said Friday 3rd May.

Sunday, 5 May brought little solace during church services held on decks everywhere throughout the convoy. Ever aware, the men bowed their heads in prayer for safe passage while remembering those lost to the seas below them.

On 6 May, with the gravity of it weighing heavily on him, his simple note would sum up the grim events of the day by writing:

Monday. One submarine at breakfast.

Nervous tension onboard ever increased as the convoy lost another destroyer the next day. It seemed as if the submarine was simply picking them off one by one to get to the troopships, and they still had some days ahead of them before reaching Le Havre.

With the wind whipping up spray, they ploughed on, zigzagging their way across the open waters, straining their eyes for any signs of periscopes when they were not carrying out drills or other guard duties. That night, too exhausted to write, Jim left his notes, falling into a fitful sleep to the rocking of the *Ellenga*.

An entirely different story awaited them the following day, 8 May, as another cruiser and a minesweeper went down. Only this time, the *Wallflower's* depth chargers found their mark, resulting in an oil slick rising to the surface of the heavy waves. The surrounding roar from the troops onboard caught Jim up in its electricity until, all of a sudden, someone pointed off to starboard. There, 300 yards from them, was the penetrating vision of another surfaced U-boat.

The *Ellenga's* depth chargers were ready for despatch, and only moments later, a series of explosions heralded their launch amid the heavy gunfire chasing the submerging submarine. Slowly but surely, an oil slick appeared in its wake. Cheers from the ecstatic men broke out all over the ship simultaneously with the first of animated choruses, seen, more than heard, coming from the surviving troopships separated by a few hundred yards across the waves.

By 3:00 pm, the British destroyer *H.M.S. Basilisk* and the armed yacht *U.S.S. Lydonia* arrived to strengthen their escort, although this did not help the *Ingleside* 2 hours later. Another submarine fired its torpedoes broadside into the vessel, which instantly burst into flames.

Maneuvered with skilful precision, the *Lydonia* pulled alongside to rescue whatever crew could be saved, discovering many were already dead, wounded or in the water waving desperately to be picked up. Those who remained trapped, unable to escape the lost vessel's lower decks, journeyed with her into the depths.

That night, picking up his pencil, Jim thought about what he would write in the notebook resting on his thigh as he leaned against the wall of the billet. He found it hard to believe they were in the middle of all this…the world had seemed so civilised not so long ago.

In the moment's quiet, Jim wrote:

Wednesday. Extra guard arrived after sinking submarine and also we sunk one ourselves within three hundred yards.

Through the night, the sea remained relatively calm except for the gentle motion of the zigzagging steamer until Reveille woke them for their ablutions at 5:30 am. This day, Thursday the 9th, proved to be more of the same, only this time the U-boat surfaced and trained its torpedo on the *Ellenga*.

Watching from the deck, the men braced themselves for the impact of the rapidly approaching blur of the torpedo until the momentum of the neighbouring destroyer drew her into its path, taking the full force of its explosive impact. Instantly, the destroyer's magazine in the bow's storage bay ruptured in a colossal explosion of fire and black oily smoke, shattering her hull like eggshells beneath the waves, immediately causing her to list. A rueful hush descended on the troops along the entire ship, in the knowledge they were the ones targeted.

In last-minute timing, the *Basilisk* rammed the submarine as it attempted to submerge in the attack's aftermath, causing it to limp away, though still intact. The eager men onboard the troopships watched the spectacle unfold as the *Basilisk* and the *Wallflower* worked together, dropping their depth charges until finally bringing an oil slick to the surface, the death knell of the U-boat and its crew.

It had been a week since they had left Suez and how they had survived this far, no one knew.

Restricted by the cabin's gloom at night, Jim's writing became scratchy, to say the least, but he managed to write his notes tighter and a little neater, accompanied by his hot and painful ear, the beginnings of an inner ear infection:

Thursday 9th. One of convoy got struck by torpedo meant for us. She was two hundred yards from us.

The ensuing few days brought more drills and duties, U-boats and suffering:

Monday night 13th May. Five of convoy left.

Even more so the next day as he added to the line:

...two of which got sunk next day.

Jim briefly took in the French coast as the *Ellenga* approached Le Havre Port the following morning. In the next hour, he would be administered Aspros upon his admission to the hospital for a driving infection of his inner ear, a swollen Otitis Media, while awaiting transfer by train to the 2nd Australian General Hospital (2 A.G.H.). He had barely seen enough of Le Havre to write on the back of a postage stamp, and now, just after 9:00 am, the milder revs of the engines indicated the *Ellenga* had arrived in port, miraculously in the company of the *Ormonde* and the *Tofua*.

It was not until 7:30 that evening that Jim was finally transferred to the waiting train with the other troops. Here they continued to wait for a further 2 1/2 hours until the train's whistle sounded their departure at 10:00 pm.

Journeying the few hours through the night found the men sleeping upright, wrapped in their blankets, heads supported by haversacks with their kits sent on to the baggage section, ready for detraining at Le Havre Camp in the early hours of the morning.

Stiff and in searing pain, Jim was transferred on 14 May straight into the 2 A.G.H. at 5:00 am in the cool chill of the grey dawn. He would remain in this hospital for nine blurry days before being transferred to the 1st Australian Convalescent Depot (1 A.C.D.) for another seven. Here, mail from home astonishingly caught up with him.

Re-reading his few diary entries in the less debilitating days that followed, Jim relived every intense moment:

Left Suez on Tuesday 30th April 1918.
Port Said Friday 3rd May.
Monday 6th May - 1 submarine while at breakfast.
Wednesday 8th May - Extra guard arrived after sinking submarine and also, we sank one ourselves within 300 yards.
Thursday 9th May - One of convoy got struck by torpedo meant for us. She was 200 yards from us.
Monday night 13th May - 5 of convoy left. Two of which got sunk next day.
Reached Port 9am. Disembarked 7:30 pm. Went straight onto train and left for Le Havre at 10 pm.
Reached Havre early Tuesday morning and went to hospital at 5 o'clock with sore ear.

Later, an unofficial listing of vessels sunk in the Mediterranean during the time of Jim's crossing would reveal:

30/04/1918 – The Kaliope off Alexandria.
01/05/1918 – The Nikaloas off Egypt.
05/05/1918 – HMS David Gillies, Naval Tug.
08/05/1918 (Wed) – the Ingleside off Algiers.
8/5/1918 – SM U-32, a German U-boat depth-charged in the Mediterranean NW of Malta by HMS Wallflower, an Arabis Class Mine Sweeping Sloop.
10/05/1918 – the Hinda off Libya.
11/05/1918 – the Sant Anna off Italy
12/05/1918 – the Omrah off Sicily en route from Marseilles to Alexandria.
12/05/1918 – SM UB-72. A Type UBIII Submarine was depth charged in the English Channel with the loss of 34 of her crew.

> Left Suez. Ap, 30th Tues.
> " P. Said. May Fri 3rd
> Monday 1 submarine
> while at breakfast
> Wednesday, extra
> guard arrived after
> sinking Submarine
> and also we sunk
> one ourselves within
> three hundred yards
> ~~Tuesday night~~
> Monday night
> 5 of convoy left
> two of which
> got sunk next
> day.
>
> Thursday 9th. One of convoy
> got struck by Torpedo
> meant for us. She was
> two hundred yards
> from us.

Some of Jim's notes during the convoy between Suez and Le Havre.
From personal collection.

An unidentified British steamer sinks after being torpedoed by an enemy submarine. AWM C00598.

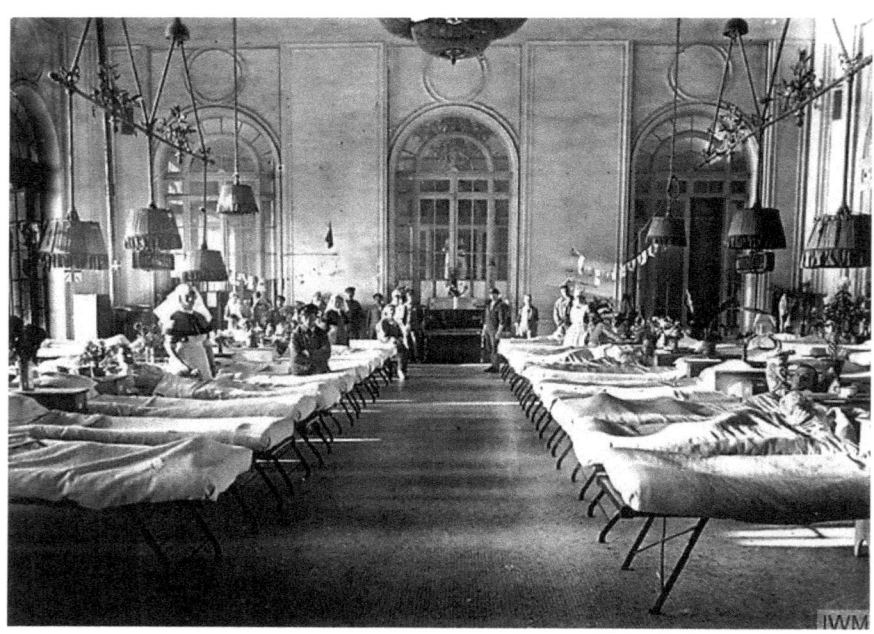

No. 2 Australian General Hospital, Le Havre. Photograph courtesy of the Imperial War Memorial.

CHAPTER 3

Fovant

"It is just twelve months today since you enlisted, and it is a week off five months since you left here but it seems like many years to me since I saw your dear face."

Jim's Crossed Rifle Badge from Fovant, 1918.
From personal collection.

LETTERS FROM HOME FILLED JIM'S mind with images of evenings in their shingle-roofed cottage, lit by the muted glow of the cut-glass kerosene lamps, as the family bent over their greeting cards, writing intently. The visions appeared so vividly that Jim could briefly smell that warm, organic aroma of the burning kerosene-soaked wick. How he missed them.

He had received several letters, including two from his mother, Adelaide, and Francie, his ten-year-old sister, in the past seven weeks since his arrival in Fovant on Salisbury Plain, England, all in time for his 19th birthday on 7 July.

Jim's release from hospital was followed by two weeks of subsequent training at Australian Infantry Base Depot (A.I.B.D.), Le Havre,

France. Lorries had transferred the 82 men to Le Havre Port on 14 June under the command of Captain Fraser with 27 of them destined for the 9th Training Battalion at Fovant. Among them were Jim, Harry, Bill, Ted, Ernie and Tommy. The 16 June then saw them embarking for Southampton, England, on the Majestic Class British Battleship *H.M.S. Caesar*.

Ed's sojourn across the Mediterranean on the *S.S. Indarra* was arranged on his release from isolation, arriving at 9th Training Battalion's camp, Fovant, 12 days ahead of the others. Much to their surprise, Ed materialised to greet them in a loud and happy reunion with prospects of many stories waiting to be shared.

Now, reading through the letters, Jim's mother's greeting card first, he absorbed all her news, feeling the warmth from her loving heart and her anticipation that his ear infection had improved.

Chermside
July 20th, 1918

My Dear Boy,

Just a PC hoping it finds you quite well and I trust you got over to England in time to get leave with the rest and I hope you had a good time. I hope your ear has got quite better again. I had a letter from Mrs Bray today asking me when I was coming down for a holiday. She said that this is the worst winter they have ever had down there. The frost is terrible there. I believe Joe Halls is going to be married shortly to some girl he met while he was in Brisbane last year. It is just twelve months today since you enlisted, and it is a week off five months since you left here but it seems like many years to me since I saw your dear face. I hope and trust God will take care of you and bring you safely home to me someday. I do trust in Him that He will answer my prayers in everything I have asked of Him. Have you got my parcel yet? I have sent two.

Best love to you from your loving Mother. xxxxxxxxxxxxxxxxx

Picking up Francie's card, he re-read it yet again:

Chermside
July 20th 1918

Dear Jim,

I hope this PC will find you in good health as it leaves us all well at home. Bert has gone out with the Scouts to Cedar Creek camping tonight. Dad, Ciss and Eve have gone to a Cantata at the hall in aid of the Red Cross. Mrs Geo Lemke has a baby boy and Mrs Gunston has two baby girls (twins).

I hope you got to Blighty for your holiday.

Best love from Frances
xxxxxxxxxxxxxxxxxxxxxxxxxxxx

Captivated by Francie's neat writing, Jim's mind wandered to earlier days spent at Cedar Creek, where he had camped with the scouts as a young boy himself, though now the memories seemed more like a lifetime ago. He imagined that dank, vegetative smell of the creek as if he were there once again, and just reading about the hall filled him with the sudden sense that he could feel its floor beneath his feet.

Pulling his mind back to soldier life half a world away, Jim thought of the busy nights he had spent writing, sending family and friends greeting cards of many places he had never dreamt of seeing until now. He had bought many British postcards while training and on leave in England, including one of Holyrood House with King George V attending a Military Parade, a close likeness to his parade when he and the men were saluted by the king themselves.

He had enjoyed some leave with Harry, Ted, Bill and Ernie, spending time in London soaking up the sights on the postcards, including Westminster Abbey, Buckingham Palace and Hampton Court Palace, just to name a few.

There was even time for a photo of the five of them in clean, fresh uniforms, each wearing the 41st Battalion's colour patch on their upper sleeves and their boots smartly polished. Jim and Bill were sitting in the front with their legs casually crossed while standing at ease behind them were Harry, Ted and Ernie. Ted was resting his left hand comfortably on Jim's shoulder, a sign that they were mates always. The portrait had been taken as a postcard at the camp studio in Fovant before Ted, Bill and Harry left for France; Ted on 7 August, followed by Bill and Harry on the 8th.

Sitting on the edge of his bunk with his fountain pen scratching busily, Jim began writing his words of greeting on the back:

'L to R sitting. J.H. Rainey, W. Mitchell.
L to R standing. H. Larsen, E. Marsh, A. Murr.
Kindest regards & best love to all from all five.

Having run out of room at the bottom, Jim added his own wishes across the top:

Best love to all from Jim. xxxxxx

He would send the photo home with his scorebook when he had finished his rifle practice for Marksman First Class this week.

***

Jim's talent for shooting was forged from two beginnings: four years of Cadets at school, but ultimately, providing food on the table as the eldest boy in their family of eight and assuming all the responsibilities the position brought on that rung of the family ladder. It was a simple life. Not only did shooting feed the family, but it was a necessary life skill for a man on the land. A rifle was an expectation among his every-day possessions, and there were not many he knew back home who could outshoot him.

Proud of his competent shooting, Jim wanted to prove himself as a marksman, stepping up from being a 'crack shot' out in the bush; shooting a possum out of a tree was a useful ability but did not qualify you as a marksman.

Jim waited for the others to finish their detail as he re-read the typed introduction on the first page of his freshly printed scorebook, fascinated by the concept of recording shooting results. Sure, he had counted his shots during his cadet training at school or when he and his mates had been shooting at a knot on a tree, but this was altogether something different. This was legitimate competition.

CEASE FIRE! filled the air with the range sergeant's booming voice just as the last shot rang out in ever-diminishing pulses through Fovant's rolling vista. Here, the training men busily attended their weapons in the silent presence of the massive chalk military insignias cut into the emerald hillside.

It was 26 August 1918 with their first detail of Practice 1 at 100 yards under perfect conditions. Jim's rifle was the famous Lee Enfield, the breakthrough rifle of its time, officially known as the Short Magazine Lee Enfield Mk III or S.M.L.E. - 'Smelly' for short. Its superior rapid firing and effective bolt action rifle made it the most revolutionary rifle manufactured in the world to date. Capable of firing 15 shots per minute, the gun provided a shooter's 'dream range' of 550 yards, although lethal to 3,000 yards if you were good enough, and sported a detachable 17-inch bayonet, vicious in every sense.

Never before had Jim owned a world-class rifle such as this, let alone fired one so renowned. He had a Martini Henry at home, which was revolutionary enough, but the Lee Enfield was the elite of gunsmithing. And this one was his for the duration, serial number and all.

Now, his target was Second Class Elementary, otherwise known as the Bull's Eye, with a 4-inch inner target. The prone detail's five rounds would be fired over their makeshift cover of sandbags in Fovant Rifle Range's presently calm conditions, each shot worth five points…*and* under the added weight of that gleaming, fixed bayonet. Jim nominated his shots as perfectly central without the need to allow for conditions…no crosswind, no mirage and zero elevation. His scores proved him right. Lifting his binoculars, he was satisfied to see he had landed a tight group as dead centre as he had expected, giving him 25 points. As a shooter, he had competed against himself all his life, and now he could prove his skill; he had just clover-leafed three shots.

With scores recorded and checked, they moved on.

On arriving at the 200 yard range, the wind flags showed gentle movement without any complicating crosswind. The knee-high grass slightly swaying between the firing point and the targets conveniently identified the strength and direction of the wind's downdrafts.

This was Practice 2 - his target, a second-class figure resembling a man's head and shoulders. They would have five shots lying prone with bayonets fixed, and, on the order, the air at the firing point filled with the grinding snap of 20 bayonets simultaneously locking into place.

Jim's pulse was calm, and he felt naturally complete in the moment, almost as if he were home, while men settled into position to the familiar muffled sound of shuffling bodies. His first shot drifted out from the head of the figure to land within the inner ring.

Adjusting his position slightly, he moved his hips barely enough to re-align the muzzle of his rifle but enough to make all the difference, laying naturally in line. His elevation was 225 over the 200 yards.

Taking a breath in, the rifle's muzzle dropped slowly as his body reflected his breathing, mindful not to hold it longer than necessary. Exhaling gently, the muzzle of the Lee Enfield rose into place, once again, exactly where he wanted it. His next four shots hit their mark, key-holing two of them to give him a score of 19/20.

Their next range was the last for the day: Practice 3 at 300 yards, five rounds, firing over cover with bayonets fixed. Again, they had the 'head and shoulders' configuration inside the two circles, and, again, Jim key-holed two of his shots, a respectable group scoring him 17/20.

This Marksman Practice was scheduled for the next two days, so when they resumed training for Practice 4 the following day, it was a prone 400 yard detail, only this time they were taking cover. Conveniently, the 400 yard targets were up on the hillside 100 yards behind the 300 yard range, clearing its targets. They did not have to move, but simply raise their elevation onto the targets beyond.

Practices 5 and 6 were both at 200 yards with bayonet fixed, although the latter practice was executed as a 30-second rapid fire of five shots fired over cover. In this discipline, the rifle would remain unloaded and the pouch unbuttoned until the order *RAPID FIRE* was called.

The resulting group was almost as good as he had hoped; he had dropped one shot to 5 o'clock, but 19/20 was respectable enough. He was shooting again, even if that meant preparing for destruction beyond his wildest imagination.

Practice 7 was still at 200 yards, only this time, standing while taking cover in a trench and firing over it with bayonet fixed…again, rapid fire. Jim counted his rounds as he fired for a perfect score with a picture-perfect group: 20/20. Thankfully, his shots had not fallen short from the misgivings of a heated barrel or, worse still, the bolt jamming, mishaps he could do without at this stage of his qualifying practices.

On the range sergeant's lofty orders, the men moved to the 300 yard range for Practice 8 which Jim had prepared himself for by absorbing the conditions and checking his breathing. The day was particularly dull but calm, making the target slightly darker. If conditions held, this could be a good result.

It was time. The men took up their standing positions with magazines loaded at the ready. Taking cover with bayonets attached, they locked rifle butts into their shoulders to prevent the recoil from breaking any collar bones or shattering unfortunate teeth. Jim aimed low, countering the bayonet's weight, which was known to affect the Mark VII ammunition's trajectory, causing it to rise, according to his training and scorebook's advice. His first round hit its mark. Again, the same for his second shot, continuing until he had a close replica of his previous group with a total of 17/20.

Following the command to *CEASE FIRE!*, the men remained in their positions at 300 yards for a further ten rounds of standing rapid fire while taking cover, once again with their rifles unloaded and pouches buttoned until *RAPID FIRE!* was given. Only then would they unbutton their ammunition pouches and load their five rounds in each magazine, again with bayonets fixed. Jim's result was a pretty group of nine nicely compact shots, giving him a score of 28/30, with a 'flyer' exactly where he nominated it out at 8 o'clock.

There were two last Practices today, 10 and 11, both on 400 yards, with Practice 10 consisting of five rounds prone without bayonet under very dull conditions. In due course, the order, *OPEN FIRE!* roared ahead of the first volley of shots. Jim had finished double-checking his elevation, which he had raised to 425, comfortable with no wind to speak of and knowing his zero was effectively spot on.

His first two shots should have felt better, but his third shot sent a tremor to his gut. He continued improving resulting in a dead-centre shot on his last round. Removing his magazine Jim cast an enquiring glance at his equipment; he was going to finish on Rapid Fire and wanted to get his head in the right place for it.

On the order to *CEASE FIRE!*, the score, verified by Jim's observer, filled him with a sense of satisfaction about his bullets' groups and overall results, something that had not gone unnoticed by others along the range. He had dropped a couple to 15/20 over 400 yards, but that was satisfactory enough.

Looking along the firing point, elbows, shoulders and jaws were getting increasingly sorer, as were his, the right side of their jaws bruised from the recoil's thumping impact. This was heavy-going training, their introduction what they could expect in the next few weeks upon their arrival in France. They had better get used to it.

For Practice 11, they remained in place for a further 30 seconds of Rapid Fire over 400 yards. Suitably timed, the range sergeant called *RAPID FIRE!* for the last time that day, followed by a volley of relentless thundering gunfire as it coursed through the countryside.

Jim's first shot went wild out to 10 o'clock, although he powered on through the incessant firing with barely a moment to aim until ejecting the last spent shell at the call of *CEASE FIRE!* and removed the magazine. Generally, he liked most of his shots apart from two, which he had nominated as a little widespread, alright for rapid fire over a 400 yard range. His resulting score of 11/20 certainly was not what he expected of a typical score, but then, this was not a typical detail.

Rifles were made safe, scores verified, and gear removed from the firing point under the expectation they would return to the 200 yard range tomorrow at 10:00 am.

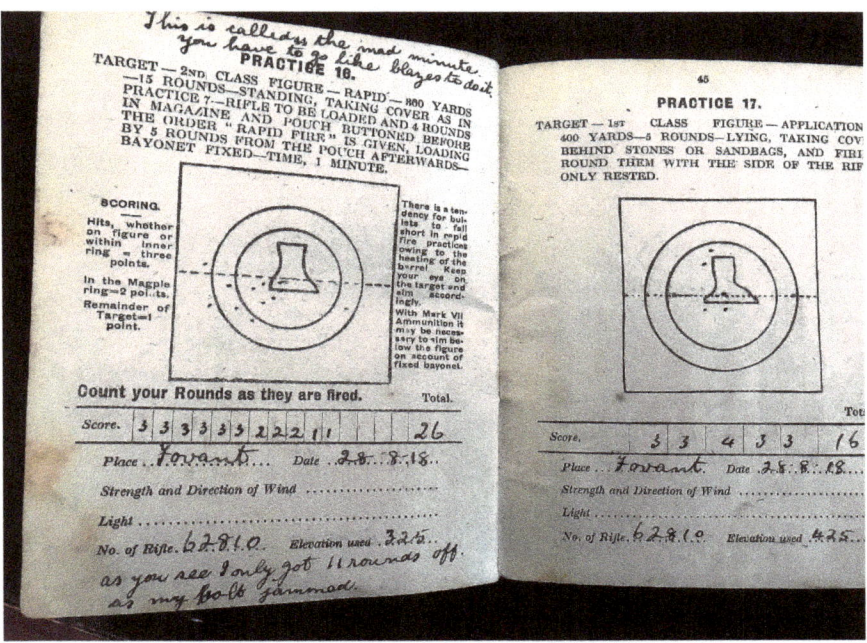

28 August 1918. The 'mad minute'. Practices 16 and 17 of Jim's General Musketry Course. Photograph courtesy of Bryan James.

Resuming rifle practice the following day saw Practice 12 executed in two parts, both of which were at 200 yards. Part 1 was two magazines of five rounds, prone with no bayonet, only this time it would be for the chance of a 'possible' of 40/40 points and wearing a gas mask. Part 2 would come shortly after, engaged in a trench.

Conditions were calm in the mid-morning of 28 August, with just the occasional lilting breeze drifting across the empty range. So when Jim and the rest of the company were given the order to *ENGAGE GAS MASKS!*, they knew conditions were on their side, at least.

Hearing his breathing inside his head, Jim listened for the order to *TAKE YOUR POSITIONS*, still watching for any change in the wind conditions as he settled in.

Shortly after, *OPEN FIRE!* followed.

Jim nominated his shots, methodically landing them in the centre of the head and shoulders, continuing effortlessly after changing magazines. There was a shift coming in the breeze from his left, but he could get the next shot away before it came through to his target. He knew not to shy at the last shot, but two flyers had beaten him the day before, which he did not want to repeat. His aim was careful as he squeezed the heavy trigger, aiming slightly off for the breeze.

As the shot left the hot barrel, the breeze was already dropping. Had it dropped enough to affect his shot? It had.

Jim's last round's point of impact landed at 9 o'clock, just barely off the main group, although the tight group between the neck and chest was perfect. Mentally calculating his qualifying scores at this point, he knew he was on the verge of qualifying for Marksman 1st Class without any further qualifying scores, unlike many others.

The range sergeant's *CEASE FIRE!* resonated across the range, followed immediately by *REMOVE GAS MASKS!* and specific instructions transferring them into the forward trench for Part 2, standing and firing over cover.

Arriving at his position, Jim relaxed, leaning against the trench wall, loading his magazine to prepare for the five rounds of rapid fire: 30 seconds of intense gunfire with only five seconds of exposure per shot.

In moments, their thunderous volley rang out on the sergeant's command, gun smoke filling the air and noses of the men along the trench. When the scores were transferred to scorebooks along the firing point, Jim's final score revealed a total of 18/20.

Remaining in the same trench, they would take cover with fixed bayonets for five rounds, where Jim soon scored 19/20, followed by another qualifying score of 28/30 for his 45-second rapid fire, then 15/20 at 300 yards.

Ten shots of rapid fire at the same range came next, followed by more standing, taking cover, rifle loaded with four in the magazine and the can opener, his bayonet, in place. Their time limit was one minute, known to the troops as the 'mad minute'.

With his barrel already scorching, there was a chance his bullets could fall short, so Jim had mentally prepared himself. So far, he had sustained no irregularities, but today, when the incessant firing split the English Summer's charm, his Lee Enfield's bolt jammed on his twelfth shot.

Gritting his teeth tightly, he worked the bolt safely, but unsuccessfully…it would not budge. By the time he had finally dislodged it, the sergeant's commanding voice rang out for the last time:

CEASE FIRE!

Shortly after, Jim's calculations revealed a score of 26/45.

Later, when Jim penned a few words in his scorebook to his family, he would write:

This is called the mad minute. You have to go like blazes to do it. As you see I only got 11 rounds off as my bolt jammed.

Four hundred yards up the range, a party of men emerged when the order over the field radio cleared them to take down the targets which were then brought up to the firing point for transferring the results. Jim's qualifying score was 133 out of 150, surpassing the Marksman First Class minimum of 125. He had done it. He did not have to fire another shot.

Observing the faces of the men along the firing point as they added their scores, Jim was not surprised to spot the unimpressed or impassive expressions, while others, in stark contrast, held satisfied glints in their eyes and carried a subtle, assured poise.

As the contingent of reinforcements made their way over to the corrugated iron hut facing the range, one of the camp's photographers came to talk with the men, knowing these were contributing scores to qualify them for Marksman First Class and Crossed Rifles Badge.

Each man qualifying for marksman was invited to be photographed, an opportunity Jim quietly welcomed as he walked over to the stream to take his position; he would send this photo home with his scorebook. Looking up, he noticed the distant huts out in front of him against the perfect emerald hillside, the ideal backdrop.

Jim stood in full kit with his trenching tool, haversack to the left, water bottle to the right, all hanging from his leather belt, and the ammunition pouches on two leather straps, one slung over each shoulder under his epaulettes and secured at his belt. His pockets were weighed down with his wallet, cigarettes, knife, scorebook, pencil, payroll book, handkerchief, compass and any other bits and pieces he would take out later.

Facing the photographer, he placed the butt of his Lee Enfield, Serial No. 68210, on the damp ground beside his right boot, his eyes as good as level with the tip of the bayonet; he and the rifle were in full war mode as the photographer lined up the frame.

Adding a further message the following night to his family back home, Jim wrote across the empty practice pages:

I never fired at either of these practices. If you count up you will find I passed as Marksman. I got 133 points out of 150. Marksman means 125 points or over. So you see I have done justice to my old time sport.

Best love Jim.

The package destined for home included the photograph of the five mates, his scorebook, and his marksman photo taken at the range the day before, tucked inside the cover to surprise them all. *Pte J.H. Rainey (3653), Fovant, 28/08/1918*, was all that was written on the back.

Jim would later send his Crossed Rifles Badge home, imagining the family unfolding the delicate wrapping to reveal the crossed rifles, embroidered rustically in bright yellow on a patch of khaki material.

The badge remained unblemished, never to be sewn onto Jim's uniform...and for good reason. The enemy sought those badges like a prize, rapidly eliminating anyone wearing the coveted icon ahead of anyone else. Subsequently, the prestigious badge would be kept perfectly safe at home, wrapped in purple tissue paper for posterity.

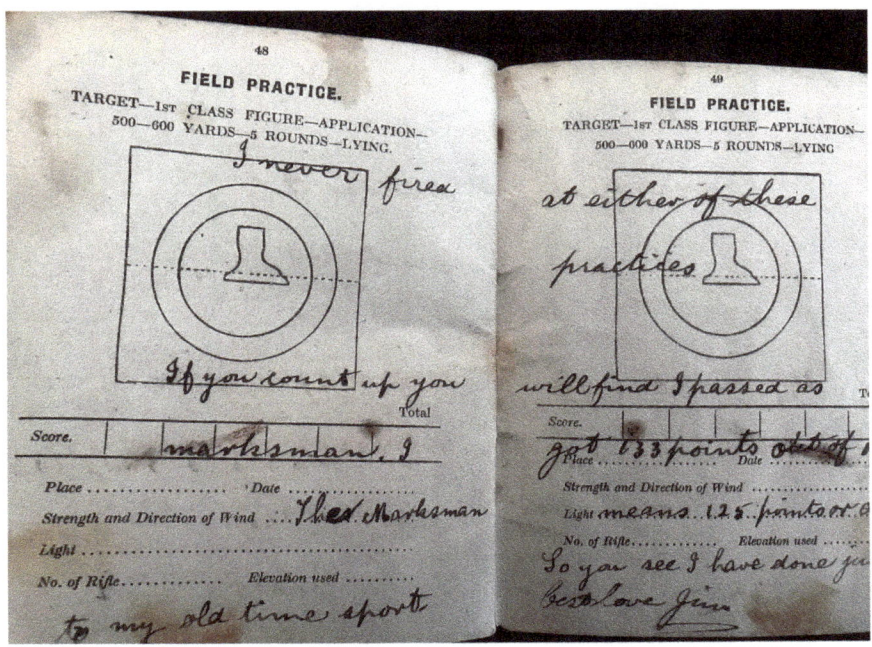

Fovant 1918. Marksman's page in Jim's scorebook. Photograph courtesy of Bryan James.

Pte James (Jim) Henry Rainey 3653. Fovant, 1918. Photograph courtesy of Raymond Pepper and Chermside Historical Society.

L to R sitting. J.H. (Jim) Rainey, W. (Bill) Mitchell. L to R standing. H. (Harry) Larsen, E. (Ted) Marsh, E.A. (Ernest) Murr. Fovant 1918.
Photograph from personal collection.

1918 Codford No. 7 Training Camp. AWM C01288

1917 Rifle practice, Fovant. Photograph courtesy of the State Library of Victoria (H85.55/160/65).

13 August 1918. 41st Battalion Guard of Honour being inspected by King George V at the opening of Australia House. AWM D00003.

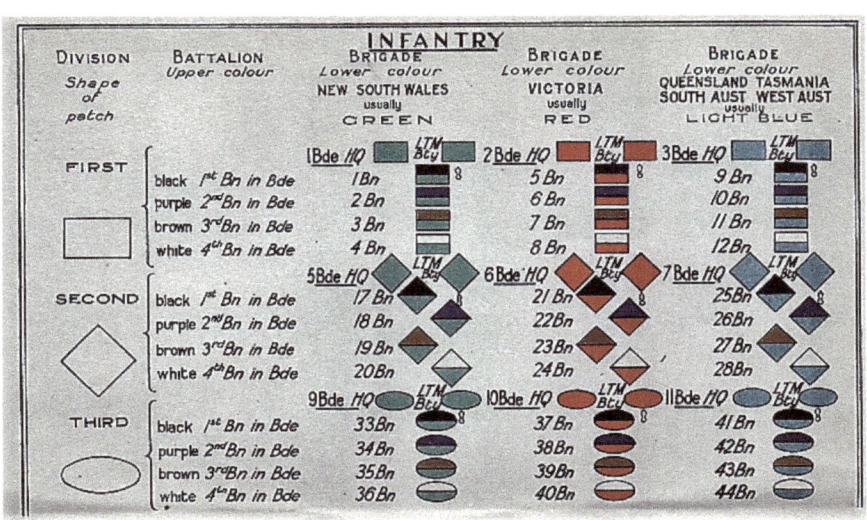

Colour patches chart of the 3rd Division. Courtesy of the Western Front Association.

CHAPTER 4

To the Front

The men presented in complete fighting order with steel helmets and entrenching tools as clouds rolled in over the battlefront ahead; a formidable vision of valour born as the fire ignited within them.

Colonel Alexander Robert Heron DSO CMG of 41st Battalion. AWM H00042.

AS JIM AND ERNIE DISCOVERED, proceeding immediately to France was not destined for all of the reinforcements. Ted, Harry and Bill were among the staggered increments of troops who had already crossed the English Channel, which was equally as fraught with U-boats as the Mediterranean. The other two stayed; Jim until 13 September undergoing further intensive sniper training.

In the grey English dawn, he marched out with Ed and Tommy amid the synchronised columns to rousing cheers from Ernie and the remaining troops when the embarking reos left Folkestone, England, for Le Havre. The sight of the surrounding transports escorted by this number of destroyers and seaplanes filled his heart with complete awe; the intensity of it would stay with him his whole life, no matter how long...or short.

Disembarking at Le Havre 9 hours later brought the savvy street merchants converging on them with chocolates, fruit, French dictionaries and other useful books on speaking French while the troops waited for lorries to transfer them to Australian Infantry Base Depot (A.I.B.D.), Le Havre.

In the distance, a British Sopwith Camel tailed a German Albatross relentlessly as they sparred in the skies above the French countryside, bringing shouts of encouragement from the gathered troops watching on with great interest. This was Jim, Ed and Tommy's first glimpse of a dogfight, so the excitement rippling through the atmosphere soon swept them up. Triplanes and biplanes had become familiar sights to them, but today, the biplanes held the air.

Dogfights were a frequent sight and the element of lucrative wagers, so when the Albatross began trailing smoke, the men resounded with cheers until the moment of impact issued forth a plume of black oily smoke from the ensuing explosion, then the camp simply erupted.

Overnight, the three mates were Taken On Strength into the 47th Battalion and assigned to an eight-man bell tent before enjoying a hearty meal of hot beef stew, fresh fruit with cream and steaming tea in the timber dining hall.

Finally, the next day, they were Marched In with full packs at A.I.B.D. Rouelles, Le Havre, rejoining the 41st Battalion where they boarded a train for the rear lines of the Front.

Those 24 hours with the 47th brought Jim a sense of belonging, but none more so than returning to the 41st. This was his unit. This was where he belonged. He was back with his mates, and they would fight alongside each other just as they had envisioned from the day they enlisted 14 months earlier.

In the meantime, though, there was work to be done. They would undertake a 12-mile route march returning to Rouelles via nearby

Tincourt Village. Attempting to ease the monotony of this morning's showery training march, Jim turned his attention to ticking through tactical responses before letting it subtly glide on to this afternoon's scheduled intercompany cricket and football matches. Many of the men on the training march with Jim were passionate footballers, although he was a self-confessed cricket enthusiast looking forward to signing himself up for an over or two of cricket.

As the battalion continued its rhythmic pounding along the sodden road, a stretcher bearer in one of the field ambulances watched the reinforcements gradually disappear into the mist and rain. On each of the man's battered sleeves blazed a red cross identifying his non-combative role. He was returning to the carnage of the Front, tiredly aware that the time was coming for these men. Oblivious to their onlooker in the ambulance, the battalion marched on, with the result that the unit's War Diary would record *No stragglers* that day.

As anticipated, the afternoon's matches engendered a spirited banter between the teams allowing them to freely let off steam, healthy for the men's camaraderie and morale. They were slated to compete in the Battalions Brigade Sports in a couple of days with some considerable sporting reputations at stake, that's if they were still here.

Jim's thoughts often drifted to the battles where his old schoolmates had been wounded. The 'push' Harry, Ted and Bill had been engaged in stretched across the French battlefront from Villers Brettoneux to Peronne, resulting in 21 officers and 194 other ranks being killed overall in those two months. The wounded, including Ted and Bill, consisted of 55 officers and 998 other ranks; 40% of the 3rd Division's wounded would not return to their units for another three months.

On 8 September, the four battalions advanced the Front Line approximately 12,000 yards easterly toward Canal du Nord, capturing 20 square miles of territory. The ruined villages retaken were Courcelles, Buire, Brusle, Tincourt, Bouchy, Hamel, Marquaix, Hervilly and notably, Roisel, with its entire railway junctions and road communications.

Now, ready for whatever was coming, Jim and the 9th Reos' waiting was almost over.

Not far away, in an officer's hall, under guard and safe from prying ears, the C.O. of the 11th Brigade gathered for that night's Battalion Conference, comprising Brigadier-General Cannan, the Lieutenant Colonels and Majors of the 41st - 44th Battalions and 3rd Pioneers. Major Dibdin represented the 41st Battalion while Brigadier-General Cannan held the floor, dominating the room as he revealed the hard-fought spoils.

War material captured included 92 machine guns and eight Howitzer guns with vast ammunition supplies. Also seized was a significant storage dump, including 35,000 coils of barbed wire, thousands of rolls of wire netting, picks and shovels with other tools, and approximately 80 transport wagons of many descriptions, including cookers and ambulance carts, all of which the fleeing enemy desperately attempted to incinerate, unsuccessfully.

Third Division's next push would extend between Vendhuille and Mt St Quentin to the old Front Line. This area would take in Bony, Claymore Valley, Gillemont Farm, Quenet Copse, Claymore Valley, Quennemont, Ronnssoy-Bellimont Road and most importantly, Mt St Quentin and the canal. Preparation had to be short, but the emphasis was on the fresh 9th Reinforcements being ready. Special Night Training Operations were tabled at least one night a week, with a practice advance arranged for 26 September between Courcelles and Bussu, on ground closely resembling the actual battleground itself. Aerial surveillance would relay for intelligence, with ten Mk IV tanks providing cover ahead of the advance as they deepened the Line.

Their advance would be in conjunction with the 27th American Division, with battalions moving into their positions by routes reconnoitred the night before. Routine Orders would be issued in the meantime, but Marching Orders were scheduled for 27 September, supplying the necessary routes and areas for the despatch of the reconnoitring parties. Otherwise, aerial intelligence would provide more traversable routes should the approach be unsuitable. Specialist training for the battalions was to begin immediately, and with that, the meeting concluded.

Short lectures were presented during smoko to prepare the men for their Friday night training operations, reminding them that the battalions would not be required to parade the following morning; Brigade sports would be held throughout the day instead.

As it happened, Saturday's enthusiastic sports resulted in Jim and the rest of the 41st Battalion letting out a mighty roar of triumph, having won the sporting tally on aggregate. The copious amounts of friendly yet spirited jibing between their rival battalions continued into the evening celebrated with a concert by the Australian entertainment troop, the 'Cooees'. At least for a while.

The light-hearted show was abruptly interrupted by the blaring siren warning of an imminent air raid. Caught in the searchlight, the enemy Albatros took a direct hit as the anti-aircraft guns trained on it sent the plane plummeting in a fiery stream.

In a sudden burst of sparks, the plane's flare supplies and coloured signal lights ignited in a vibrant cascade of colour hurtling towards the earth, a similar fate for several others of its squadron, as well as one of the British planes. With the excitement now having run its course and the risk of any further air raids averted, the concert resumed heartily as the satisfied men returned to their seats for the remainder of their uninterrupted evening.

Sunday morning's Church Parade was attended punctually, accompanied by a background quaver of 'Big Berthas'. These were the 16.5-inch Howitzers of Germany's heavy artillery in the distance, filling the air with their devastating thunder. The sound of their opposing presence continued tauntingly during the Battalion Parade Ceremony as medals were issued to the 20 men who had won distinctions at Amiens the month before.

In the following days, Jim and Ed found themselves hospitalised with gastroenteritis, the misfortune bringing its own surprise; a familiar voice calling Jim's name as Bill Mitchell put a broad hand on his shoulder. Bill and Ted had been in hospital recovering from shrapnel wounds received in the battle near Peronne, with Bill soon transferring out, leaving Ted to recuperate. As it happened, the three would be discharged together, although Bill's return to 'A' Company subsequently separated them when the fighting started. Harry would soon join Jim in 'B' Company on his return from the Front Line trenches, while Ernie remained behind in the Machine Gun Depot at Parkhouse, England, prompting pledges from all five to rendezvous when they could.

Meanwhile, Jim and Ed would join Norm Huddy and Bill Chapman, waiting to be Taken On Strength into 'B' Company by Sgt Duley before rejoining the battalion for Monday's 8-mile route march to Tincourt's battered village.

Norm was a sapper who had come over on the *Themistocles* in 1917. Trained in tunnelling and explosives, Norm was inspired by General Herbert Plumer's famous quote prior to the detonations of Messine Ridge in April 1917:

> *Gentlemen, we may not change history tomorrow, but we'll certainly change the geography.*

Under Plumer's orders, the tenacious sappers had tunnelled beneath the unsuspecting German Lines at Messines, setting explosives in such volume that the resulting blast instantly blew the top off the ridge immobilising approximately 10,000 Germans. The resounding explosion not only changed both history *and* the geography but was supposedly heard back in England.

Bill Chapman, a 25-year-old Scottish-born labourer from Perth, had enlisted a year before Norm. He had seen his share of action, having since recovered from a gunshot wound to his right thigh and, more recently, pneumonia. The 5-foot 8-inch soldier would later return to Australia on the *Zealandic* with his new English bride.

All five had watched the constant flow of casualties from the Front Line as they were stretchered into the nearby huts by the Field Ambulance orderlies through the Autumn rain. Every day, the maimed and unsavable were grim realities of what they were up against, with some days worse than others. Two more of their reinforcement mates had died of wounds in that time - Wally Norton and Johnny Herbert - their losses feeding the simmering resentment towards the Bosche, a bitterness which continued to embed itself all the more deeply through them all. As their bitterness grew, so did Jim's heightened awareness that he was ready to take on whatever evil he was about to contend with, both from the other side and from within.

Now, the four soldiers rejoined their battalion on parade in the cold September drizzle, receiving their orders that the route march would be fully packed under a weight of approximately 85 pounds and in complete marching order. All officers were also to march fully packed, with the only exception being mounted officers.

Barely audible, the lightest whisper spread unnoticed through the assembled battalion as Major Heron's voice carried clearly across the parade ground with their orders for this morning's battalion route march. Companies would proceed to Tincourt returning via Buire-Doingt in this order: Headquarters, 'A' Company, 'B' Company, 'C' Company, with 'D' Company as rear guard. Reports would be made to the head of the column. The only personnel to remain off-march would be Company Orderlies, two sanitary men and three cooks per company.

Eleven years older than Jim, Major Alexander Robert Heron had initially enlisted with the 27th Light Horse, now finding himself with a string of military honours to his name, including the Victoria Cross, commanding the 41st Battalion.

Within 20 minutes, the companies were re-assembled at their starting point. Their marching out state depicting the columns were ready to leave had been rendered to the Battalion Headquarters, and they were moving off to the marching tune, *Blazes Away*.

Distant bombardment of artillery fire and shelling continued to dominate the horizon as horse-drawn artillery 'limbers' cantered their way through to the Front on the adjacent roads. Ambulances negotiated their way back past engineers rebuilding the cratered roads sabotaged by the retreating Germans, repairs being made in earnest for the volume of oncoming traffic.

Keenly focused on keeping step, Jim strode through the pain emulating through his feet and ankles, which were prone to aching just as abysmally at night. As he marched, the orders Heron had announced on parade echoed in his mind. Halts would be regulated by Headquarters at the head of the column, while the companies maintained the strict marching discipline of 100 yards between Headquarters Company and each unit.

The Specialist Training night manoeuvres they had commenced in the past week involved 2 hours per session being spent in gas respirators, bringing the reality of the Front closer. Tomorrow night's training was for them all - Lewis gunners, signallers, stretcher bearers, runners and batmen; the lot. Their operations would include scouting and patrolling to prepare the men for the gruelling task ahead.

By day, the battalion practised rapid rifle loading and covering fire, trench warfare, gas training, and bearing and picket, otherwise known as B&P, entailing site markers to confirm the direction and accuracy of artillery targets. The B&P Card placed on the stake recorded the coordinates, height, bearings with drawings, and its general location on the map. Ultimately, the technique proved remarkably accurate as an artillery regiment on a theatre or divisional grid ranged large numbers of heavy artillery, firing simultaneously on the same target with devastating effect.

Visions of their training at Codford Bombing Range where they had followed the bearing and picket to destroy a long-range bunker, triggered a surge of adrenalin throughout the troops as they anticipated seeing their training soon being put to the test. The Officers' Conference tonight would hopefully deliver more specific plans tomorrow.

Monday, 23rd, saw the 41st Battalion awaken to again no word on their Marching Orders. Instead, the battalion left camp for a route-march to Bussu and Moislaines, returning via Mt Saint Quentin, a distance of over 10 miles, finishing with a routine foot inspection. Jim's feet had hardened with all the marching, overcoming any blisters he'd endured throughout the past 14 months, although he still needed to rub his calves at night to get the blood flowing through his aching muscles.

A conference was held later that night to discuss the day's work and preparations prior to their Marching Orders of the 27th. Tactical training would continue as per the syllabus, focusing on saluting, scouting-patrolling and formations, musketry rapid loading combined with bolt manipulating practice, platoon drill rifle exercises, and keeping touch and direction.

Jim's morning began with half an hour's Battalion Parade in the rain at the usual 08:30 am, followed by rifle exercises, gas training, bearing and picket, finishing with Platoon Drill. Their training continued daily until the men heard the words they had been waiting for; *Marching Orders*. Today was 27 September, and they were good to go.

Lieut. John Grant Smith addressed the expectant companies accompanied by the padre, who would, in turn, preside over those who would be buried on the battlefield in the coming days, both those of the 41st Battalion and others. Smith was known for the skilful handling of his troops, having displayed tenacious bravery during the battle of Hamel as Officer in Charge (O.C.) of his platoon. His Company Commander had been wounded, resulting in Smith taking command and successfully capturing the enemy's position, including three machine guns and several unlucky prisoners.

During his next stint at the battle of Herricourt, Smith's bravery and skill in command saw the capture of all their objectives with an additional five machine guns and 70 prisoners. A natural leader, the man was an inspiration to his men in the heat of battle.

Today, on their call to the battle lines, Smith would lead them. Their objective, the ultimate mission:

Capture the Hindenburg Line.

It was heavily fortified by German defence and machine gun posts that were about to become the enemy's last stand. The men presented in complete fighting order with steel helmets and entrenching tools as clouds rolled in over the battlefront ahead; a formidable vision of valour born as the fire ignited within them.

This afternoon, they were moving out at 5:00 pm on the Moulin Rouge-Hamel-Marquaix Northern Road, then guided on a more traversable route once reaching the newly retaken Front Line ruins of Roisel. Here, the companies would bivouac the night in banks with Battalion Head Quarters. Smith explained their orders.

On the morning of 29 September at 5:00 am, the 27th and 30th U.S. Divisions were expected to breach the Hindenburg Line and capture the Green Line.

Third Division would be positioned on the left, the 5th on the right, taking the new ground all the way to the distant Red Line. In conjunction with the divisions, the 11th Brigade and the 10th Brigades would capture and mop up the divisional area, signalling their progress by launching Verey Light flares accordingly:

2 Greens each from 'D' and 'B' Companies -"I have captured Beaurevoir Line."

2 Reds from 'A' and 'C' Companies -"I have captured Red Line."

2 Greens from 'D' Company - "I have mopped up Battalion Area in Beaurevoir".

Four tanks were allotted to the 41st Battalion to capture the Beaurevoir Line, four to take the Red Line and two more to seize Knoll 135 before moving south of Beaurevoir. Whippet Tanks would operate with 'A' Company and fly a green flag with the identifying number of its Section to avoid being mistaken for enemy tanks. When flying a tricolour flag, the tanks would be returning to refill; if broken down, a diagonal flag of yellow and red would fly.

From the air, 15th Wing R.A.F. would drop smoke bombs as cover, preventing enemy observation from higher ground of their advance to the Green Line. For identification, the planes of the 3rd Squadron were painted with black panels on the underbelly 3 feet from the fuselage, its role being contact, counter-attack and dropping smoke bombs.

Alternatively, the planes of the 8th Squadron were identified by black bands on the underside of the tail and would coordinate with the tanks, reporting their locations and progress while disabling enemy anti-tank guns with machine gun fire and bombs. All runners would show any messages from the Front to all batteries they pass through and remove all signs once a battalion had left the area. Battalion Orders specifying their task would then be provided once the area was reconnoitred. This was just the beginning.

Troops were reminded that the Continental Time system would be initiated tomorrow night at midnight, with AM/PM replaced with 24-Hour time being four complete figures. Instead of 1210 am, it will be 0010 hours, 3:25 pm will be 1525 hours, and Noon will be 1200 hours. The time for midnight will now be either 2359 hours or 0001 hours. Having been instructed, the troops were mindful of adopting this new time system, although it should not affect most of them while laying some Bosche low.

With that, the column, complete with their cooks, began their march to the battle lines. Passing their starting point at 7:15 pm, the keyed men moved off fluidly from Boignt in their 8 ½-mile approach march via the Tincourt-Hamel-Marquaix Crossroads at Roisel.

Vastly congested limbers, trucks, and ambulances at Hamel significantly disturbed the column's order, holding up their progress until finally reaching Roisel, where they were met by the reconnoitring party to guide them to the reserve trenches. Miraculously, the congestion dissipated, allowing the traffic to pass steadily and the men to continue their light-hearted march to the Front Line 3 miles ahead. They were in good spirits. This was their day, and they were ready.

During one of their ten-minute halts, another German plane 'buzzed' them closely in its endeavour to bomb them, though completely missing its mark to hit some unfortunate mules instead.

Finally, after entering the complex trench system and following the 41st Battalion light signs - fuel cans with '41' punctured into each side - the companies reached their bivouacs, little more than earthen bunks in the walls of the sandbagged trenches. Surrounding them were the skeletal remains of the forest, mute witnesses to the food carriers bringing hot tea later at midnight.

Jim and Harry were in position with 'B' Company out on the left, immediately behind the 27th American Division. In the moments of ensuing silence, the two mates reached out and shook hands in a way neither of them could remember having done in all their years as mates, their bond seeing them side by side even in war.

Their mothers were convinced they could get themselves in and out of trouble together, so these next days, or even hours, would reveal whatever truth their words held.

RETURNED WITH A CREED — 55

Codford Training Camp Bombing Range. AWM P01688.015.009.

29 September 1918. Australian sergeants seek instruction prior to
the offensive against the Hindenburg Line. AWM E03392.

30 September 1918. Australian reinforcements marching to the Front Line near Bellicourt. AWM E03513.

1 October 1918. Australian infantry passing along a sap towards Guillemont Farm during the Hindenburg offensive. AWM E03418.

Harry Larsen 3589, Fovant 1918. From personal collection.

CHAPTER 5

Battle of the Hindenburg Line

This was a God-awful place where the American dead lay in deep, grotesque piles, and the wounded desperately attempted to drag themselves to shelter; utterly God-awful.

Bodies of 27th American Dvn troops laid out for burial after heavy losses at the Hindenburg Line 29 September 1918. AWM E04942C.

IT WAS AFTER MIDNIGHT ON 28 September 1918, and a shell was coming.

The realisation of it dawned only seconds before the mustard gas shell landed against the wall in the trench, exploding into a cloud of onion-smelling yellow gas. 'B' Company, under Lieut. George Sidney Dodds' command immediately scrambled to engage masks. From 1:00 am, the night became bombarded with the intermittent shelling of these lethal exploding canisters, instilling their own form of terror at the very thought of the creeping acid burning the eyes, throat and lungs and blistering the skin before its poisonous smell could be even vaguely detected.

Jim and Harry had acted swiftly, although the evil vapours already swirled eerily around them. The baptism of fire began, observed by a number of rats scurrying along the parapet to drop stealthily into the trench, seeking shelter in its hidden crannies.

Still more 10.5 cm shells dropped out of the darkness along the entire length of the trenches, continuing intermittently until 5:00 am. Under this heavy concentration of gas, the stoic troops remained fully masked throughout the night, the apprehension and restricting apparatus preventing any remote prospect of sleep.

Casualties remained surprisingly low from what they observed, except for one officer who had copped the full brunt of the gas with the shell having landed at his feet. In the least time, he was writhing in pain, his eyes and throat on fire from the choking gas as a medic in a respirator appeared swiftly to lead him away into the gloom with a wet towel covering his rapidly blistering face and eyes.

German planes persisted in their night raids, combining with long-range shells targeting the rear to immobilise the support lines positioned there. The real possibility remained that smoke from the kitchen fires may have unintentionally flagged their locations.

Reveille and a welcome breakfast of porridge and hot tea arrived at 5:30 am. Cooks carrying the canvas pack of dixies and tea on their backs dispensed the meals among the bleary-eyed troops as respirators were gratefully removed after an intense night of laboured breathing.

Half an hour later, a party of the officers and Non-Commissioned Commanders (N.C.C.) began a forward reconnaissance, some proceeding as far as Benjamin's Post amongst the American Line in an attempt to strengthen their meagre knowledge of the sector.

According to the maps, there was a discrepancy in their position. The American Front Line had been mistakenly defined as nearer to the Catelet Post-Benjamin Post Sector than the Gillemont Farm-Quennemont Farm system. On the strength of this revelation, new Brigade and Battalion Orders were issued later that morning in conjunction with the revised battle plan and in collaboration with all officers, tank officers included.

The 41st Battalion would be positioned in the left front of the four battalions comprising the 11th Brigade and flanked by the 38th Battalion. They would utilise the success of the American Division out in front to ultimately reach the Green Line by the various points respectively, advancing strategically at 11:00 am from the Green Line to the Red Line.

Their initial advance was to be made in a line of platoons with instructions not to participate in the fight for the Green Line. Instead, they were to await further orders on their arrival, maximising their advantage with the four tanks, two trench mortars, four machine guns and 8mm field artillery. With their new orders now in place, the men were equipped and supplied with full rations during the afternoon.

29 September 1918

Reveille at 0530 hours preceded a breakfast of pork and beans ahead of the oncoming thunder of guns that was about to unleash at 0600 hours. They had rested well through the night without the constant threat of gas shells, although a considerable amount of gas was still lying out in the gully. Along the Line, Jim, Harry and the others were nervously alert and never more battle-ready, adrenaline coursing through them as they waited...*and* waited. Although Harry had shared his 'baptism of fire' with Bill at Peronne in August, today was no less harrowing.

Thoughts of home crept into every mind along the Line while a shuffling movement nearby caught the immediate attention of others. Several heads turned to discover one of the officers making his way through, issuing rum allocations to calm the hotbed of fraying nerves.

Under the tails of 8th Squadron's Sopwith Camels were the identifying markings of their black bands, making them clearly recognisable in the brightening morning. As intended, their surveillance disguised the approaching hum of the Mark IV and Whippet Tanks.

Rum rations were just settling in the stomachs of a thousand adrenaline-charged men when, precisely at 0600 hours, the Australian barrage opened up like hell itself. A torrent of shells and earth rained down ahead of the advancing Americans, and the percussion of the exploding shellfire beat against the men's chests and bodies as if it were a solid wall penetrating their very being. The creeping barrage of shells covered 2,000-3,000 yards along a Front spanning several miles, with an 18-pounder battery to every 25 yards, silencing all else. Among those rendered inaudible were many larger guns, hundreds of machine guns and innumerable Lewis guns.

Bracing themselves against the trench walls as the ground shook around them, they watched the 800-American line move ever forward through the battle scene of fire, skeletal trees, and barbed wire silhouetted through the smoky morning, an unforgettable, haunting vision.

At 0715 hours, the bombardment finally ceased. Jim and Harry gave each other a reassuring nod and waited with 'B' Company assembled in the N.W.-S.E. Line. This was their turn.

Their objective moving forward from the trenches at 0730 hours, was to reach the Green Line at 0900 hours. Here, they hoped to get in touch with the 38th Battalion positioned to their left. They would then proceed to take the Hindenburg Line, 3 miles away, between Vendhuille and St Quentin - 3 miles of death.

On the order, 'B' Company climbed over the parapet, plodding through the debris and littered shell cases, their advance assured as the seven brigades of field artillery pushed along the four marked roads, led by their tanks. Although they were not the first 'over the top', they had every confidence in the 'Yanks' capturing the outer trenches of the German trench system.

Distant planes put down the smoke screen ordered ahead of their approach as Lieut. Smith observed the troops moving toward the heavy machine gun fire. The morning mist grew denser, adding to the low visibility from mustard gas and smoke lying throughout the gully. The poisonous fumes surrounding them forced the men to keep their gas masks on, hampering their advance enormously.

On crossing the gully to the foot of the slope towards Benjamins Post Trench system, they could hear the enemy machine gunfire fiercely engaged, its rounds peppering the earth around Jim and the approaching troops. Lieuts. Smith and Dodds, with hundreds of others, pushed on through the fog and gas amid their growing concerns that the Americans had neglected to 'mop up' the Green Line once captured. Their fears were soon realised.

As suspected, the Americans had overlooked clearing out the bunkers containing hundreds of Germans safely hidden within their tunnels. Instead, the inexperienced troops had moved out in front to pursue the Red Line, a grave mistake with catastrophic consequences.

Eight hundred American troops had moved forward of the German trench system, only to be mowed down within 15 minutes by an enemy swarming from the bunkers behind them. The screams of the Americans being slaughtered in the fog beyond their reach were drowned out by the relentless firing of the enemy's machine guns.

The 41st Battalion's advance took them 2,000 yards to Benjamins Post Trench system through unyielding bombardment and artillery fire under the orders not to become involved in the fight for the present but to wait for further orders.

Calls of *Stretcher bearer!* were heard amid the chaos with a couple of the tanks now clearly broken down. One was on fire with its men desperately trying to escape, only to be engulfed by the flames. The tank had struck a Plum Pudding bomb, which stalled it, rendering it a helpless target for the unrelenting heavy artillery fire.

Unbeknown to Jim, Harry was struck in the left shoulder by a gunshot, followed similarly by Lieut. Brewer a short distance away but dying where he fell. Harry was evacuated to the remains of a farm building being used as a field hospital before his transfer by the 9th Field Ambulance to the 37th Casualty Clearing Station. He would spend the next three weeks convalescing in the hospitals at Etretat and Le Havre.

Presently drifting in and out of consciousness like a bad dream, Harry could hear the active enemy machine guns from the opposite ridge making progress for his mates painfully difficult, especially out on the left front along the Ronnssoy-Bellimont Road and Claymore Valley Trench systems. Here, men were dropping sporadically under the heavy artillery barrage. This, along with machine guns and snipers, made it impossible to advance according to the plan. Tanks had reached the crest further out on the right, maintaining contact with the 41st, although the southern advance was much less disrupted than the northern.

By 1050 hours, Jim and 'B' Company had reached the ridge, with the further loss of Lieut. McHauley, who was wounded, the battalion having suffered heavy casualties, including the fallen Lieut. Brewer. Jim had lost sight of Harry in the fog near Benjamin's Post but learned later that he had been hit and stretchered out.

Lieut. Flannery reported to D.I.G.A. by Runner:

From 41st Btn

Have reached ridge A26B23. Lieut McHauley wounded. Lieut Brewer killed. Heavy casualties. In charge of 1 & 3 Platoons. No contact from/ on either flank. Tank Commander PJ reports strong M.G. positions 250y in front. Tanks attacked and 5 knocked out. Casual advance. Enemy live at 27A intact. Am returning to get touch with flanks.

Flannery Lieut
10:50 am

Strong enemy machine gun positions held fast directly in front, and five stonkered tanks, disabled early in the engagement, loomed defencelessly in the obstructing fog, resulting in a disconnected advance towards a firmly intact enemy. Rations were short, but the battalion was at last in touch throughout the four companies, sheltering in whatever cover and shell holes they could reach, awaiting further instructions.

Mud and warm blood sprayed the troops as bullets from the heavy gun and artillery fire rained down on them, kicking up the earth around their cover. The carnage from the enemy's gunfire continued for the most prolonged time, making it clear that the Front Line had to be retaken with the doomed Americans still out in front.

Observation of the attack's progress was impossible owing to the thickening mist and increasing numbers of gas shells bombarding them, and as midday approached, Lieut. Carruthers of 'B' Company reported their position:

To 41st Btn

Am still at F24 lower square 50.60. In touch with 38th Btn. In touch to rear with 42nd Btn. Casualties 2 killed 2 wounded (walking) 10, Officer Clark gassed. Some shell gas is being sent over/around us.

Lieut Carruthers B Coy
11:10 pm
[As in message have had no word from front or rear. Some Boche on Ridge to our left front before BONY.]

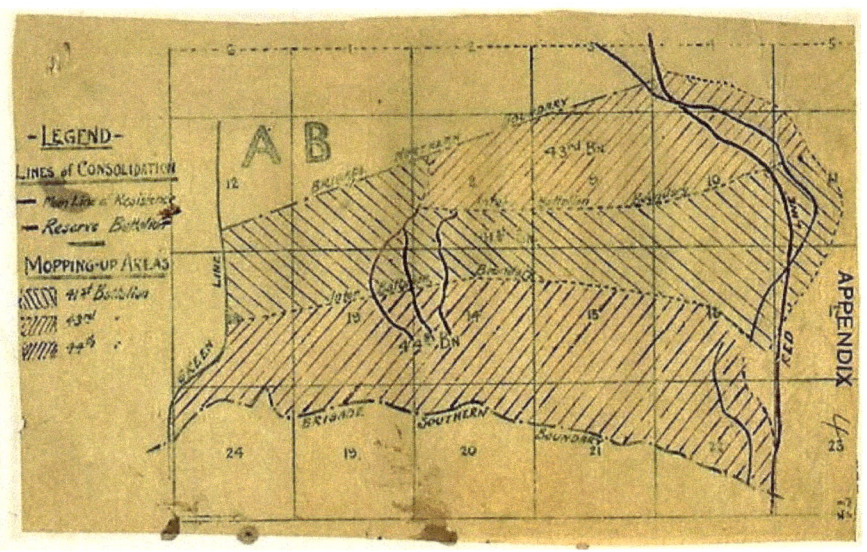

Battle lines for the 41st, 43rd and 44th Battalions. 29 September 1918. AWM RCDIG1004546.

Pockets of fog and gas gradually lifted to reveal the shocking carnage of hundreds of American soldiers lying butchered wherever Jim looked. The chilling sight was evidence that they would have to push on through this wave of death in their advance to the main trench of the Hindenburg Line with its maze of storerooms and fortresses.

Their tense waiting continued as more Americans began to materialise, staggering through the bloodbath in small groups. They reported being overwhelmingly repulsed at the Gillemonte-Quennemont Line, with mass casualties rendering them helplessly disorganised.

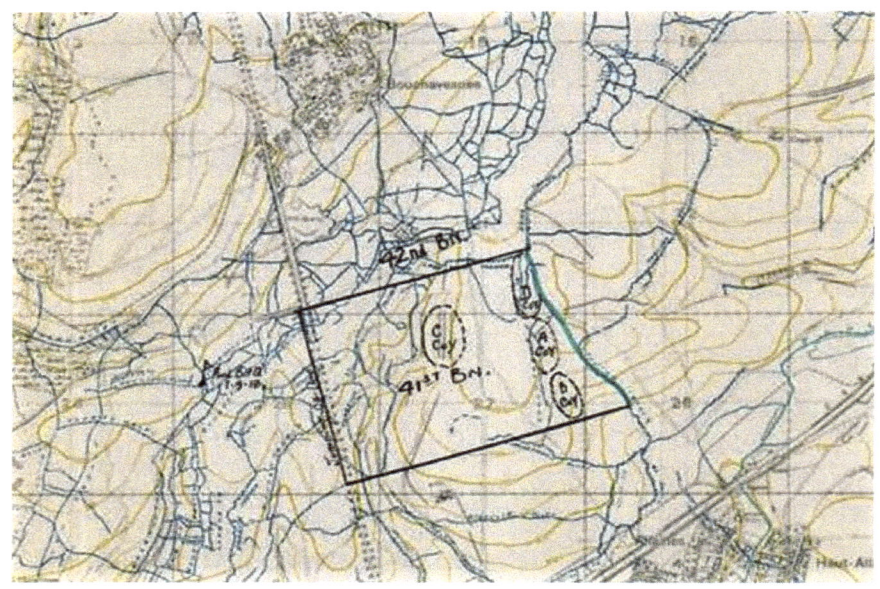

Positions of the 41st Battalion's A, B, C and D Companies during the Battle of the Hindenburg Line. Jim was in B Company. The 27th American Division made it to the Green Line but neglected to mop up causing severe losses to the Americans. AWM RCDIG1004547.

Lieut. Flannery was ordered to send patrols to reconnoitre the machine gun positions and snipers surrounding them before sending the battalion forward, however bad the cover of their positions. In response, the Bosche ahead of Bony kept up a brisk, relentless fire from the ridge to Jim's company's left front, causing many casualties among the patrols.

One platoon advanced to Quennet Copse and began working along the trench towards the enemy, only to be met with vigorous bombing resistance. Here, the extent of heavy barbed wire obstacles also rendered the trench impassable. The battalion only moved about 200 yards forward, with the fire from enemy machine guns and snipers proving too strong to overcome in daylight without artillery assistance.

One Lewis gunner climbed out of the trench and, firing from the hip, swept the enemy machine gun positions with gunfire only to be shot through the head by an enemy sniper. Shortly after, Lieut. Dodds stood up, gathered his men and moved forward, only to meet his end in the same way. The casualties from the morning just kept coming...nine officers and 80 other ranks so far.

On the left, the 38th Battalion faced similar conditions. The order came to postpone the advance temporarily against an enemy which appeared to have taken every measure possible to debilitate the protective advance of the tanks.

German prisoners were being taken systematically and escorted to prison cages located further behind the Lines. During a routine interrogation, one of the prisoners stated his field battery had special orders to deal with tanks: 77 mm guns, anti-tank rifles, light trench mortars and machine guns. All were using armour-piercing bullets and every last one was being used against them. The following urgent order rallying the Field was issued by the 11th Brigade at 1340 hours:

PRIORITY

Aeroplanes report flares lit on green Line East of GOUY ST, MARTIN and NAUROY. Appears Americans have made green Line but have not mopped up. 3rd Aust Div will advance to green Line. 44th advance on right. 41st advance on left. 43rd close support. 42nd reserve. No Tanks available. All Americans in vicinity and those overtaken will be absorbed by Btns. Corporate with flanks. Move immediately.

From 11 Bde 1:40 pm

During the afternoon, following the Commanding Officer's (C.O.) instructions, all surviving Americans of the 27th Division (about 100 men, including a 1-pound gun team) had fallen back to 'B' Company's position. Twenty of them were absorbed by the company, with the remainder subsequently merged with the other companies, swelling the battalion numbers.

While this was undertaken, the company took shelter in hastily dug positions, shell holes and whatever else was available. Lieut. Lawson left his cover endeavouring to save the company sergeant, lying in an exposed position some 70 yards in front, but was instantly killed by a heavy shell that exploded near him.

Sgt. Galloper, who was further along the trench, scribbled an urgent despatch to Headquarters advising that U.S. troops were holding Claymore Trench but could not be reached in daylight due to sniper activity and machine gun fire along the front and from Bony.

Galloper's report read:

To 11th Bde

Patrols from my left Coy report U.S. Troops holding CLAYMORE TRENCH. They cannot be reached in daylight. Any movement on our front draws sniping shots and M.G. fire from Trench system in front and from direction of BONY. We hold. QUENNOT COPSE. In trench on both flanks and to rear. Tank report. FLANNERY did not withdraw as stated in report. This practically means I have no working tanks at present.

From 41st Btn 1:30 pm
B Galloper

With orders now received, they were to advance and clear up the enemy fire on their left towards Bony. All four companies, 'A', 'B', 'C' and 'D', moved forward and captured the hostile battle positions under intense heavy artillery fire and shelling, as fierce fighting ensued.

Around 0600 hours, at great sacrifice, the troops re-occupied Trollop and Triangle Trenches, Quennet Copse and only a small part of

Guillemont Trench. The men isolated out on the left by sweeping gunfire were obliged to remain at the Scarp in the miserable rain. These were the outer trenches of the main Hindenburg Line, the trenches the Americans had not cleared on their way through upon reaching the Green Line.

At nightfall, an effort to get into Guillemont Trench was successful with the result of the isolated platoon now re-established, numbers of Boche killed and five machine guns captured. It was the most extensive trench for even the most seasoned men: 12 ft wide and 12 ft deep.

On the back of this success, a Company Commanders' Conference was held at 0830 hours, and it was decided to attempt capturing the entire trench system the following day. Firstly, though, hot meals and rations would be distributed among the troops around midnight.

Later into the night, the whole battalion crept silently into the darkness and rain, moving ever more closely to the seemingly indomitable main Hindenburg Line Trench before positioning themselves for the morning's attack. They had not received any water with their rations and badly needed it.

Lying in the boggy, putrid shell hole, waiting for the morning's advance, Jim's thoughts briefly returned to home and the typical morning he imagined them enjoying. It was Tuesday there, with the scent of flowering bottlebrush filling the warm air, Spring nests, new calves...*laughter*.

In stark contrast, the rain continued to fall ceaselessly through the drawn-out night, as did heavy shells directed at the weary Australians, blasting the landscape in and around the shell holes where they sheltered. This was a God-awful place where the American dead lay in deep, grotesque piles, and the wounded desperately attempted to drag themselves to shelter...utterly God-awful.

* * *

30 September 1918

The 11th Brigade's Line ran from Top Lane on the western boundary to Road Junction linking with Stave Trench on the eastern boundary. The 11th intended to capture the Hindenburg Line in the morning, continuing its northerly attack from the east and west grid line. This action saw the 41st Battalion in the frontal attack, securing this sector by mopping up in an easterly direction between the grids.

Now, with only rations for a meal and the meagre amount of water left in their canteens, they remained ready. They *had* to be.

At 0600 hours, the Australian bombardment split the morning with its thunderous war cry as the creeping barrage moved forward at a rate of 100 yards every 5 minutes for the first 15-minute half. Behind its cover, advancing in one formidable line, was the mass of the 41st, 42nd, 43rd and 44th Battalions' troops as far as Jim's eye could see. Cloaked by the solid shockwave of the sound itself, he felt as if he were a physical part of a moving monolith. He did not 'hear' noise so much as he felt its density swallow him whole.

Under orders received the night before, the battalion successfully took the whole sector, engaging no resistance from the enemy except for a few bursts of machine gun fire at long range. In their hasty evacuation during the Australian assault, the Germans abandoned some of their wounded, who were later aided by the Allies.

Successfully capturing the Line yielded 28 machine guns (light and heavy), one 77mm gun and one anti-tank rifle, besides large numbers of rifles and two of their own Lewis guns, which the enemy had used against them during the initial stages of the attack. The battalion was then re-organised, and Jim's 'B' Company proceeded with its orders to mop up Stave and Claymore Trenches, accomplishing contact all round after establishing posts in Claymore Trench by as early as 0900 hours with no casualties.

At 0950 hours, Lieut. Grant Smith sent his despatch to *DIGA*:

Trench systems in A19a are mopped up and Posts are established.

In touch left Flank with 38th Bn right Flank with D Coy. In touch with Reserve Coy and also with forward H.Q. Stn by Lamp.

No Casualties this morning. Detailed casualty state herewith. We did not get any water last night and want some.

Coy HQs A19.a.30.60
Grant Smith Lt
'B' Coy
9.50 am

Troops were on the lookout for traps set by the Germans, evidence which Bill's 'A' Company had encountered while seizing numerous machine guns and anti-tank rifles in their sector of the captured trench. Additionally, many useful German maps were conveniently souvenired. Bill did not make it to 'A' Company's section of the trench, though, having taken another burst of shrapnel to his leg and stretchered to the same abandoned farm ruin as Harry for transfer by field ambulance.

Word finally arrived at 'B' Company that not only was their own artillery continuing to force the Germans into retreat, but the French had also now captured the western end of the sector. Adrenaline from this magnificent Australian and American conquest vastly empowered the troops. The Allies had *captured* the main Hindenburg Line.

The 42nd Battalion reported action in the Hindenburg back system where their patrol encountered parties of Germans, resulting in one of their own being captured, although 'C' Company worked progressively along Bony Avenue with little resistance.

Lieut. Secombe sent out a reconnoitring patrol in conjunction with Jim's 'B' Company at 2000 hours, joining patrols going out 2-hourly to patrol right to left, as did the 33rd Battalion, who also patrolled their immediate right.

Lieut. Heron issued his despatch to Lieut. Wood that the 41st Battalion was in position on the left flank from Stave Trench system to Paul Trench, with three companies in the foremost trench in the shadow of their operating tanks. There was no sign of the 34th Battalion. At this point, Heron requested hot tea for the men while Lieut. Smith, temporarily in Company H.Q., despatched a Situation Report, a 'sitrep', to 'B' Company revealing the current positions:

1st Oct 1918
TO: 'B' Coy
Normal.

No Enemy activity except for intermittent shelling with some East chiefly directed against our left rear. Our Patrols went out at 8pm-10pm-12midnight and discontinued on 34th Btn going out at 1:30 pm to establish Observation Posts towards BONY. Patrol Report Attached.

X

X   34th Out Posts
CLAYMORE TR
38th Btn   ~~~~~~~~~~~~~~~~~~~~~~~~~~~   'A' Coy
*   S ʃ   'B'   Coy   41st Btn*
*   T ʃ   No 6   No 5   No 8*
*   A ʃ   Platoon   Platoon*
*   V ʃ*
*   E ʃ~~~~~~~~X~~~~~~~~~~~~~~~~   'C' Coy*
34th Btn in advance at 1:30 am   Coy HQrs
*   ◊ <-<-<-<-   GRID*
6:30 am
Smith Lieut
O/C MB Coy HQrs

Illustration drawn by Lieut. Smith at 6:30 am on 1 October 1918 during the battle of the Hindenburg Line. AWM Appendix 582 of RCDIG1004547.

Still more heavy rain fell unabated throughout the night into the early morning of 1st October while Jim's 'B' Company enjoyed gratifying sleep in the dry German dugouts, waking only to exchange with those on patrol as they returned. During the following fine, cool day, the company rested and cleaned up after being issued dry socks, good meals, and replenishing all battle stores.

Patrolling the newly captured Front, Jim was amazed at the sheer size of the main Hindenburg Line with its concrete system of trenches and dugouts. Hell, the timbers in its construction alone were 2 feet square. It was immense.

Until now, the barges in the St Quentin Canal tunnel had billeted hundreds of Germans safely at any given time, with those now remaining futilely endeavouring to 'hole up' in its diminishing safe harbour. As he patrolled, Jim could hear the nearby gunfire and shell blasts at the canal, which was currently being cleared of those desperate pockets of the enemy that remained within its shelter. Other than that, there was significantly less shelling with only periodic shots directed at the nearby roads and crossroads - none of this underachieving enemy fire essentially caused the 41st Battalion any concern.

Stories began to circulate of body parts of German soldiers being used in the German cooking pots to feed their troops. Many would not believe a word of it, not having borne witness to the results of bomb blasts. Anything airborne was bound to inadvertently land in a cooking pot at some time, but those insisting on the notion were not ones to let the truth get in the way of a good yarn.

While morning patrols were busy, Lieut. Park despatched his sitrep to Lieut. Heron:

To: C.O. 41st Btn, 34th - Confirming telephone message.

Captain Peters BONY AVENUE report timed 9:15am that Lieut Horden and a Sgt of the 3rd Pioneer Btn had not returned from BONY. They had gone up DIRK VALLEY-LE CATELET ROAD

> *North East to the outskirts of BONY going through the cover which they forward. Badly damaged by our fire.*
>
> *They reached the first house – no enemy movement was observed and no Machine Gunfire. They were not interfered with in any way. They then returned along BONY AVENUE and requested to Capt PETERS at 14C63 at time above mentioned. I am pushing Capt. PETERS' Coy to BONY and will replace his Coy in BONY AVENUE by 'B' Coy. Lieut O'DONNELL who will support Capt PETERS if necessary.*
>
> *Parke, Lieut 9:38am*

All around Jim, the grave parties went about their gruesome task of collecting the vast numbers of American and Australian dead, removing their paybooks and identification for replacing with identifying tags for burial. Once recorded and buried in this temporary location, they would be presided over by the padre and left safely resting, pending re-interring in a formally consecrated location when time permitted. Unless further heavy fighting returned, they could lay securely identified in readiness for that day.

Tens of thousands of others had lain peacefully only to be churned into oblivion as battles raged back and forth over relinquished territory, including their graves. The Tomb of the Unknown Soldier and commemorative monuments would later bear homage to their memory, their bones forever belonging to 'no known grave'.

Private Verdi Schwinghammer's entries of the 42nd Battalion detailed the shattering account of 29 September 1918 at the Battle of the Hindenburg Line:

> *That night we advanced in the pitch darkness to near the Front Line and lay down in shell holes in Company of hundreds of dead Soldiers. The dead Americans were piled feet deep here. It was raining heavily and we experienced a terrible night and I thought we would never see morning. Shells were falling thick amongst us and we were covered*

with dirt from the shells as they exploded in the mud. We lost a great number, wounded and killed, that night.

The German bunkers were well kitted out, even powered in some localised areas with one of the most remarkable luxuries being a single bed and bedside lamp in an officer's quarters. Souveniring was greatly indulged by the more seasoned soldiers over the next 24 hours, while others were left sickened by the notion.

After considerable time, Jim and his exhausted platoon Fell In with the others in their respective companies at 1700 hours on 2 October 1918. In their immeasurable exhaustion, it could easily have been a month rather than days since they had filled these forsaken trenches to finish the job upon them.

Passing the yellow flags of the latrines, the men filed unhurriedly through the evacuation lines as they exited the trenches in withdrawal to the old bivouacs where they would gratefully find hot meals waiting for them. Along the way, the runners ('scamperers' as they were typically known) were lighting the 41st Battalion's light signs positioned beside the battalion's colours flying from a pipe lodged in the trench wall.

Simultaneously snaking throughout the separate one-way sector of the ingenious trench system, newly arrived reinforcements from the Back Lines, including Ted, made their way to the Front, where they took their positions, relieving the weary troops.

Lieut. Heron later noted that one of the thoughts filling the fatigued minds of the retiring men was receiving a hot meal…but more imminently, the waiting train that would deliver them to the Back Lines at Warlus.

Allied tanks and infantry troops preparing for action near Bellicourt. AWM H12514.

A captured German concrete dugout in the Hindenburg defences near Bony. AWM E03591.

Allied soldiers at the entrance to the St Quentin Canal near St Quentin. AWM H15944.

Australian Graves Detachment at the Hindenburg Line. AWM P04541.001.

CHAPTER 6

Warlus

No amount of sporting camaraderie could mask the change in the atmosphere, though - trouble was looming.

29 September 1918 Australian engineers repairing the sabotaged Corduroy Track to Bellicourt. AWM E03630.

BY 0800 HOURS, THE 41st BATTALION had risen to Reveille, washed and shaved in time to assemble for a hot breakfast of porridge and pork with beans, washed down nicely with hot tea. Today, 3 October, they would march approximately one mile in platoons, from Hargicourt to Templeux le Guerard, where they would remain until the morning of the 5th in shelters they were to yet build on their arrival.

Doggedly trudging along the muddy, potholed road, the bedraggled columns of men passed the wreckage of limbers with their noble teams of horses, silent in death, and trees mere remnants of themselves amongst the moonscaped region.

Arriving in a comparably short time for such a gruelling route march, Jim and the troops welcomed the wholesome distraction of erecting the timber frames and panels that would house them while waiting to board the light train for the deeper echelons of the Back Lines.

Templeux was in ruins, the destroyed village shattered by unrelenting bombardment while being retaken by the Allies two weeks earlier. Between a nearby stone house and the train station lay the village's Communal Cemetery, presently the site of sombre activity as another Graves Detachment prepared more graves for the dead still being retrieved from the rubble. In time, like so many other villages, Templeux's abundant outskirts would accommodate the consecrated ground for the vast numbers of those yet to be re-interred.

A tan brick two-storey building with its steeply pitched roof remained miraculously untouched. Painted in white capitals on a blood-red background high on the side of the building was the name of the village: TEMPLEUX. The church's wrought iron gate hung forlornly against a once thriving private hedge, now aesthetically embellishing the ruins of the once charming chapel behind it. The roof was caved, typical of every other building in the village, leaving only the bare, skeletal remains of these torn and crumbling vestiges.

During their two days at Templeux, the men managed to build sufficient shelters, as well as latrines, officers' and mess huts to house the swelling numbers of troops as the Front Line encroached ever forward through relinquished enemy territory.

There, in the earthy damp of the drizzly Autumn morning, the distant skies brought an engaging display of three Sopwiths on aerial surveillance, taking masterful control above the broken countryside. Clouds of smoke sporadically studded the grey sky as German artillery failed to 'down' the skilfully elusive biplanes.

An eventful hour later, 'B' Company Fell In amidst the 41st Battalion awaiting their return march to Hargicourt, where they entrained for Peronne en route to Airaines. During their march through the sparse French pastures to Hargicourt, up to 60 artillery horses could be seen casually grazing where they were left to spell unmolested between battles. Miraculously, the horses remained within a short distance of the Front Line's rear camps, roaming freely through the fresh regrowth.

It was 5 October, and what the men were about to see from the train windows during their journey would empower them. Lieut. Heron reported later in the battalion's October Summary of watching the men's interest spark as they comprehended what they were looking at the further they travelled. His report reflected his empathy for the troops:

> *On the 5th we travelled by light railway to Peronne and from there by rail to ARRAINES. (sic) A most interesting trip, the first 4 hours of which were through territory we had helped to capture via CHAULNES and VILLERS BRETTONEUX, and as the men recognised their old camping grounds in the early stages of the great offensive, naturally great interest was created.*

Peronne had seen brutal fighting at the beginning of September, where numbers of the 9th Reinforcements had been killed among volumes of others. This was Ted, Harry and Bill's 'baptism of fire' and where Jim's brother-in-law, Steve, was wounded.

The troops now observed the transformation of a peaceful Peronne safely back in allied hands. And it did not stop there. The route was taking them through the shattered ruins of Chaulnes, Rosieres a Santerre and Amiens, villages that had been under enemy control until very recently. Cheers and howls from the jubilant men peeled spontaneously through the carriages as they passed through mile after mile of the rolling, devastated countryside. The further they travelled, the more the troops began to grasp the enormity of their advance since 8 August...it was staggering. For some, the emotion was overwhelming.

Testimony to the onslaught, the desolate ruins of Lamotte-Warfusee's formerly alluring church, now blended with the endless others destroyed, prompting the realisation as they neared Villers Brettoneux that this had been their Front Line only weeks before.

Villagers in Villers Brettoneux and its surrounding farms, where encouraging numbers of townsfolk were back in their homes, hailed the triumphant troops as the train clattered onwards. Appearing in doorways of the rubble-strewn buildings came people of all ages joyously calling out *Merci!, Au Revoir!*, with the men onboard replying equally as enthusiastically.

Approaching Amiens, villagers along the way had also made their way back into their homes in an attempt to rebuild their shattered world. Pausing in the process of whatever they were doing, they waved and cheered the passing troop train, with the jubilant troops waving back heartily in the promise of a new life ahead for France.

When the locomotive finally chugged to a halt at Airaines, the men disembarked, ready for their 3-mile march to Warlus and their awaiting billets. Every officer had been given a bed, and the men were assigned to cots with mattresses padded with plenty of straw. The battalion's Mess, located in a local chateau, also offered plenty of fresh meats, fruits, and vegetables to be enjoyed daily; odds were good for a pleasant stay.

Focus was also applied to the constant vying of the men's competitive spirits by introducing Billet, Guard, Cooker and Platoon Competitions. In even more good-natured rivalry, the Rifle Range conducted shooting competitions, with one of the matches held by the Army Rifle Association (A.R.A.) scouting for elite riflemen potentially worthy of entering the prestigious Bisley Shooting Competition.

Every afternoon was devoted to sport: rugby and soccer teams trained for the Divisional Championships, in addition to a boxing tournament slated for Abbeville. Typically, the sports meetings commenced at 1400 hours, with the competitive athletics not only engendering morale and camaraderie, but also fitness and strength.

Sprints and long-distance running of 100 yard heats, 220 yards, 440 yards and a half mile with their associated finals were precursors to the Relay Race and the odd random 3-mile Cross Country. Jim was not inclined to compete in the Cross Country as his feet and ankles suffered from a condition evidently stemming from the souls of his feet. He could cope with the pain, although putting himself through a Cross Country run was not his idea of a fun afternoon of sport. If Ted and his ever-growing long legs were here, he would have undoubtedly been one of the 20 men in the platoon who would have entered the race. But it was war, and he was in a separate unit; they, like so many others, would get together eventually.

As it happened, No. 3 Platoon won the Cross Country to the supporting roars heard from all directions, predictably on the back of winning bets.

Apart from the shorter races, Jim felt more of a candidate for the heats of the 1-mile Bicycle Race and the Final but happily slotted into the Tug-of-War as well as any novelty events such as the Siamese Race, Alarm Race, eight-man team Land Boat Race and the Elephant Race. A perfect example of having a spring in his step was undeniably Ed Barnett, who was naturally entertaining to watch in both the Long Jump *and* High Jump.

Cricket matches were also immensely popular with its convenient practice in bomb-throwing techniques, livening the competitive atmosphere and more Jim's style. Preferring cricket above all sports, playing in battalion team matches quickly became his favourite pastime, next to his rapidly improving photography.

No amount of sporting camaraderie could mask the change in the atmosphere, though - trouble was looming. Fewer numbers of reinforcements were arriving from Australia, making it necessary to reduce the number of battalions in each depleting Division from four to three. In the 3rd Division's case, it was the 42nd Battalion that was selected for disassembly and absorption into the 41st.

Jim, Ed and 39 others were not unexpectedly transferred from 'B' to 'D' Company, while another 32 were transferred into 'A' and a further 40 into 'C'; the 42nd would join the 41st Battalion as Jim's old 'B' Company. The 42nd Battalion had defiantly opposed relinquishing their identity by taking strike action. It was only on discovering they would *all* remain together in the one company that the men begrudgingly agreed to the transfer.

Their more pressing concern, now, was changing the colour patches from the 42nd's familiar purple over blue to the 41st's black over blue. In a sympathetic effort, the 'Brass' laid their options on the table: the

41st's patch may be worn in place of the 42nd's; the 41st's patch may be worn over the 42nd's; or the 41st's patch may have an oval hole in the centre worn over the 42nd's to expose a portion of the concealed patch beneath.

The majority of men chose the second condition, with the object being to preserve the whole of the 42nd's colour so that a faded portion would not show when the men were allowed to *go back to their old unit*, a hope not altogether lost. Lieut. Col. Heron's report acknowledged this great battalion in recognition of its service, with further appreciation of the battalion's collective grievance, too:

> *The 42nd did not take too kindly to this change, but their old Company identity is being maintained by each Platoon being comprised of the remaining members of the four old Coys.*

Like many other battalions facing the same crisis in the A.I.F., the 42nd's absorption had been hard-fought, yet despite their anguish, they settled dutifully into their new place within the Division when the day finally arrived. The historical event was held on 24 October, with the 42nd appearing on the Parade Ground for the first time as 'B' Company of the 41st Battalion, its sister Queensland battalion.

The 41st Battalion's general tasks were to return the battalion's discipline and smartness to its earlier high standard, the objective of their training here in Warlus. This result could only be achieved by strenuous, energetic work aided by the urgent equipping and clothing of the men.

Concluding the day's work, the companies formed up and marched past their Company Commander (C.C.) for inspection, an impressive sight earning them commendations from General Cannan.

For the first time in France, the 41st Battalion's 'D' Company deployed a Short Guard contingent of ten, Jim included, to Head Quarters, demonstrating the men's general smartness and testifying to their collective efforts and class.

Under these formalities, their unified cadence had been sharpened to precision from parades, 1-hour ceremonials, endless drills and route marches, all making their transition at changeover a joy to watch. 'D' Company Guard had not gone unnoticed with its pleasing accuracy. Lieut. Col. Heron, himself, was particularly interested in the overall improvement of the battalion's polish, satisfied that today's evidence was proof enough.

Lieut. Col. Heron later wrote in his October report:

I have never seen the Battalion looking better. The physical standard of the men has much improved. One would not recognise the Soldiers in Warlus today as the tired men who left the Hindenburg Line on the 3rd of this month.

Several days later, a designated Range Practice was held between 'B' and 'D' Companies, as per the Army Rifle Association (A.R.A.) guidelines, where Jim's results recorded him first in 'D' Company's best ten shots, with his score of 78/80 placing him fourth on aggregate out of the 70 shooters comprising the two companies.

The following day's Routine Order released the best ten shots of the A.R.A. Platoon Competition, with Jim's 'D' Company second to their newly revamped 'B' Company, marksmen and all. It was not a forlorn hope that Jim could perhaps shoot at the prestigious Bisley Competition in England among the elite of the Army's finest shooters, but he would have to beat the likes of Robert Wilkie.

Wilkie was a farmer from Cedar Creek, Queensland, a 'crack shot' even at rapid fire, and recently presented with the Military Medal for bravery at Hamel. His courage and devotion to duty and his comrades as a stretcher bearer earned him the esteemed award, having administered first aid under heavy enemy fire before moving the wounded to safety. In April the following year, he would volunteer for Grave Detachment duties, eventually returning home on the *Port Denison* in September.

Aside from Reveille at 0530 hours, ablutions and breakfast, mornings for Wilkie, Jim, and the others generally began at 0830 hours with a half-hour parade, followed by physical training and games until 0930 hours under the instruction of Major Cohen. The grinding regime continued with a further 4-hour Battalion Parade from Monday to Saturday unless the weather was too bad, subsequently reducing the drills to company training on their respective parade grounds. Even Sundays were arduous, with Church Parades followed by 1-hour Ceremonial Parades, all proving to have a steadying effect on the men. They were there to remain in top shape.

Typical of the syllabus was half an hour's Salute Training, where the men practised passing an officer, marching up to and addressing an officer, as well as being seated or standing when approached by an officer. Another critical component of this exercise was identifying the numerous flags flown in a motorcade. It was crucial in understanding who was arriving in the camp.

Half an hour's gruelling gas training was then held on the open training course of the rifle range, where dummies hung, three per section, on two extended frames 50 yards apart. Halfway between the two structures were cardboard targets, Army Rifle Association-style, mounted on timber braces. Applying respirators to keep the body familiar with all subsequent movement while wearing them, they would charge and attack, heading for a line of low benches representing their objective...the enemy trench.

Frequently practising their timing and fluency on this obstacle course under gas shell 'bombardment' kept their wits honed in readiness for battlefield duress. The more natural the manoeuvres became, the more coordinated the men stayed in overwhelming circumstances.

Rifle practice was always an expectation with its drills and rifle exercises, competitions and rapid-fire to determine the best shots in each company. Like the well-initiated Robert Wilkie, Jim understood that apart from the integral mechanics of Range Practice with its care of firearms, the crucial tactical elements of cover, discipline, control and visual training armed the men with the skills to read the onslaught and implement damage of their own. Equally as important, the more they trained their trigger pressing, elementary aiming, visual training and judging distance, the sharper their precision became.

Not only did skirmishing, guard and sentry, and bayonet training fill their days, but the persistent routine drills continued. If it wasn't Battalion Parades, it was Battalion Inspections by the C.O. or Brigadier General Cannan. And if it wasn't inspections, it was route marches; 12 miles of them. The route taken on 25 October incorporated Warlus, Camp-en-Amenois, Hallivillers, Belincourt and Belloy, returning finally to Warlus. This day saw 'C' Company judged the march's best company.

It was during one of these route marches that Jim's feet inflicted unbearable suffering, causing him to Fall Out under Lieut. Dimmock's command to seek the medical officer at the rear of the column, where he was diagnosed with 'flat feet'. He was one of four men who sought the medic during the march that day: the other three included two with diarrhoea and one who was injured.

Overall, the battalion enjoyed the perfect Autumn weather throughout their first month at Warlus, with the men's health generally good and the utmost care being taken in preventing the Spanish Influenza. Quenching the troops' appetites with the fresh, plentiful arrays of food, fruit and vegetables afforded by the battalion's healthy finances assisted enormously in improving the men's immunity against the unforgiving influenza spreading in alarming proportions.

Templeux le Guerard 3 October 1918. AWM E03788.

Light rail used to transport troops to and from the Front, France 1918. Its convenient lightweight fabrication provided the ability for rapid assembly and deconstruction. AWM E02768.

2 October 1918. German prisoners at the clearing station, Abbeville.
Photograph courtesy of the Imperial War Museum. IWM Q9353.

A Peronne street sign reading 'Roo de Kanga', characteristic of the Australian Diggers' humour. AWM E03412.

Warlus – Rue d'Airaines. Photograph courtesy of Info Bretagne.

Abbeville – Photograph courtesy of Info Bretagne.

CHAPTER 7

War is Over

The men in their lines glanced at each other in confusion, daring to believe what this could mean.

11 November 1918. A crowd of civilians and Australian soldiers gather in the Vignacourt Town Square on Armistice Day. Officially, the troops weren't informed of the armistice until three days later. AWM P10550.089.

IN WARLUS, JIM WAS ON BATTALION Parade, ready for inspection. It was 1058 hours on 11 November 1918, and the dull rumbles of the Howitzers' sporadic heavy firing could be heard beyond the horizon. As the men stood to attention, an increased pummelling of distant fire came from both sides, no longer erratic but vicious. Then, without warning, a protracted silence followed.

Jim remained still, listening for the anticipated bumps and thuds travelling to them from the Front Line, but none came...none from either side. General consensus decreed there was a good reason for the silence, whatever that reason may be, until fervent peels of church bells rang out through Warlus and its surrounding farms, continuing in uncharacteristic momentum.

Glancing at each other in confusion, the men in their lines dared to believe what this could mean. Chiming bells resonated through the countryside as people came from everywhere, running along the adjacent roads to the village, calling out excitedly to each other.

Responding to the distracted side glances through the lines, the parade sergeant snapped the troops' attention back to more disciplined matters, reminding them that current proceedings were business as usual. What they did not know was that just before dawn, as the men slept, an armistice had been signed in a train dining car at Le Francport near Compiegne, France, ceasing all hostilities from 1100 hours today. By noon, War Correspondents everywhere had wired the historic announcement to the papers back in Australia, their transmissions reaching home around 9:00 pm Australian time.

Peace was no guarantee under this shaky truce, though, requiring the troops to remain in full combat mode as if there had been no armistice signed at all. Battalions would not be officially informed for another three days in the possible event of the German Army reneging, reducing the Armistice to ashes as a result. Except for the buildings draped in French, British and Australian colours and townsfolk celebrating ecstatically, the troops and nurses remained uninformed for the next three days, presuming nothing but longing for everything.

In the meantime, the 41st had a significant march planned for 14 November 1918, involving much preparation. She was to be the leading battalion in the main body of the 11th Brigade - the Advance Guard to the 3rd Australian Division. They would be flanked on the right by the 4th Division and the 5th Division on the left.

The 43rd would form part of the 44th Battalion for this exercise, then Vanguard to the Advance Guard later. Two sections of the 11th Trench Mortar Battery were allotted to 'A' Company and would join the 41st Battalion at Metigny.

Instructions were issued that the battalion would route march to the crossroads via Laleu and Metigny, passing the starting point at Battalion

Headquarters at precisely 0800 hours. Dress was Full Marching Order and in the following Order of March: the 41st Btn Band, 'A' Company, 'B' Company, Pipers, 'C' Company, 'D' Company, Headquarters. On arrival at the crossroads, the 41st would carry out an Outpost Scheme by Company Commanders (C.C.), placing the men in outpost positions.

Not only were the gathered divisions immense, but impressive, the product of seemingly endless drills, parades, and route marches, all contributing to their instinctive accuracy. Their flawless exhibition was in the order of the A.I.F.'s greatest pride.

Rumoured to be the precursor of a march into Germany, it was suggested that 50 men would undertake this meritorious display until the notion was abandoned as unnecessary.

Two days later, Lieut. Heron stood before them on parade. It was 16 November, two days after the official announcement that war was finally over, but the news he was about to give them would take the wind completely out of their sails.

On behalf of Major-General Gellibrand, Heron began to read the following orders:

> *Owing to the organisation of the Army of Occupation having been fixed at four Divisions for each Corps, it has been necessary to detail the last formed – the Third Division – to remain in FRANCE when the Australian Corps moves forward.*

> *I do not doubt that this decision will be a bitter disappointment to all ranks of the Division. During the past two years we have fought, suffered, endured, and yet have to forego the satisfaction of standing as conquerors on German soil. We remain in FRANCE, but it will be as representing the A.I.F. and it will be by our discipline that we can add to the reputation of the whole.*

> *Australia has paid full price for her share of the victory and for fighting to a finish wherever we have been engaged. It is for us who survive and who remember to see to it that, one and all, we remain worthy of our*

fallen comrades to the very end. Whether we go or whether we stay, I have answered for it that the Third Division will be 'in the line' where wanted.

Jim's 3rd Division was destined to be the last to leave France, and ultimately, the 41st Battalion itself would represent a large percentage of the A.I.F.'s last boots on French soil.

Disappointment was painfully evident among the men by the predictable expletives rising from the parade in the falling rain. Others stood quietly, remembering lost brothers and mates. As long as they remained in France, the men still considered themselves connected with them, not abandoned to be forgotten on these foreign battlefields, especially so near Christmas.

Around this time, Jim and some of the boys took four days' leave to venture into Paris, where they visited the Eiffel Tower, The Louvre and the many magnificent cathedrals. It was during one of the cosmopolitan city's tramrides, he spotted a young French girl the same age as his little sister, Francie, entertaining the surrounding passengers with her laughter. The amusing vision stayed with Jim long after their return to camp, prompting him to write early Christmas cards to the family, particularly Francie's unique gift card he had bought in Paris.

On the front of the freshly printed card he had chosen for his parents was the simple greeting, *Remembrance*, with the Rising Sun emblem of the A.I.F. directly above. And there, inside the card opposite the verse was the 41st Battalion colour patch of black over light blue, the words *Christmas 1918* nestled beneath it.

The verse inside read:

> *To you, our own dear loved ones,*
> *Way o'er the other side,*
> *We wish the best and brightest*
> *To bless this Christmas tide.*
> *And tho' perforce 'somewhere in France'*
> *In body we must stay,*

In spirit we shall cross to you
To share your Christmas Day.

Jim's neatly written words to his parents reflected those of so many others, only with a weight lifted from his shoulders with the Armistice signed, ensuring a truly Merry Christmas, after all. Jim's simple yet heartfelt message read:

To Dad & Mum,

With best wishes for a Merry Christmas.

From Jim xxxxxx
41st Battalion, A.I.F., France

The card Jim had bought Francie was elegantly embroidered with an iridescent blue dragonfly settled on a bunch of pink flowers, the very thing a young girl would adore. Her small, brightly lit face had instantly filled his mind the moment the exquisite card caught his attention, imagining her excitement on receiving such a beautiful thing.

With his thoughts having come so easily with visions of her happiness, Jim was soon recapping his fountain pen:

Dear Francie,

A pc to let you know I am still thinking of my little sister. The first thing you will do when you get it is run over and show it to Hazel I suppose. Well, Francie, how are you getting on at school? I'll bet you get a bit more cheeky every day and don't learn half as much as you did when you first started. I was on a tram the other day and saw a little French girl that was just like you. She was about your age and made as much noise as you used to. She had everyone laughing. Well goodbye and best love, Kiddie.

From your loving brother Jim.

P.S. Don't forget to write to me like you do to Emmel & Steve.
xxxxxxxxxxxxxxxx

Across the English Channel in a billet during his two weeks' leave in Blighty, 27-year-old Fred Stenner from Bowral and the Rainey's family friend, was also writing New Year wishes to Jim's parents, George and Adelaide, on a booklet of postcards he had bought especially for them. The cards would give them an idea of where he had been stationed despite the strict regulations forbidding any mention of camp locations. Fred would return to the 49th Btn on 30 November.

His message was short but enough:

To Mrs Rainey and Mr Rainey,

Wishing you a Happy New Year 1919. These are a few views of the place where we are camped. They are of the place before it was knocked about by the Germans.

From Pte F.E. Stenner (135)

Rifling through the cards one last time, Fred took in the many scenes of the Citadelle el l'Eglise, Panorama el Tour de Mont-Fort, Le Pont el l'Hotel des Postes, Clacher de l'Eglise el faubourg Saint-Medard, Le Pont la Citeadelle el l Eglise Depart du Bateau pour Hasliere, Le Prieure and Le Pont la Citadelle el l'Eglise; every one familiar to him and yet strangely unrecognisable to see them undamaged.

Throughout camps everywhere, a pilgrimage had begun. In the crisp late Autumn night, men made their way to the night post's chutes, dropping their parcels of greeting cards and envelopes through cavities in walls into the hessian bins inside.

Within 100 yards of the men focused on posting their Christmas mail, the Australian Corps News, dated 18 November 1918, lay in numerous military files outlining the Armistice's conditions. It spoke of the considerable reparation costs Germany faced for all damage done, the cost of keeping all troops in the Rhineland, and the restitution of the Russian and Rumanian gold confiscated by Germany.

In addition, Germany would evacuate from Belgium, Alsace-Lorraine and Luxembourg within 14 days and East Africa within a month. They were to hand over all military installations intact, their armada, planes, guns, all stores of food, and more immediately, *all* prisoners of war.

Sabotage was a grave concern with the yet-to-be-surrendered German Fleet at Scapa Flow, including battle cruisers, battleships, light cruisers, destroyers and submarines. German warplanes were also at risk before reaching the British Air Force's inventory, along with the arm's artillery boost of 30,000 machine guns, trench mortars, 5,000 heavy mortars and field guns.

And the Brass's fears were not unfounded. Germany would blatantly and unashamedly scuttle 52 of their 74 vessels in front of the British Navy during the handover in six months' time, with German mechanics vengefully nobbling anything still remaining: plane engines, troopships, lorries...the lot. What was not sabotaged inclined suspicion.

Lightening the atmosphere, though, was the anticipation of a commemorative dinner arranged for the 25th of this week, celebrating the 2nd Anniversary of the 41st Battalion's arrival in France. An ornately decorated notice bearing the words, 'God Save the King', depicted an Australian scene with entwined Eucalypt branches, two laughing kookaburras, a koala, kangaroo and a sassy possum; Jim's favourite shooting story involved a similar sassy possum.

As expected, the menu was enticing to the enthusiastic soldiers, and in all good spirits, the men of the 41st agreed that it was *bloody tops* for the battalion to be honoured so memorably, including those lost along the way and any presently convalescing.

Harry had recovered enough to man the Supply Depot temporarily while he awaited early embarkation to England, accompanying Bill, who had now been Taken on Strength back into 'A' Company sporting a scar on his leg the size of an egg. Ted also joined them for the dinner from his unit, although Ernie remained in Parkhouse, England, in his Machine Gun Detachment. Otherwise, a good night was expected.

In a well-lit hut, 40 yards from the night chute, Lieut. Heron was working dutifully on his report, beginning with the battalion's arrival in the back area of Warlus, where he, too, was comfortably billeted.

As he eyed the report submitted by Chaplain Major Mills, the gravity struck him that a chaplain had one of the toughest jobs of them all, given the present burial quotas. The dedicated chaplain had detailed the conditions of the Front during last month's battle along the Hindenburg Line, and having had the fallen moved to graves nearer to the edge of a nearby wood, where he had presided over a total of 84 burials.

In the medical sense, Heron had noted that little use had been made of the Blue Light Room, this being the Prophylactic Ward for the treatment of venereal diseases. The considered explanation was that the essential preparations and preventatives for venereal disease, including anal gonorrhoea, were conveniently available in all the towns, and Warlus was considered pretty safe. Nonetheless, calomel tubes were available, with only a resulting few being issued in treatment.

One hundred and thirty influenza cases had been accounted for in the six weeks since the battalion had arrived in Warlus, all safely recovered until the last few days when three perished from bronchial pneumonia. The sick men and their immediate contacts were isolated as far as possible, although this luxury often proved to be impractical, restricted by a shortage of billets. While still causing trouble but declining with the assistance of perfect sunny days, the reduced number of influenza cases provided the ideal opportunity to re-inoculate the men who were due for it.

Baths were located at Allory, a considerable distance of 5 miles via Martigny, requiring the men to bathe, on average, every eight or nine days. In between bathing days, ablutions were carried out in the designated area with bowls, buckets and wooden tables provided. Otherwise, all was satisfactory from the hygiene perspective.

Naturally, the signing of the Armistice was a strong point, withheld for an additional three days due to the uncertainty of the Germans upholding the agreement, with all officers waiting anxiously for the result of the presented terms while training continued as usual. Aside from the villages throughout the country being draped in flags and regalia, Heron stated:

> *Consequently, there was no outward sign of rejoicing on our part, although we all felt greatly relieved that our chances of fighting again were practically nil.*

Bending his head again, Heron recommenced his writing, referring to the excellent lectures discussing post-war problems that had been willingly attended. The men supported the informative lectures in the genuine interest of anxiety and nervousness, handling the awkward, 'elephant-in-the-room' conversations they may face once they returned home and alcohol dependence.

He further acknowledged a letter of great appreciation from the Monseigneur, the Bishop of Amiens, thanking the 41st for the Guard of Honour, buglers, and full band provided to assist the Requiem Mass held at the cathedral in honour of those killed on the battlefield of the Somme. His inspiring words asserted that nothing could have been finer than the appearance of the Guard of Honour or more impressive than the playing of Chopin's Funeral March by the 41st Battalion Band, nor as unforgettable as the sounding of the 'Last Post'.

On the lighter side, Heron noted a cinema show that had entertained the battalion for ten days with two shows daily, besides visits from the Y.M.C.A. entertainers with their party of ladies.

Proposals regarding demobilisation and repatriation had been presented to the brigadier and were being energetically discussed throughout the battalion. They included a comprehensive educational scheme, the Australian Corps School (A.C.S.), whose development was yet to be determined by its influence on the battalion, ahead of the Peace Treaty's eventual signing and engaging this hard-fought peace.

Reflecting momentarily on the anticipated dinner to celebrate the battalion's 2nd anniversary in France, Heron considered General

Cannan's remarks to him one morning following the splendid route march of the 14th:

> *I would not hesitate to put this Battalion up against anything in the A.I.F.*

At last, the long-awaited recognition Heron and the other officers had strived to achieve for these determined and honourable men of the 41st Battalion had been served.

Heron's concluding paragraphs would later include the outcome of the dinner towards the end of the month, but for now, he would finish the evening's notes with the battalion's delay in leaving France. Delayed but imminent, demobilisation was coming:

> *Everyone shared the regret that they could not go home as a complete Unit and were anxiously waiting to return home at the earliest possibility, now that the prospect of future employment as a fighting force is nil.*

Front of the card Jim's mother, Adelaide, sent him following Armistice Day, 1918. From personal collection.

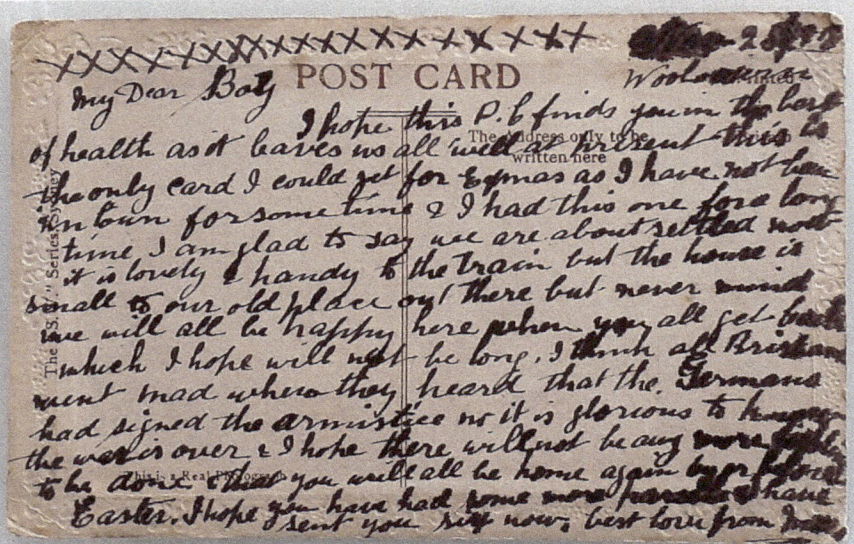

Jim's mother's Christmas card to Jim after Armistice Day 1918. From personal family collection.

Jim's embroidered card to his ten-year-old little sister, Francie. From personal family collection.

After the armistice. Australians undergoing bayonet training in gas masks at the Australian Corps School. AWM E01673.

The start of a 440 yards foot race in France. AWM H03965.

CHAPTER 8

Christmas, 1918

"I think all Brisbane went mad when they heard that the Germans had signed the Armistice so it is glorious to know the War is over and I hope there will not be any more fighting to be done and that you will all be home again before Easter."

Jim's 41st Battalion Christmas card to his parents. From personal family collection.

OVERHEAD, THE WEATHER SHOWED signs of turning, holding off just long enough for Battalion Parade so the men could make their way to their Repatriation Class for the rest of the morning. The rain did not ease overnight, though, so Jim found himself shooting in even more cold rainfall the next day at Rapid Fire Practice for 'Best Rapid Fire Shot'.

Falling effortlessly into his natural rhythm, Jim made the top ten best shots out of 40 shooters in the morning drizzle, followed by a march to the Allery Divisional Baths. Here, 'B', 'D' and Head Quarters

Companies, as well as 60 other ranks who were Marched In that day, enjoyed their rejuvenating showers and a fresh set of clothes.

Under the onset of recently increasing cases of influenza, Jim soon became one of those casualties suffering a raw, raspy throat accompanied by severe aches and fatigue, made altogether worse by parades in the showery Winter mornings. The next morning, 6 December, was no better, bringing its accompanying blast of increasingly icy winds.

Marched Out from Sick Parade under the buffeting of this merciless freezing gale, Jim was transferred by the 10th Australian Field Ambulance to the Red Cross Hospital, a splendid converted French chateau in Warlus. Here, he joined Ted Marsh, also recently admitted for the same unpleasant reason.

While December was not the coldest Winter month, recent days had produced nothing but hard frosts, driving rain and that continuing howling gale, the perfect breeding ground for swift flu outbreaks that also brought the threat of deadly bronchial pneumonia. Vast numbers of soldiers admitted to hospital had died from complications that heavily attacked their lungs and depleted their immunities regardless of the nourishing food, although Jim was earnestly endeavouring not to become one of them.

Within the stone walls of Warlus' nearby cemetery were fresh graves of those who had succumbed to the brutal flu, a stark reminder of its severity. Also, not lost on the men was the war's even darker side; lying among the cemetery's dead was a British soldier executed by firing squad for desertion in 1916.

Barely able to breathe and dosed to the gills on whatever the medical staff could give him, Jim was transferred to the 3rd Australian General Hospital (3 A.G.H.) in Abbeville a week later, leaving Ted behind to rejoin the 41st Battalion in just a few days.

A significant hospital on a flat stretch of ground, the 3 A.G.H. was over an hour's rambling drive from Warlus. The massive hospital camp of the Australian Army Medical Service gave the appearance of a small town, consisting of roomy tents in efficient rows of canvas and fly ropes.

In the middle of the consortium of marquee wards were the timber wards, Nissen Hut wards, the well-primed operating theatre, X-ray department, pathology with microscopes, dentist and dental workshop, hospital offices, living quarters, Quartermaster's Stores, kitchens and post office, all powered by the newest commodity; electricity.

Each timber roof bore a chimney, evidence of the warm comfort of the wood-burning stoves within, where hot water simmered in kettles at the ready on continually heated stovetops. Beyond their warmth, cots lined the walls beneath the glass of the broad 'push-out' windows, directing ventilation and light through to those recuperating below.

Tent wards were established around three rows of hospital cots, the middle row strategically occupying the spaces between the line of central uprights, headed by a medical station table and chairs, all ventilated by mighty sweeping ceilings designed to remove any stale or hot air through flaps operated by ropes. Vases of flowers festooned ward side tables, while outside flag poles flew the British Union Jack and the hospital's red cross, clearly visible from the intersection out at the main road. Two guards were posted on Sentry Duty here at all times, identifying drivers bringing the sick through the hospital's entrance.

Hovering throughout the wards as they performed their duties, the seemingly inexhaustible nurses, dressed in grey with their white full-length aprons brandishing a red cross, were adored for their strength and tireless devotion. Their very presence was the flint re-igniting hope.

Now in the French Winter of 1918, as Jim, 19 years old, lay feverishly in bed fighting the Spanish Flu's aggressive symptoms, a second wave swept through the population. Attending to him as he fought through his searing fever were those same dutiful nurses.

Victims across the globe were dying within days, sometimes only hours, of developing the highly infectious and deadly disease, their lungs filling with fluid causing gradual suffocation. Two other privates who had sailed with Jim on the *Ormonde* had died from influenza more recently, one of them suffering the added complication of exposure to the harsh elements in the trenches.

The voracious disease rippled its lethal tentacles worldwide, resulting in over 50 million deaths globally by 1919, including 15,000 deaths in Australia in addition to her losing 60,000 of her valiant sons to war.

Over two weeks later, on 22 December 1918, Jim was finally discharged from hospital and returned to Warlus, where he was Taken on Strength, rejoining the 41st. He was back in 'D' Company, where he was surprised to find Bill and Ted happily bearing the news Ernie had recently arrived from Parkhurst and was Taken on Strength into the 5th Machine Gun Division. Unfortunately, news of Harry's recent departure to England dampened the joyous occasion.

Overnight delivered heavy Winter rain with frost, and snow was anticipated in the coming days, raising hopes for their first White Christmas. Still, the newly implemented education programs in the Army schools Jim had now been introduced to were progressing splendidly, and 'D' Company cleaned up in the Billets Competition, keeping their buoyant morale even lighter.

Later that day, the atmosphere was stirred by an invitation extended to anyone wishing to compete in a Public Speaking Class debate on the 'Nationalisation of Sports and Theatrics': 'B' and 'C' versus 'A' and 'D' Companies. Numerous men would later be designated for ongoing debate teams, but today, those chosen prepared their witty case arguments ahead of another entertaining evening for their rowdy, encouraging audience.

Crisp, sunny weather remained until midday when it turned on its worst display, with relentless rain inundating nearby villages. In an effort to relieve the swamped streets, drainage schemes were implemented and completed by the morning of Christmas Eve, allowing flooding in the village to subside. In addition to this great success, encouraging news came that preparation for Christmas Dinner was going apace, topped by the troops being treated to an even larger than normal mail delivery.

Jim had already received some Christmas packages from home, which included a Christmas cake laced with brandy, a tin of Billy tea, two pairs of socks, knitted gloves, chocolates, cards and letters, but today he managed to receive some more. One letter from his mother said it all, giving him the feeling of life at home after Armistice Day:

Nov 28th, 1918
Wooloowin

My Dear Boy,
I hope this P.C. finds you in the best of health as it leaves us all well at present. This is the only card I could get for Xmas as I have not been in town for some time and I had this one for a long time. I am glad to say we are about settled now. It is lovely and handy to the train but the house is small to our old place out there but never mind. We will all be happy here when you all get back which I hope will not be long. I think all Brisbane went mad when they heard that the Germans had signed the Armistice so it is glorious to know the War is over and I hope there will not be any more fighting to be done and that you will all be home again before Easter. I hope you have had some more parcels I have sent you by now.
Best love from Mum xxxxxxxxxxxxxxxxxxx

While Jim read his mother's slightly ink-blotched writing, he realised he had been looking *ahead* to Christmas, not necessarily looking *forward* to it; it was his first Christmas away from home. Christmas was a time for being home with family, but it would be another 12 months before any of the men would share that luxury.

Having penned his 41st Battalion Christmas Cards with careful planning to the family, neighbours and friends, including Harry's mother, Jim absorbed their relief and his mother's, not just his own. The signing of the Armistice carried their one greatest hope; their boys' return.

Knowing that his brother-in-law, Steve, had been shot in the left shoulder during the fighting near Tincourt in early September, Jim knew they would send him home on the first available ship once he was able enough to travel, which by now should put him a third of the way home. This in itself was encouraging. Better yet, being the colder time of the year, they might send him back the quick route via Suez. Either way, he would spend Christmas at sea.

More immediately, though, according to tomorrow's routine order, Christmas morning required them to front for Church Parade conducted by Chaplain Major Mills at 1000 hours, followed by a march into St Maxent, where a sumptuous Christmas dinner would be held at the Chateau de St Maxent for the men at midday. The Christmas feasting was staggered to accommodate the numbers and duties involved; the sergeants would dine lavishly at 1700 hours and the officers, even more so, at 1900 hours.

Waking to a hard, icy frost with the promise of the clearest sunny day, their perfectly peaceful Christmas morning was a stark contrast to the one they would be having at home, where the stifling heat fuelled electrical storms bursting forth in torrents of rain. And then, of course, there were the ceaseless, sticky flies…how the men missed it all right now.

In light of this, the troops had been treated to a hearty stew for Christmas breakfast before being issued two packets of cigarettes, a cigar and some chocolates, soon followed by their wintry Church Parade, where the men stood at ease in their greatcoats listening to Chaplain Mills, some intently, others distractedly.

An hour later, amid the dispersing columns now filtering through the spacious manicured gardens, Jim, Ted, Bill, Ernie, Ed and Tommy stepped out of the biting Winter cold into the warm, festively decorated Chateau de St Maxent as the peel of the midday bells rang out across the French countryside from the ancient stone churches. Ernie had joined them from the 5th Machine Gun Company to share Christmas with his old mates, joyfully celebrating together.

Their astonishment at the chateau's exquisite decorations was reflected in their faces. Holly and mistletoe hung everywhere, colourfully adorning the overhead beams amid the many Australian, British and French flags draped from the opulent walls. The holly-laden tables, too, were bountifully laid out with nuts, fruits, exquisite French chocolates and delectable pastries among the many enticing treats enjoyed immediately by the eager men.

Warmed by the roaring fire in the chateau's magnificent fireplace, Jim was pleased to see the promising spread anticipated on the decorative menu. Christmas dinner looked like it was going to be an absolute treat: turkey and goose with all the trimmings, beer, plum pudding, and the most decadent plethora of French delicacies. The menu's fashionable retro style matched the 41st Battalion Christmas Card Jim had sent home, its array a delight to the eye:

Australian Soup
Baked Goose
Roast Turkey
Braised Beef Cutlets
Cabbage
Butter Apples
Plum Pudding with Sauce
Variety of Fruits with Cream
Hazelnuts
Tea, Beer

True to expectations, Jim enjoyed his beer first, followed soon after by baked goose, turkey and beef cutlets with a generous side of cabbage and gravy, every bit as enjoyable as his mother's longed-for cooking.

Although the spirited atmosphere in the welcoming mansion was filled with youthful verve, the men could not escape their gratitude that this would be their only Christmas here. Many among them were persevering through their second, third or fourth Christmases away from their long-suffering families. Lasting peace would bring them all home to share the joy of next Christmas around family tables everywhere, an expectation that burned within them since the signing of the Armistice.

Festivities continued beneath the chateau's grand ceilings for 3 hours. Not only were generous servings of the revered plum pudding doused in brandy sauce heartily enjoyed, but second helpings of buttered apples and other luscious fruits served with cream as well. And their raging appetites were ready for any and all of it.

Several beers later, with fond, spirited tales energising the joyous Christmas atmosphere, the men stood, raising toasts in any number of respects, the first embraced by a sombre hush around the dining hall:

To those at home, those no longer with us and Christmases at home yet to come.

Revelries were now drawing to a close as cups of hot tea were finished and beers reluctantly drained, the lieutenants' cue to issue each man with two more packets of cigarettes, a cigar and extra quantities of chocolate. These came in addition to yet another surprise Christmas Comforts Fund parcel of more cigarettes, more chocolates and a few other welcome treats later in the afternoon. It had been a considerably generous Christmas Day.

Later in the evening, an outstanding concert was held in the recreation hall to top off a remarkably enjoyable Christmas for them all. Some maintained it was one of the best shows they had ever seen, while others had been so well-oiled by the time they left the chateau that they missed the entertainment completely.

Concerts and free time contributed to the blissful atmosphere as the 9th Reos enjoyed the warming fires of recreational halls, chateaux, family homes and billets everywhere. Although it was not the White Christmas they had all anticipated, the troops made this glorious Armistice Christmas in France an occasion to remember.

Soldiers who had been billeted in households on their arrival in France had become so fond of their French families that they now shared Christmas with them in a welcoming family atmosphere as if they were their own. For these men, returning home would prove as painful as leaving their Australian families - helpless, splitting grief.

Boxing Day's glittering arrival reverberated with the crunching of hard frost under a thousand Australian boots as the men headed into Abbeville to take full advantage of the rare holiday atmosphere. Their sojourn took Jim and his five mates into the friendly village, a lively walk along Avenue du Rivage past the familiar stone walls, quaint farm buildings, chateaux and churches, all delightful scenes that never tired them. Their festive season's merrymaking still rendered them relatively replete, consuming little this day except for occasional French chocolates, the wonder of all delights.

Anticipating the 'Cooee's' mid-afternoon performance arranged in the hangar, the mates knew they would need to return early enough, perhaps even hitching a timely lift in a lorry, to join the vast audience imbued in true Christmas spirit. Tonight, there would be no brass band under Lieut. R.R. Wood as they had headed to the 3 A.G.H. in Abbeville to entertain those invalided and the staff who cared for them.

Daybreak on the 27th brought a high wind accompanied by light drizzling rain, backed up with more of the same on the 28th, resulting in the cancellation of their usual route march just as the companies reached the starting point. The weather ultimately reflected what little interest the men could summon, although classes continued in the warmth of the huts under an expectation of snowfall as temperatures rapidly plunged.

Even more rain followed the next morning, accompanied by a steady gale coming in from the west to usher the morning's parades and classes. Characteristically, the men were wrapped comfortably in their trench coats, thwarting the biting wind.

Scheduled for another afternoon performance, the 'Cooees' unavoidably cancelled due to the particularly harsh weather. Instead, a significant number of officers and men, including Jim and his mates, obtained leave to Oisemont, Abbeville and other places of great attraction in the vicinity, improving the afternoon's amusement considerably.

Again, on the following day, continuing rain fell heavily, resulting in the Church Parade being cancelled for the first time since the men came out of the Line. Instead, a lorry from the Divisional Motor Transport Company arrived during the day for the battalion's use, testing the men for their motor driving skills under the A.C.S. Educational Scheme. Jim, especially eager to learn this new skill and eventually be tested, understood automobiles were here to stay and wanted to learn all he could about them while he had this rare opportunity.

As its low rumble drew nearer to the Base Depot, the troops eyed the heavily built khaki Standard 'B' Series Liberty with its folding canopy over the cab and tied-down canopy behind, its battered sides indicating the truck had seen some work. It was one of those simple excitements that gave him hope for the future to utilise these new skills back home, although he still had a bit of thinking to do. A definite plan was hatching, regardless.

A few hours later, with driving lessons finished at St Maxent for the day, the afternoon brought them time to ramble along the village streets and local surrounds, freely engaging in the generous local activity. If they were lucky, they might even get another lift back in one of the passing lorries for the price of some cigarettes, although for now, Jim and the others were just glad of the freedom.

According to the next day's systematic routines, 50 men each from 'B', 'C' and 'H.Q.' Companies were sent to the baths, with each man immediately issued a clean change of clothing. The quality obtained was better than usual, so it seemed hopeful that more of the same could be expected. 'A' and 'D' Companies would take their turn in the coming days.

In light of more unexpected developments, a suggestion had been made by 2nd Lieut. Percival George Whiteside, which sparked keen interest. Holding a meeting to determine the men's interest in photography, Whiteside signed up 16 members seeking to improve their skills, Jim, Ted and Bill included. Forming a committee of the 41st Battalion Camera Club, the keen photographers discussed their experiences to reveal some interesting film developing.

In time, Whiteside wanted to see the newly formed Camera Club venture out on a field trip, a few days that could rekindle lost interest in their mundane routines and perhaps enable their memories of France to flourish as the countryside began to heal.

And so, with the morning came the eve of a new year, bringing the promise of peace and goodwill to a world torn into chards. Volunteering to assist with the erection of a Nissen Hut on the Village Place, Jim joined the team of Division Engineers who had already commenced the morning's work on site. Others from the 41st also volunteered for the project under the able supervision of the Padre, bringing the miraculous metamorphosis of the hut from stacked to standing in remarkable time. The transformation was outstanding.

Later in the afternoon, Jim and his four mates, along with many others, were given leave to visit their local haunts, where the stroke of midnight naturally drew out the various parties of revellers parading the streets singing with great gusto. It was also no surprise that what they were singing was anything but hymns.

Jim was not concerned that he would spend the first day of 1919 with the mother-of-all hangovers. Like most soldiers hell-bent on getting some mileage out of their therapeutic intoxication, he was getting his euphoria's worth right now and blocking out the rest as coloured lights rocketed into the heavens above.

Contrary to orders, the forbidden coloured signal flares, or Verey Lights, lit the sky as church bells chimed midnight, celebrating the old year's passing. Transfixed by the illuminations as he wrote the last entry in the War Diary for 1918, Lieut. Col Heron's thoughts wandered to nights along the Front Line where the Verey lights illuminated the skies:

> *These pyrotechnic displays were also illuminating the sky in the villages for miles around and reminded one vividly of many a night spent in or near the Line.*

Chateau de St Maxent where the 41st Battalion enjoyed their Christmas lunch 1918. Photograph courtesy of Infobretagne.

British Army soldiers inspecting some of the streets in the ruined village of Bellicourt. AWM H15943.

Edward (Ted) Marsh 3644, Fovant 1918. From personal collection.

CHAPTER 9

New Year of Peace

Again, farewells rang out to the waving troops as the rain began to fall gradually heavier on the columns marching in rhythmic formation, destined for Gamaches Train Station.

A sculpture of a kangaroo and joey made from snow. AWM P10700.001.

JANUARY 1ST, 1919, WAS A general holiday with Battalion Leave enjoyed by those well enough to visit Abbeville, St Maxent and any number of the soldiers' favourite haunts in the neighbouring areas. There was much to be thankful for, and the clock was ticking...*loudly*.

For those hungover, the tight heads and sick stomachs confined the heralders of the night before to bunks or wherever they happened to find themselves, even in random barns amongst numbers of curious sheep.

Those French wintry mornings of January's first two weeks were always going to be intensely cold, shrouding the men's immediate world in crisp frost until light rain solidified into ice, the precursor to the anticipated snow falling later in the month. Not only was the bitter cold unforgiving, but the hard frosts could not thaw enough before more snow fell, intensifying the icy air even further.

Invariably, the carefree inner boy in each man was released, and fierce snowball fights broke out spontaneously. Neither Jim nor any of his mates had seen snow until this Winter, so the novelty soon had them packing the frozen powder into projectiles, snowmen, shapely Mademoiselles, and even a kangaroo with joey.

Route marches were maintained in fighting order, and parades had continued throughout the month, conveniently aided by the chilly air rejuvenating the soldiers during their training. On one of those frosty mornings of the first week in January, the 8-mile route march took them along the Doudelainville-Fresne-Oiisemont Railway Crossing fork roads, returning finally to St Maxent in occasional scuds of drizzle.

On their return, they discovered their afternoon would be spent erecting a Nissen Hut at nearby St Maxent for a recreation and lecture room, a venture they were enthusiastic about merely for keeping warm. Typically, the regime of the troops remained much the same as the Peace Treaty still had not been signed, nor would it be until 28 June 1919. Nonetheless, it was announced on parade that regimental censorship was officially discontinued from 1 January 1919.

Unsurprisingly, there was a sudden increase in disciplinary actions, including a private striking a sergeant in the course of a heated exchange. Disciplinary cases of Absent Without Leave (A.W.L.) escalated from the occasional one or two to four or five at a time, as was the evident lack of eagerness shown in the results of the Billet Inspections and Cookers. 'D' Company's fastidious 'edge' was still in comparatively good shape, but none were putting in that final polish they had only weeks earlier. Now, that same clipped 'edge' was just enough to be considered passable.

Then finally, the day arrived when the anticipated announcement was made on parade regarding leave requirements. At last, peace really was returning without the troops being required to carry their weapons and ammunition while they were on leave. The day had come:

In order to provide better comfort, the members of this Brigade when going on leave will not in future carry:

Ammunition, Rifle, Gas Respirator, Steel Helmet, Entrenching Tool Head, Helve and Carrier (Sic), blankets. During the winter months, the latter may be carried if men so desire to improve their comfort in the train and en route.

Further reference was made to leave being taken in Paris, revealing that the Australian Y.M.C.A. had extended its operations to the Hotel Windsor along Rue de Petrograd. Troops were reminded to present themselves to either the Hotel Florida or Hotel Windsor for accommodation, meals, hot baths, social rooms, concerts and tours, which would be gladly given at all hours, an opportunity Jim would not miss.

No sooner had the news been received when the heavens opened, delivering a downpour that culminated in the assembly being promptly cancelled so troops, protected in their trench coats, could move on, arriving conveniently dry at their allotted classes.

Sudden heavy downpours continued during the following days, resulting in rugby games and parades, including Sunday's Church Parade, also being cancelled. Alternatively, educational classes held at the A.C.S. provided some fine debates on various topics with additional lectures on photography conducted by 2nd Lieut. Whiteside of the newly formed Camera Club.

Standing 5 foot 11 inches, the Engineer from Warwick towered over many in the class, especially Jim. Whiteside had recently been authorised to undertake a six-day field trip on 26 January, taking them on an assignment to photograph the areas throughout the Hindenburg Line where the 41st had fought four months earlier.

Four months did not seem anywhere close in the minds of these men…it felt more like a lifetime ago, yet as close as yesterday. The emotional scars, haunting dreams and crippling nerves all contributed to a heaviness in their spirit that no amount of Australian larrikinism could shift.

In its welcome distraction, the field trip announcement filled the hut with energy as the details were revealed. They would take one of the lorries and make their way back through Templeux Le Guerard, Hargicourt, Bony, Bellicourt, Mt St Quentin, The Canal, Malakoff Farm, then return to Warlus via Ronssoy and Jeancourt.

During the coming days, the men's luck with the weather changed for the worse, alternating from 1-hour route marches in cold sunshine to that of high winds and rain with anticipated snow. The one redeeming factor was that the next day was payday, and a visit to the Glass Works at Martainville had been arranged for the troops by way of a short march.

Located just over 2 ½ miles from St Maxent, the Glass Works had proven to be a top-rated attraction, with only the uninitiated who had not enjoyed its intricate treasures. The perfume bottles and figurines stunned even the hardest of men, and the 'Boudoir Boxes' were found adorning many of the hotels and homes throughout the men's and nurses' intermittent stays during their leave.

Soon after, with their interests amply satisfied, the troops explored the village further, taking their time before finally making their way back to camp for the evening.

Assigned baths continued over the next few days, involving the rostered companies marching to Huppy 4 miles away, so with Jim now in 'D' Company, it was presumed their turn could be expected on the 11th as long as the routine held.

French authorities had recently made it clear to the hierarchy that British troops, including rowdy Australians, were not complying with travel protocols on the railways but deliberately flouting regulations; unacceptable behaviour that would cease. Officers and nurses were to travel in first class, Non-Commissioned Officers (N.C.O.s) second class and privates were third class…assuming there was even room left in third class.

In contrast to the typical parade and route marches of the 9th, the officers attended a demobilisation lecture to prepare them for decamping. The process was in its early beginnings at last, with those embarking to Australia to be fully kitted with all the necessary items.

Each man would be issued the standard shave kit, two pairs of breeches, braces, boots, leggings and putties. In addition, they would also receive their badges, 'Australia' titles, identity disc, a holdall, sewing kit (housewife), kitbag, razor, towels, socks, singlets, two pairs of drawers, jacket and hat through to a fresh greatcoat, all of which would be issued during their quarantine stint at Rouelles, the origin of their inauguration to France.

Some very hard frosts continued to hold incessantly in the prevailing days, resulting in the village ponds freezing over an inch thick. Gliding on the frozen ponds and crashing in all manner of ungainly stacks soon replaced football as the frozen ground rendered the games impossible. However, it was ruled that the losing teams of any unorthodox rugby games would receive the 'booby prize', a tin of bully beef.

Similarly, route marches were made increasingly difficult by the frozen road surfaces, but a surprisingly brisk pace continued in spite of this adversity.

Troops would also be issued their weekly fuel allowance (firewood) for heating the indoor stoves, requiring each man to give his hut number and sign for the respective issues from the Quartermaster. It was here they could also arrange replacements for any bowls missing from the ablution amenities. Too many had mysteriously disappeared, inconveniencing numerous soldiers who were looking forward to a shave and a wash. As a result, the removal of these bowls from the ablution tables was now forbidden.

Within days, a distinct and unmistakable buzz filled the mid-January air, announcing the transfer of the relevant troops to the A.C.S. at Le Champneuf, 20 miles west of Abbeville's rural countryside dotted with its stone buildings and churches. Today, Jim would farewell his old mates: Ted would later be transferred into the 3rd Aust. Division Signals Company, Ernie into the Salvage Unit, leaving Bill to remain in the 41st. Jim, instead, accompanied Ed and Tommy, transferring to the A.C.S., where they were soon joined by the entertaining 28-year-old motor mechanic, Charles Gladstone Arthur, from the 17th Battalion.

By day's end, the four had been transferred into Australian Corps Headquarters until Taken on Strength into the school the next morning. Here, the A.C.S. Army Instructors were committed to the men's rehabilitation and training them in the industry's latest technology. Not a stone was left unturned or an opportunity squandered; 'Tomorrow' was here and within their grasp.

In the greater scheme of rehabilitation, Charlie was transferred into 'Jeumont', where he would hone his trade with salvaged lorries, amongst other industrial casualties of the war, and refresh his driving skills. Ed was also expanding his plumbing trade training with the compliments of the 'Jeumont' Technical School, the sister school to Jim and Tommy's 'Rue' where they were receiving their Junior level school education. Under present orders, they returned to their huts through the drizzling rain to collect their belongings, ensuring their billets were respectably clean on leaving, to meet back punctually at their Assembly Area by 1000 hours for transfer by lorry.

On arrival at Champneuf, it became clear there were a couple of further schools commencing: the Brigade Education Class (including Mathematics and English) at Rambures and the Brigade Telephone Mechanic School at St Maxent. All schools were driven by the Demobilisation Program to repatriate the soldiers, now referred to as students, who were falling in at their respective lecture rooms to begin their studies as per their syllabus. Today, there would be no parades.

During the remainder of the month, students presented daily in clean fatigues and greatcoats in preparation to march to the baths available to them at their respective times:

Officers (1315 – 1400 hours).
Other Ranks (1400 – 1500 hours).
P.O.W. Coy's time (900 – 1030 hours).

Sports were also keenly encouraged at Champneuf, in the open area fringed scenically by the sand dunes and the pine forests. The demand for golf clubs had increased to such an extent that orders demanded they be returned immediately on completion of the final round as supply was limited and demand was significant.

In the interest of playful antics, an errant football was released on parade by 'no one', causing such a degree of enthusiastic engagement that parade was swiftly rendered a complete debacle. The riotous disorder came to the sheer dismay of the C.O., who shook his head bemusingly while the parade sergeant bellowed at the melee of khaki before them. That said, there was a lighter side to witnessing the troops indulging in the heartening camaraderie, a scene that would not be forgotten for more than one reason.

Regardless of the uplifting mood this refreshing entertainment brought, it was soon decreed that kicking footballs within the 'lines' was utterly forbidden, resulting in footballs being issued strictly for competition matches in future.

One of the majors commanding the A.C.S. was Major Alexander Paterson, tipped to become Lieut. Colonel. Identified as an intelligent officer of excellent military knowledge in the field, Paterson's proven handling of men not only earned him the Military Cross but placed him in the spotlight as capably equipped to command the battalion. His empathy and command instilled respectful and abiding behaviour within the ranks.

By now, the men had been instructed to advise their families back home to address their mail accordingly; for Jim, it was to the *Australian Corps Central School (41st Btn – Rue School), France.* As a reminder, the Routine Order further affirmed that letters were not to be posted in civilian Post Offices...strictly the base's Post Office conveniently positioned near the Barber's Hut.

As it happened, prices had been set at the barber with a 'straight back and sides' costing 1 franc for officers, .50 francs for other ranks and a shave worth .30 francs; on that score, Jim was happy to shave for himself. Evidently, the prices were the same wherever the men were posted.

Changes were constantly implemented as more men filled the camp, Charlie Arthur's arrival included. And so it happened that during the sharp, bitter winds blowing mercilessly on 18 January, the remainder of the 41st Prisoners of War (P.O.W.) Company were Marched In from Abbeville. Their arrival coincided with the first troops of the demobilisation rollout, marching out in the middle of this bleak, freezing Winter to farewells from all corners of the camp.

Three days after the P.O.W. Company's arrival, the boys of '1915' Quota marched out in the grey dawn on their way to England for transfer to Australia. Again, farewells rang out to the waving troops as the rain began to fall gradually heavier on the columns marching in rhythmic formation destined for Gamaches Train Station. The crunching of hundreds of trampling boots grew further and further distant until they finally faded out of sight in a shroud of rain, leaving an ever-present hush falling across the camp.

Heavy frosts preceded light snowfalls in almost blizzard conditions throughout the coming week ahead of the welcome arrival of 130 stoves from Corps Head Quarters. Subsequently, no lectures or parades were held the following day. Instead, the men fitted 90 per cent of the stoves throughout the school.

While January continued bleakly and the men were still a far cry from home, demobilisation remained a slow, encouraging burn within thousands of hearts. The men simply had to wait their turn. Others had found love, bonded with their adoptive French families, and were torn between two worlds as they struggled against the dread of each encroaching moment, the pain of leaving drawing infinitely closer.

Unidentified students and German prisoners at work in the
Carpenters Shop, Australian Corps Technical School. AWM E05024.

A group of unidentified students at work in their Motor Mechanics
Shop, Australian Corps Technical School. AWM E05036.

A group of unidentified students in the Plumbers and Tinsmiths Shop, Australian Corps Technical School. AWM E05037.

A group of unidentified soldiers in the Electrical Generating Room at the Australian Corps Technical School. AWM E05015.

CHAPTER 10

Australian Corps School

"Australia has never produced anything finer than this army in France and nobody holds her divisions in higher respect than the enemy."

Unidentified students in the Engineers Machine Shop at the Jeumont Australian Corps Technical School. AWM E05028.

"THE AUSTRALIAN CORPS SCHOOL HAS evolved into a magnificent institution. It has assumed the proportions of a small military college with highly trained instructors.

Each Division sends 20 officers and 45 men for every course. The training embraces all details of infantry education, machine gun, Lewis gun, trench mortar, bombing, bayonet fitting, intelligence, signalling, cooking, and sanitation.

It has acquired a very high standard of efficiency and discipline, and organised recreational sports are also compulsory. Under a system of competitive work by the divisions it turns out keen Soldiers and is of a high value as a preparatory school for officer candidates from the ranks.

The men here learn not merely how to become good Soldiers but also military pride. There are battalions, many of which possess now battle flags richer in emblazoned honours than many British regiments could boast before this war. It has become a reputation of the Australian Army that it can do anything well which it undertakes.

This reputation built up by the Divisions in the past, is fostered at the school by every possible means. The results of the good work of this little Australian military college in the field is visible to a great extent in the magnificent health, spirits, and soldier-like qualities of the Troops in Line.

A finer and more efficient army of its size was never sent into battle.

Every man in the force believes he can go anywhere and do anything like the veterans of Wellington. The leadership of the officers is of the same high standard as the fighting powers of the men.

The work of the Australian Technical Troops - Mining and Field Engineering - is admitted by the best Judges to be equal to any in the British Army.

Australia has never produced anything finer than this Army in France, and nobody holds her divisions in higher respect than the enemy."

AUSTRALIAN CORPS SCHOOL,
FROM THE COMMONWEALTH OFFICIAL WAR CORRE-
SPONDENT.
An excerpt from The Sydney Morning Herald
Tues, 29 January, 1919.

Lieut. Arthur Edmund Dimmock set about preparing Jim and the class, including Ed, Charlie and Tommy, for the completion of their Demobilisation Forms, the first step towards going home. He had been through the Battle of the Hindenburg Line with them, and now, he was to deliver them the rehabilitation that would see them returned to Australia as civilians once again.

As their instructor, he sat behind his desk in the process of roll call, ensuring every man was present. The timely forms recently arrived via the A.I.F. Postal Service lay at his left elbow. The instructions were simple; the forms were to be completed under his direct supervision, pressing each soldier to ensure that the information recorded was complete and accurate as part of a simultaneous event throughout the A.I.F.

Following roll call, each man was called to collect his Repatriation and Demobilisation Form 534 under strict instructions not to commence writing until directed. There were questions that required some explaining, and it was critical their answers were accurate and truthful, with no detail overlooked.

On their completion, the forms would be returned to the Repatriation Department for the exclusive purpose of the Demobilisation Section, A.I.F. and the Civil Repatriation Department in Australia to issue quota and draft numbers.

Each quota generally totalled in excess of 1,000 troops aboard ships accommodating over 150 officers and more than 2,600 other ranks per embarkation. Drafts were the off-shoot of quotas, smaller contingents comprising up to three officers and often over 70 other ranks.

At 5 foot 6 ½ inches, now marginally taller than when he had enlisted, Jim was eye-to-eye with the blue-eyed lieutenant as he collected his form.

Arthur Dimmock had been 32 years old when he enlisted on 7 December 1915, having seen his fair share of action since then, including fighting alongside the trusty 41st Battalion at the Battle of the Hindenburg Line. Although battalions were scheduled to return as per their enlistment dates, 1914 and 1915 enlistments first, Dimmock was destined to remain a little longer yet to 'harry' this lot.

Under careful instruction, A.I.F. troops throughout every camp in Europe and the Middle East were launching into their forms, completing their paybook and regimental numbers, full names, decorations, permanent address before enlistment, proposed address after demobilisation, date of birth, rank/unit/division, and date of leaving Australia; all the general information expected on an A.I.F. form.

Typically, the form then involved more detailed questions...usual occupation before enlistment, last occupation before enlistment, and name and address of the employer. This third brought the troops to the next important question, *Have you a promise of employment?* Answering *Yes* only applied if your employer gave a definite and affirmative promise to keep your position open for you, not extending to a drunken promise but a definite proposal, to be perfectly clear. All possible steps were taken to ensure that this particular question was answered truthfully as future choices re-entering civilian life depended upon it.

Instances where the boss was holding their job for them but had died, leaving the business in other family members' hands, required the soldier to immediately write and ask them if his old job would still be there when he arrived back. If that were the case, they would write: *Unsure – awaiting written reply*. Otherwise, if returning to work there was unlikely, they needed to write *No*.

When they were ready to move on, the Lieutenant read out Question 12...*If physical disablement prevents the soldier from engaging in his usual occupation, what other occupation does he propose to follow?*

Dimmock had suffered gunshot wounds in the thigh and shoulder himself, which continued to give him trouble, but he, like many thousands of others, was living on the adrenaline of finally getting home. The answer given here was designed to assist in preparing the soldier for work outside of their usual occupation if an injury prevented it. The Army simply needed to know what that occupation was expected to be. As their fountain pens scratched their respective answers, Dimmock was aware he was yet to complete his own form, with the prospect of returning to Chemistry when he arrived back in Nanango, the thriving Queensland country town.

Question 13 asked if the soldier required assistance from the Australian Repatriation Department to obtain employment or locate *him in an occupation*. The next question, which was entirely optional...*Are you a member of any Trade Union? If so, which?*

As the last of them finished their writing, Dimmock went ahead with Question 15...*Is an early return to Australia desired?* Before too much enthusiasm was expressed, he pointed out that this meant they may have to pay their own passage home if there was no reasonable explanation why. So, that would be *No* unless they believed their health or some other legitimate reason required consideration.

There were those whose brothers would sail before them, so it was their greatest hope they might embark together. Tragically, all too many had discovered they were the sole survivors from a family of brothers, so their requests were made in all good faith.

Dimmock had known of brothers belonging to different units before leaving Australia, having requested to sail together and been granted permission. Nothing was impossible. It warranted consideration but was not guaranteed. They would explain this in their answer on the form, fill in the additional Form 537 for early repatriation, and patiently await further notification.

Adequately supplied with the 537s, Dimmock instructed those interested to collect one from him when they had finished. Again, clear and truthful explanations were stipulated, prompting a reminder of the penalties for declaring false requests.

Question 16 required the state they belong to and their federal electorate in BLOCK letters, which finally brought them to the signing of their signature on the far right of the form. Signing in the wrong place meant filling in another form, something no one cherished, so Dimmock would sign as their witnessing officer after they had signed correctly in front of him.

This was all they needed to complete Form 534. The rest was for the A.I.F. Education Service to determine the educational support the school could provide in assisting with the men's future occupations. In conjunction, the medical officer dealing with any of the men's injuries or incapacities would coordinate with the school to develop suitable, innovative programs.

Schooling would continue until their Demobilisation Cards were issued, allocated with their respective quota numbers and associated drafts. For those remaining, they would learn of their ships and embarkation dates in turn as the embarking quotas progressed. This was expected to take some time, but they were on their way.

The next step in this prolonged process involved Form 535...the Application for Discharge in Another Country other than Australia. Some had good reason to stay in Britain, those with family there, for instance, although others were planning on remaining here in France or another country instead of returning to Australia.

Either way, it was made clear that the interests of Australia would have first consideration rather than any man's personal agenda, with discharge outside of Australia being granted sparingly under select reasons and only in exceptional cases. Under no uncertain terms, any who were considering skipping their position in the A.I.F. to remain in the country would be unequivocally termed 'deserters'.

Three men from the Australian Corps School (A.C.S.) would complete Form 535, while elsewhere throughout the 41st Battalion's 9th reinforcements who had signed up together, a further ten would fill in the same form in their bid to remain in England. Ultimately, they had family here, so now was an excellent opportunity to make good on this offer. In this classroom, though, Lieut. Dimmock began to explain the conditions of the application:

- *That they weren't to have dependants in Australia, or at the very least, the dependants were to be agreeable to the soldier being discharged elsewhere.*
- *That Australia wasn't his domicile country and that on arriving in Australia, he would then be required to leave Australia to return to the nominated country for discharge.*
- *That he was able to maintain himself in the country in which he wished discharge or intended to go after discharge.*

- *That the countries in which discharge was to be granted were confined to the United Kingdom, some places en route via the normal course between the United Kingdom and Australia (Eg France, Egypt or Colombo).*
- *That the Govt. of Australia was absolved of any further repatriation liability to him, his wife, widow or any of his dependents, including remuneration to cover the cost of the voyage, pay and sustenance during voyage and pension rights.*
- *Plain clothes or subsequent allowance would be given subject to provisions as the 30s [shillings] per suit of plain clothes; cap or 21s [shillings] 9d [pence] per overcoat.*
- *Deferred Pay payable on discharge was to be settled as 30 per cent on discharge, 35 per cent after one month with the balance after 3 months from date of discharge.*
- *Upon discharge, all military arms, equipment, uniform and clothing in his possession were to be returned to a designated place as directed by the Director-General of Repatriation and Demobilisation.*
- *A medical examination prior to discharge was essential for recording the Applicant's condition.*

Dimmock's immediate concern was to organise those returning to Australia within the limited time they had and prepare their quotas and drafts. Those remaining in Britain were not quite so urgent, but these applications still needed to be lodged quickly for processing.

It was on a freezing, sunny Winter morning just a few days later, that parade brought the curious news of an unassuming visitor's arrival, a visitor who would be attending battalions far and wide to hear the combined voices of the troops, both in their experiences and current ambitions. Many neither knew nor had heard of the tall, spectacled stranger, although he hoped to learn a considerable amount about them and the battalion that day.

In his modest, committed manner, the young reporter amiably declared to the gathered troops of the 41st Battalion seated in the long recreational hut that he had been covering the infantry and its engagements from the Gallipoli Landings to the demobilisation process.

His visit today at the A.C.S. was to research the 41st Battalion to learn more about their experiences both in the Line and now as students of the new education classes. These classes drew particular interest as they were expressly developed for the men's repatriation into civilian life on their impending return to Australia after four years of immeasurable suffering and sacrifice.

Each man listened with interest as Captain Charles Edwin Woodrow Bean, War Correspondent and Press Representative, addressed them. As he spoke, an unseen door opened itself in front of them, revealing a future, liberating them from their world of war and leading them into an immediate new world with hope and prospects.

Charles Bean's support of the A.I.F. Education Scheme in 1919 bestowed the vision the men needed, encouraging a keenness in each hopeful, weary soldier.

From the writings of Charles Bean:

The Camp of the Australian Corps Military School among the sand dunes between Rue and the mouth of the Somme was used for the secondary and commercial School (sic), known as the Corps Central School, to prepare 500 Officers and men for the matriculation, accountancy and Civil Service examinations in Australia.

It opened on 11 January and in April, the exams were held. It was a matter of national concern that the results, excellent for so short a course, should be recognised in Australia.

A second school was opened in a refurbished glass factory fitted with trainloads of damaged machinery abandoned by the Germans. 4-6 weeks classes were organised in 18 trades for 500 students at a time.

They were billeted around, many extended their attendance and 2,000 in all passed through. Both schools joined together on 6th May and were shipped together in July for Australia on the Main.

Students at work in the Fitters Workshop. AWM E05032.

Students and prisoners in the Wood-Working Shop. AWM E05022.

Students and prisoners in the Blacksmiths Shop. AWM E05033.

Students in the Joiners Shop. AWM E05075.

Ernest A. Murr 3656, Fovant 1918.

CHAPTER 11

Champneuf Farm

As Jim looked around him, it was not so much the macabre scene that caught his eye, but the lone inverted rifle with its bayonet plunged deep into the regained soil, a solitary symbol of farewell.

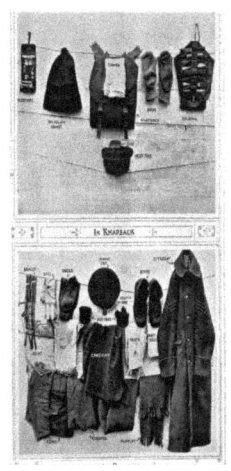

The soldier's kit. Photograph courtesy of Encyclopaedia 1914-1918 Online.

THE WINTRY CHILL MET JIM, Ed and Charlie on their return with the Camera Club to Champneuf Farm after surveying the bleak, torn battlefields and ruined villages.

Bill and Ted had accompanied them from their units, all accomplishing their individual assignments over the snowy, shell-cratered battlegrounds littered with barbed wire entanglements and reliving the torturous moments that haunted their sleep. Beyond their raw emotions was an honesty between them, a natural energy that enabled them to walk silently together yet know each other's thoughts, their movements individual yet synchronised.

In the peaceful Winter quiet, the men absorbed the carnage and might of the war's full magnitude that ripped open countries around the world, leaving them bleeding and desolate. The villages around them – Bony, Ronssoy, Guillemont Farm, Tincourt, Mt

St Quentin, Bellicourt, Peronne – God, was there any sign they had ever *been* villages at all? They thought they had become insensitive to it, but no...thousands of crosses proved otherwise.

Jim's eyes adjusted to the gloom inside the ruined farmhouse that had acted as the Field Dressing Station during their assault on the Hindenburg Line in September. Harry had been stretchered here with a bullet in his shoulder and Bill with his leg open to the bone.

All that was left of one wall was rubble strewn through the gaping cavity of the house, although a fair part of its roof remained reasonably intact. Tables used for dressing the wounded were still in place, lanterns once lit with fuel to aid surgeons and field ambulance staff to dress gaping wounds were left behind, and discarded remnants of supplies and blood-soaked clothing littered the floor.

Whiteside rallied the men as they meandered towards what remained of the barn's outside wall, peppered with machine gun damage and surrounded by drifts of dense rubble, a perfectly eerie backdrop. Jim and Ted positioned themselves in the backline of the photo; Jim out on the left behind Ted, with Bill over on the right after hastily rejoining the group with Ed and Charlie. It was unsettlingly quiet.

Percival Whiteside stepped through the wire cordon sectioned off for horses when the Line had moved further forward. Moving into the extra space gave him the distance he needed with the light available for an ideal group shot.

With the group now settled into position, Perce checked his settings. Satisfied that he had calculated well enough for a good result, he looked down over the viewer, adjusting the frame until the group was perfectly centred. On the count of three, Whiteside pressed the shutter lever, confident of a fair shot. His enthusiasm was infectious as the group disbanded to move further around the ruins for their next best photo opportunity. War now offered a new and creative perspective.

A nearby shell hole scoured by heavy rains yawned grimly under its sentry of a distant avenue of emaciated trees. As Jim looked around him, it was not so much the macabre scene that caught his eye, but the lone inverted rifle with its bayonet plunged deep into the regained soil, a solitary symbol of farewell.

It was 1 February 1919, their final day near the Hindenburg Line before commencing their return via Ronssoy. Absorbed in the scene, a thought came to Jim. Considering his words carefully, he approached 2nd Lieut. Whiteside, presently lining up the scene of two stonkered British tanks that had strayed unwittingly into an old British minefield. Formalities had been left aside in favour of casual interaction, so there was no expectation of saluting when Jim came alongside.

Jim waited while Whiteside explained the scene before them: British tanks blown to bits by our own Plum Pudding bombs originally laid for the enemy when this had been the front line during the Spring Offensive in April 1918, the irony of friendly fire. Whiteside added that eight men carried dummy tanks, each constructed of life-size, painted timber profiles, into position like Egyptian goddess's sedan chairs, creating the illusion for distant watchful eyes that the force had more tanks than it did.

Whiteside had not forgotten Jim had approached him for reasons of his own, though, and soon discovered his unexpected thinking. Jim's driving needed practice, so he sought permission to drive some of the way back to Champneuf, explaining this was the perfect opportunity to put his skills to good use after his driving lessons at the school. And the decision was soon made. Jim would drive to Amiens, where he would swap back with the driver, Reggie, for the remainder of the trip while Whiteside sat in the back with the others, enjoying the camaraderie.

Rallying the rest of the club, Whiteside announced they would have their rations now, and then Jim would drive them halfway home. He pointed out their luck was in – what with them sharing his company – so he wanted to hear all the best jokes and any stories they had to tell. Jim and Reggie were to work out their arrangements between themselves as the group made their way to the lorry where their rations waited for them, under instructions that they would have half an hour break and leave at 1300 hours.

Half an hour later, the men were returning to the back of the waiting lorry right on cue as Jim and Reggie busied themselves with the crank handle in front of the Crossley 25/30. Curious, Reggie asked Jim where he had learnt to drive. On explanation, he agreed that being rained out of their parades and sports for a few days was a plausible enough reason that they should be kept out of trouble by learning to drive a 'B' Series Liberty Lorry around St Maxent and Martainville.

Reggie's voice was drowned out by the engine roaring into life as they leapt into the cabin. To both their satisfaction, Jim avoided grinding the gears, demonstrating he was far from a learner in his skilful handling of the truck. Although the Crossley was capable of 55 mph, the drive to Amiens would take almost two hours, averaging a speed of 48 mph over the sodden roads as Reggie shared his expertise of the light airfield tender. A sturdy all-rounder, the Crossley was widely used by No. 4 Squadron, Australian Flying Corps (A.F.C.) for transporting aircrew, aviation fuel and parts, and housed a four-speed transmission with reverse, a five-bearing crank engine and dual rear wheels. Listening intently, Jim absorbed Reggie's impressive knowledge of the transport, developing his experience and confidence with each passing mile.

As the outskirts of Harbonniéres came into view, an immense boom caught Reggie in mid-sentence, startling the men in the rear of the truck, who immediately believed the lorry had hit a mine. The blown tyre threw out the Crossley's balance, and before it had slowed to a stop on the roadside, men were already leaping frantically out of the back.

Jim's practice changing a tyre during his training came in handy now, beginning with removing one of the spares stowed on the running board beside him. Reg had never actually changed a tyre out in the field himself, but Jim seemed to have it all under control, fully aware this misadventure now zeroed the focus on him to prove his abilities.

Hunkering down next to him to assist with the loose wheel's rotation, Reggie spotted the culprit as Jim pointed out the ragged chard of bomb casing protruding from the tyre. The wheel change took roughly 20 minutes, so after a welcome smoke, they continued on their way.

An hour later, stopping among the familiar ruins, the men stretched their legs while Jim and Lieut. Whiteside swapped places as arranged. Questions about how the Crossley handled in the mud and the blown tyre saga generated an exciting discussion until a quietness gradually filled the canopy. Jim finally found restorative slumber, his head bowed onto his chest for the rocking sojourn home as the French Winter night closed in on the weary travellers.

On their freezing arrival at Champneuf, with cameras in hand, the men now discovered that all applications for leave were to be submitted for the adjutant's signature no later than 1800 hours the next day, 2 February – very little notice, although enough for some.

Men taking leave would be inspected for any prohibited German or Austrian souvenirs, such as automatic pistols; selling them contravened regulations. Random inspections would be carried out in Le Havre, with any man found to be possessing contraband returned to his unit immediately and his leave cancelled or, in some cases, arrested pending further investigation. The possibility of being dishonourably charged for theft or some other charge was a significant deterrent in itself.

These new regulations were in readiness for the first demobilising troops transferring to England, their departure now ever more imminent. Accordingly, all school staff personnel who embarked from Australia on or before 31 December 1915 were required to parade in clean fatigue dress at the Orderly Room by 0915 hours on 5 February to supply their demobilisation particulars.

As these first demobilising troops assembled, the 41st P.O.W. Company marched along the road to the camp's exit, having completed the construction work of the school ahead of Capt. Mulholland's scheduled visit later that day. Over in the stores behind them, the recently received electrical supplies were being arranged and laid to commence the lighting installation in the camp's newest additional buildings. All ranks were warned against tampering with the lighting installation:

> On no account will unauthorised persons control the block switches in huts. These switches were for repair and circuit control exclusively by Staff under the direction of the Engineer Officer.

Lamps were not to be interfered with or removed from their sockets. The number of broken lamps had become so great that the demand was impossible to satisfy until the occupants were warned of a new 5 francs charge for each lamp broken in their hut.

Additionally, touching any fuse box or removing lamps from their sockets was forbidden, emphasising the safety of this 210v installation. The final word on the matter was basically:

LEAVE IT THE BLOODY HELL ALONE!

In the coming days, almost six inches of heavy snowfall descended upon the Champneuf countryside as students undertaking French studies focused on their letter writing and grammar for those hungry for commercial studies.

Parcels continued to arrive at the Army Post Office for men who had already left to return home to Australia, leaving packages that could not be forwarded. To prevent this in the future, the Army decreed that each man proceeding on embarkation would nominate another soldier to receive his parcels instead. Otherwise, all such unclaimable parcels would be handed to the Australian Comforts Fund for distribution among Australian troops.

Perfect skies shone bright and clear in the following days, bringing southeasterly breezes and the joy of skating and sliding on the local ice-laden ponds. So, naturally, seized with boyish glee, Jim and the men joined the others, making the most of these amusing antics, unheeded, ahead of the coming thaw.

Late Winter progressed with an emerging new threat. A surprise smallpox outbreak led the military authorities to recommend urgent re-vaccination against contracting the disease, especially important with the constant movement of troops risking the disease's spread.

In the wake of this unsettling announcement came a comparatively more welcome one: an Australian Corps Essay Competition, which had been in the wind for the literacy classes. The subject was 'Education for Democracy', and there were prizes for best and second-best essays.

With so many troops encamped, ensuring cleanliness and hygiene was paramount. School Order No. 41, subtitled simply 'relief', was a reminder to the men that urinating in the lines or on the ground in the vicinity of the camp was *a filthy habit and must cease*. The men's carefree attitude towards decorum continued on parade and around the camp, mandating urine buckets be placed in the lines at night for convenience. The clear message was: *Use them!*

Rubbish was another issue. Strewn indiscriminately among the bushes near the Engine House, litter prompted another order to improve the disappointing impression of the camp by placing all rubbish in the bins provided.

For Jim, such orders brought no surprises…until *this* totally unexpected announcement. The Army would be taking applications for commissions into the permanent forces, calling for interviews with the adjutant to obtain particulars. The thought of re-enlisting made Jim's blood run cold, but the Australian armed forces were about to dwindle to a bare minimum of permanent staff.

Back in Australia, in light of this opportunity, his wounded brother-in-law, Steve, was preparing for medical discharge from the 42nd Battalion, re-enlisting within 48 hours for a further two years. During that time, Steve Johnson would eventually become staff sergeant.

Endless parades in the mid-February thaw continued amid clear and mild days scattered with occasional light showers as more men were Marched Out for demobilisation. Battalion Routine Orders warned the departing troops of counterfeit notes proffered to soldiers in exchange for money, as several such cases had occurred at railway stations in London. All ranks should guard against having money transactions with strangers. Those remaining in camp were not concerned with fake notes where they were going, though: Abbeville.

Restrictions on visiting the French village were removed, with passes resuming under the same conditions as other nearby locations. Any officers and other ranks who wished to spend the night at Abbeville were to make their arrangements promptly as accommodation was limited.

In stark contrast to some free time at Abbeville, Jim and the other troops were on notice that their exams were approaching; the focus was on providing students with stationery and emphasising the importance of their attendance. The Corps Central School set the examinations to commence in several weeks on 14 April, and students arranged their studies accordingly. Every student received an inkpot and fountain pen from the librarian under the instruction that each student was to take every care with these as he would have to bring them with him into the examination room. Ink would be available in the coming days.

It had not gone unnoticed that several students were consistently absent from their classes without reasonable excuse, prompting a warning of the consequences from the Superintendent of Studies. For the second time, the Superintendent made it abundantly clear that they *are not here to shirk their work* or they would not receive the certificates required to build their futures at the end of the course. He further specified that if a man was not attending a lecture, he would continue his studies in his hut.

In the men's interests, Lieut. Blackshaw crossed to England to collect much-needed textbooks ahead of the exams, returning on the 26 February as Lieut. Nolan arrived in London to replenish school supplies.

The students' initial school concert was held in Hut F at 2000 hours a couple of nights before Blackshaw's return and hailed as a great success. Perfectly timed, the heartening mood from the concert bolstered the men's spirits as the weather devolved into a dull gloom with cold winds for the remainder of the month.

February 23rd's Routine Order brought good news for a select few. Danish or other Scandinavian men may visit their native land before returning to Australia, an opportunity too good to miss. Any eligible men should see the adjutant at 1230 hours the next day.

As entertaining as this news was to Jim and his mates, disappointment intervened when the adjutant cancelled overnight leave to Amiens. Instead, it would be available from 0900 to 2100 hours – not what the men hoped for, but it was leave.

March's dull start with sharp winds continued for the remainder of the first week, although the Spring atmosphere soon returned, bringing with it the exam timetable, which had been set down for the two weeks from 14 to 26 April:

Timetable of Examinations – Australian Corps Central School

Monday 14th April	*English*	*1400–1700 hours*
Tuesday 15th April	*History*	*1400–1700 hours*
Wednesday 16th April	*Geography*	*1400–1700 hours*
Thursday 17th April	*Arithmetic*	*1400–1700 hours*
Monday 21st April	*Book Keeping*	*1400–1700 hours*
Tuesday 22nd April	*Arithmetic*	*1400–1700 hours*
Wednesday 23rd April	*Geometry*	*0900–1200 hours*
Friday 25th April	*Business Principles*	*TBA*

The year was progressing slowly for the students at Champneuf, although 1 March brought the first day of Spring, along with the change of time to French Summer Daylight Saving, coming into force from 2300 hours the following night.

In true spirit and admiration for the skill of the school's resident photographers, many students took the opportunity to obtain Camera Club photographs of the school's workshops and surroundings. Jim appreciated the satisfying results the practice gave him, using the film supplied by the Quartermaster Store. His Kodak Eastman had turned out to be a solid investment.

That same afternoon, a large marquee stood completed, erected by the troops as a Recreation Hall for dances, pictures and lectures, a substitute for the hangar the school had originally requested. The ingenuity of the marquee finally achieved the results they were desperate for without further painful waiting.

Although the marquee was finished, the students and staff held that evening's dance in the Le Crotoy Casino, attended by local villagers and those from further outlying areas. Cinema shows would screen in the marquee on Wednesdays and Saturdays after tonight, providing compelling entertainment that Jim, Ed, Charlie and Tommy looked forward to immensely.

More entertainment followed the next afternoon as R.A.F. Lieut. Dicks made an emergency landing in his Sopwith Camel – a transfixing event for the school but utterly heart-stopping for Lieut. Dicks. Consequently, the extent of the plane's damage resulted in the R.A.F. officer remaining at the school for a week while the plane underwent repairs.

However well-intended, the school's encouragement was proving inadequate for those who had become increasingly restless in the camp during the preceding weeks, believing instead that employment was sufficient to prepare them for civilian life rather than attending school. Some placed newspaper advertisements seeking employment while awaiting repatriation. The adjutant put a stop to that, promptly releasing the order to *Cease this practice immediately*.

That crisp Spring morning had shown great promise until deteriorating into light rain that hampered the troops unloading the newly arrived stores. After remaining outstanding for two months, bulk quantities of tables and administration forms had finally arrived from Ordnance. The increasing lack of supplies was worsening day by day.

In addition to the ordnance supplies, three further marquees arrived from 3 A.G.H. for recreational purposes during the next few days, along with the newly released order that Official Time was to be checked daily at 0900 hours by the men systematically checking their watches against the external Orderly Room clock. Synchronisation was integral and would be maintained at all times.

To the hierarchy's dissatisfaction, a further inspection on 6 March showed the camp was unclean and unsanitary. Rubbish continued to be a problem, and the student other ranks' Quarters were in a *filthy condition* prompting swift rectifying action *at once*. All huts and quarters were to be kept scrupulously clean to prevent this squalor from putting the camp in *danger of a serious outbreak of disease*.

Hut commanders were responsible for designating one man from each hut to be accountable for its cleanliness and immediate surroundings, a monotonous task that did not bode well for some. Jim, on the other hand, had already manifested an orderly attitude that would last his lifetime.

The parade sergeant still administered the occasional punishment for urinating in the lines, amounting to two days' forfeited pay, along with the recurring cases of A.W.L. costing varying amounts.

Extended lengths of absence and their circumstances determined the difference between A.W.L. and desertion. Unlike the British, the A.I.F. never executed a soldier for desertion. Instead, the punishment was jail time for the duration of their service unless released back into their unit, as in the case of Fred Stenner, Jim and Emmel's family friend in the 49th Battalion.

Fred had argued drunkenness for his 18-day absence to no avail; he received a jail term of five years for the offence. Two years later on 15 March 1918, he rejoined the 49th Battalion under a suspended sentence to assist in bolstering the depleting numbers of infantry. Fred was gassed after three weeks in the trenches and hospitalised for over two months before again returning to his unit. He would finally board the *Commonwealth* and return to Australia on 13 April 1919.

Lightening the camp's atmosphere was the ever-popular weekly event held by the students, the dance at Le Crotoy, with entertainment extending further into the next day. All ranks engaged with members of the Women's Army Auxiliary Corps (W.A.A.C.s), recently renamed for their exemplary war effort. Originally Queen Mary's Army Auxiliary Corps (Q.M.A.A.C.), the W.A.A.C.s embraced their new title, particularly the unique acronym, with the corps' swelling commitment propelling the Women's Army into a promising future.

With spirits still high in camp from the recent carousing, Rev. G.E. Muschamp marched in to carry out the duties of a theological tutor.

Unfortunately, his arrival coincided with reported tardiness demonstrated throughout the ranks on the blowing of 'Retreat'. The troops were immediately on notice that they would pay due tribute by standing to attention while the bugler sounded the call, with the warning that *This will be enforced.*

The adjutant, bent on sharpening any tardy attitudes, mandated that in future, all sleeping quarters in the school were to be cleaned and ready for inspection at 0900 hours, with the men being shaven and clean by that time. Additionally, General Parade at 0900 hours would be staggered according to the first letter of the troops' surnames, beginning with A-C, followed by D-H the next day; Charlie Arthur, Ed Barnett and Tommy Edward's respective days.

Much to Charlie and Ed's misfortune, their parade was met with heavy showers, easterly winds and a thick fog shrouding the camp all day. The men stood to attention throughout the entire unpleasant process, acquainted with far worse, only now their larrikin attitudes were growing increasingly indifferent.

Later that night in Crotoy, Jim and the students held a successful and much-anticipated fancy dress ball attracting many artful costumes devised by whatever means possible, including using some pieces commandeered from empty houses. Other men creatively applied souvenired paraphernalia from the battlefield for even more unique and interesting effects.

Within days, the men received word that the School Notice Board displayed a copy of the 'Assistance and Benefits' provisions available to the soldiers returning to Australia. Further over on the same board were the results of the match between the 41st Battalion Australian Rules Football Team and the A.C.S. from 17 March, resulting in a win for their 41st Battalion mates.

To the men's disappointment, the announcement came on the 20th that The Café de l'Hotel de la Marine, Le Crotoy, was out of bounds to all troops until 27 March. But their dismay did not stop there. Leave from the 23rd was also suspended until further notice. Due to a strike in England, *no* travel was permitted for personnel on leave, demobilisation, or cadres (groups of men assigned to specific duties). This news evoked much grumbling and muttering on parade, especially from those who were next in line to return to England under their allotted quotas. For them, embarkation taunted exasperatingly just beyond their reach.

As frustrating as this news was, the delay brought the ideal opportunity for any students who had not been medically examined at the school and weren't attending lectures to parade at a suitable time for their review, assisting greatly in their demobilisation's smooth processing.

Sequential increments for parade continued to progress, with Jim presenting with those in the P–Z group from 29 to 31 March. During this parade, the adjutant again directed their attention to the numerous cases of men reporting to the quartermaster to replace 'lost' items of clothing. In future, there would be no further replacements issued without returning the old or worn-out article. Consequently, neglecting to return the item would result in the amount being debited to the requesting man's paybook.

Their fun had just run out.

41st Battalion Camera Club. Jim Rainey far left. Ted Marsh second from left and Bill Mitchell far right. AWM P01861.005.

29 September 1918. A damaged Australian Medical Dressing Station used during the Hindenburg Line offensive. AWM E05244.

Liberty Trucks of the 1st Australian Motor Transport Company, Peronne. AWM P00520.005.

Le Crotoy – the Statue of Joan of Arc and Hotel de la Marine on left.
From personal collection.

CHAPTER 12

From April to Le Havre

Their day had finally arrived; Quota 48 and Jim's Draft 98, cloaked in camaraderie and good humour, were leaving for Le Havre Camp.

3rd Division Demobilisation Quota 39 marching into A.B.D. Le Havre. April, 1919. AWM C04797.

SWEEPING IN WITH APRIL'S rejuvenating atmosphere came Brig. General Long, Director of Education, and Capt. Mulholland, Assistant Director of Education, visiting the school to interview the various classes well into the afternoon before leaving for 3rd Division H.Q.

As a result, the 11th Brigade's weekly Report on Education concurred that the education of the units was proceeding satisfactorily, regardless of the gradual demobilisation. In addition, trade lectures conducted by Sapper Ingram, 11th Field Company, proved successful, and both Long and Mulholland expressed their genuine appreciation.

The days ahead were typical of the irresistible French Spring, and on 2 April, the Medical Board arrived from 3rd Division to inspect the school's personnel, completing their duties the next day. No classes were held owing to the medical inspections, conveniently coinciding with the visiting 34th Btn Rugby Team's match for the afternoon, although not a memorable outcome for the Home Team. In the interest of competitive spirit, large numbers also attended several rounds of golf and other sports in the perfect morning.

Lieut. Adjut. Ewing released the surprising but welcome order regarding original colour patches. The order stated that upon arrival in England, any battalions who were transferred to another unit when withdrawn from the Field may wear the distinguishing colour patches of their old units. This news was eagerly received by those originally in Jim's sister battalion, the 42nd, although it still stung that the A.I.F. had integrated them into the 41st to begin with. This order also applied to personnel transferred from their original units to commence new duties at A.I.F. H.Q. and Dept of Repatriation and Demobilisation or on the permanent cadre of a training unit in England.

This appeasing colour patch announcement preceded an update on the ever-fluid demobilisation progress. In reality, Brigade Schools Rue, Jeumont and others located further away could not survive beyond the next demobilisation draft due to the receding numbers. It was no surprise when the following week's Report on Education confirmed that all Brigade Schools would discontinue that week on 12 April.

From their inception until now, these schools had proven their undoubted value, with instructors maintaining exemplary enthusiasm throughout. Students everywhere also expressed their gratitude for the Education Branch's assistance, some endeavouring to stay on as long as possible. Seven students of the Commercial School, Le Translay, had elected to continue their studies at Rue while the telegraphy class at St Maxent would continue under the decorated Lieut. Trudgian, M.C. within the 41st Battalion.

Under the Brigade's organisation, the impending draft was bringing the main educational activities of the battalion classes to a close. Jim's classes were considerably smaller than last week, although evidence suggested proportionate instructors and students would allow lessons to continue successfully during repatriation. Libraries and popular discussions had also continued as expected, although not for long.

On 16 April, the staggered roll-out continued as Quota 39, the longest serving troops of the 41st Battalion made up of enlistments from 1916 and 1917, marched out at 1000 hours from the crossroads, ¾ mile southwest of St Maxent. A week later, on 24 April, they were followed by Quota 45 comprising the 41st Battalion's Field Ambulances, Divisional Signal Company and Divisional Train Unit.

Jim, who no longer belonged to his old 41st Battalion but to A.C.S. as a student, could only watch and farewell the departing troops as the contingents moved out. Bill, Ted and Ernie were already on the move from their camps elsewhere and would meet Jim at Codford when he finally reached England. In the meantime, lessons persisted for Quota 48 and Jim's Draft 98 until their Movement Order No. 21 was released 11 days later, the last School Order submitted by the A.C.S.

Dated 5 May 1919, the order began with instructions that breakfast the next day would be at 0800 hours, followed by their midday meal at 1145 hours, consisting of their day's ration, which the men would carry. Additional bulk rations would be delivered by the quartermaster.

Finally, their day had arrived; Quota 48 and Jim's Draft 98, cloaked in camaraderie and good humour, were leaving for Le Havre Camp.

Carefree with elation, the men Fell In on the general parade ground at 1245 hours in full marching order, each carrying a blanket. At 1300 hours, the head of the column passed the starting point outside the school's orderly room as the last quotas marched out at 100 yard intervals between companies.

With that, Lieut. Adjut. W.T. Ewing wrote his final entry:

AND HEREIN THE AUSTRALIAN CORPS SCHOOL CLOSED.

Within a few hours, the troops arrived at the 11th Demobilisation Regiment Headquarters, Gamaches, where they were all directed into billets under the strict instructions that they were to be left clean and satisfactory, and no accounts left outstanding.

Every member of Jim's quota and draft was identified, medically examined, and issued their Demobilisation Movement Card 541 containing their respective quota and draft numbers. Each name, rank and regimental number, unit and quota number was entered onto an official register known as the nominal roll, and along with every soldier who had passed through this depot, Jim was questioned to ensure he had handed in all ammunition, bombs and explosives.

This procedure included his waterproof sheet, Lee Enfield rifle, bayonet and web equipment under the present Peace Time regulations before leaving for A.B.D., Le Havre. From this point, each soldier produced their freshly issued Demobilisation Movement Card while passing through the Le Havre camps and anticipated embarkations until their eventual arrival in Australia.

Preparing for the troops' arrival at Gamaches Railway Station the next morning, each Company and Head Quarters had detailed two batmen under the command of one N.C.O. to act as loading party and baggage guard for the officers' baggage being delivered by 1000 hours. The school then proceeded by train to Le Havre, departing at 1430 hours after being inspected and approved by a medical officer. By rendering the necessary certificate, the officer verified the wagons were sanitary, and all medical equipment and personnel were complete.

As the men boarded the train, Quota 48's C.O. sent a telegram ahead in readiness for their arrival at the reception camp. Along the way, the hungry men would consume their bulk rations, but only with an officer's permission.

So far, the troops' organisation had progressed smoothly, with each soldier adhering to good train journey discipline, having been drilled into them that misconduct would cause delays and dislocation of these very complex transport arrangements. Any unnecessary disruptions impacted rail and shipping, causing substantial delays for the quota and the following troops, a totally unacceptable situation.

Ahead of the train's arrival at Soquence Triage Station 4 miles from Le Havre Reception Camp, their blankets were rolled into bundles and collected, ready for handing into A.B.D.'s Quartermaster, and the men's names marked off against the Nominal Roll. Waiting lorries transferred them the 4 rattling miles to the Cleansing Camp consisting of a 'delouser', medical examination facilities and an Equipment Store, where they were lectured briefly about the procedure they would undertake.

Impressively, the Cleansing Camp delouser could process 300 men an hour, although the maximum number who had ever passed through in a day was barely two weeks earlier on Quota 39's arrival when the camp processed 2,287 men. It was in the wind that between February and June, the end of the troops' occupation in France, the facility would process over 56,000 men. The exact number would tally 56,514.

Proceeding in single file to the orderly's window, Jim and his quota each received a numbered bag and two corresponding discs: one disc for their boots, the other for their bag of personal items. One of the clerks showed the men their individually numbered racks in the undressing chamber, where each man hung his greatcoat, puttees, uniform and hat. This was also where they discarded their underwear, socks and worn-out towel in a drum before entering the Medical Officer's Station to hand over any personal items for storing in designated pigeon-holes.

Following in line, Jim moved on to the next window, where all boots and discs were handed over for placing in another compartment, the line progressing surprisingly quickly. The men's clothes were then promptly sent to one of six fumigation chambers for sterilisation at 130ºC for 20 minutes. Once finished, another orderly removed the trolley from the chamber, hanging the racks of clothes in the dressing room on the corresponding pegs for collection when the men returned.

Medically examined and showered, Jim and the others found their clothes hanging in the next room, including a fresh issue of underwear and socks for each man. Having dressed, he presented his numbered disc at the orderly's window to retrieve the rest of his belongings.

Processing busily continued as Jim's quota proceeded to the Quartermaster Store to disassemble any equipment they carried, ready for inspection. Hearing his name called, Jim strode into the store to empty his equipment onto the counter. He was one of seven being attended to by the same two efficient clerks deftly performing at their 300-personnel-an-hour rate. The first clerk categorised the items, which the second clerk then inspected for any missing articles swiftly and surely.

Here, Jim silently farewelled the last of his war equipment. In its place, he received his sea kit bag, where he would store his clothing and shaving kit for the remainder of his A.I.F. service abroad, two and a half weeks at most. Jim, Charlie, Ed, Tommy and the rest transitioning with them would later proceed to other billets within the A.B.D., the base where their time in France began nine months earlier, and no one would return to the Cleansing Camp again.

They were now paraded in front of their C.O., Lieut. H.G. Nolan, for marching out to A.B.D., their home for their last fortnight abroad in France, where the four mates and the remainder of the draft were consigned to a separate depot from Quota 48.

Once allocated their billets, the hungry men soon enjoyed hearty meals served by the cooks, and every possible measure was provided to ensure their comfort. The men were treated to gymnastics displays held by the Y.M.C.A., the latest silent movies, basketball matches with American and Interbase teams and dancing twice a week, which proved enormously popular.

During the whole embarkation process, the exemplary conduct of the ranks streamlined the proficient processing of all quotas and drafts, the first step on the long road back.

April 1919. 3rd Aust Dvn men of Quota 39 at Gamaches Railway Station before embarking for the Demobilisation Base. AWM E05161.

April 1919. 3rd Dvn soldiers of Quota 39 waiting for a train at Gamaches Railway Station. AWM E05159

Australian Base Depot (A.B.D.), Rouelles. AWM A02044.

1918. S.S. Lorina. Photograph courtesy of unknown donor.

CHAPTER 13

Adieu to France

Bystanders waving farewell lined the harbour shores while sloops and other smaller vessels accompanied the steamer with cheers of 'Au Revoir', 'Merci' and 'Bon Voyage'.

Australians drawing up a gangway for disembarkation. AWM C02574.

CAPTAIN D.F. MIDDLETON WAS the C.O. in charge of embarkation at the bustling Quai d'Escale, Port Le Havre.

As Embarkation Staff Officer, he had the immense task of overseeing the loading of the ships, compiling the personnel records, and ensuring the smooth transition of the ceaseless stream of repatriating troops, a sight that could not please him more. Every day was another day closer to going home himself, and evidence that France was quickly emptying of her khaki population.

Advance parties of two officers and 10-20 other ranks preceded the demobilising quotas 11 days ahead to enable a smooth transfer at Southampton, England, for the disembarking troops who followed in their thousands. Jim's Quota 48 advance party was now in place, ready for the quota and draft, patiently awaiting their call at A.B.D. to embark at Le Havre.

Aiding procedures were P.O.W.s who would load cargo and luggage into the hold of each waiting transport. For the moment, they were kept in a shed at the dock until loading orders were issued.

Each day, a call to the Divisional Naval Transport Officer (D.N.T.O.) in Le Havre revealed which ships were expected to arrive in port, making ready for any preparation required for docking. Lorries were then assigned to collect supplies and returning parties from whichever ship was being unloaded.

Intermittent drizzle came in briefly off the Channel that morning, 23 May 1919, as the *S.S. St George* and the *S.S. Lorina* lay alongside the dock, ready for loading. Le Havre Port Base already had the numbers for today's embarkations and details of the ships taking the troops to Southampton, so Middleton could now advise the D.N.T.O. what time to order the steam for the waiting ships. Both ships were ready for loading by 1430 hours.

Middleton called A.B.D. to tell them to move all troops out of camp at 1330 hours without any further orders. Today's quotas would come by lorries and the draft by train....Jim's Draft 98. Their Demobilisation Movement Cards showed they were all part of No. 2 Group, destined temporarily for Sutton Veny on England's rolling Salisbury Plain. From there, they would transfer three to four days later as No. 3 Group to nearby Codford. The two schools, 'Rue' and 'Jeumont', comprised No. 3 Group, also identifying as Quota 48; Jim remained in Rue School.

As the departing train blew its shrill whistle and the engine picked up pace, Jim noticed more birdlife was beginning to return to the budding trees. The Spring afternoon was as perfect as he had seen during his time in France, and the trip through the torn countryside would see them reach Le Havre in an hour. In that time, their baggage would already have been stowed on the transport by P.O.W.s, ready for off-loading on the troops' arrival in the South England port.

Rumbling on through Montgeron shortly after, the train passed the prominent French barracks of Forte de Tourneyville until finally arriving at the Quay, where embarking troops were making their way steadily up the gangway of the *St George*. However, it was the idling *Lorina* that would take Jim and his draft from France today.

Bearing twin funnels and masts, the *Lorina* was a neat, double-propellor turbine steamer, built around the same time as the *Ormonde* and decked out as a troopship when she was finally launched in 1917. As her smoke stacks plumed steady streams of grey smoke, her engines rumbled into life, sounding familiarly like the low, warning growl deep in the belly of a menacing dog.

Fifty officers and 900 other ranks of Quota 54 boarded the *St George* in a streamlined procession. After 1 1/4 hours, Jim and the troops were finally given clearance to embark, making their way to the *Lorina*'s gangway with their Demobilisation Movement Cards, paybooks and tags ready for presentation. In typically military fashion, the sea of khaki gradually cleared until only a handful of dock workers and others remained on the dock. Captain Middleton surveyed the gangway as it was lowered and removed by a contingent of 50 men, supervised by Middleton's staff sergeant.

They had seen it all before as newly boarded troops. Still, there was always cause for shouts of encouragement and whistles as the soldiers in two parallel lines of khaki slouch hats below strained against the iron traverse like a man versus machine 'tug-of-war'.

Middleton made his way back to his office to send the necessary telegrams ahead to Southampton as the *Lorina* cast off at 1630 hours to follow the *St George* amid yahoos and cooees. Middleton's closing records stated:

> *Embarkation carried out in splendid weather.*

A small tugboat skilfully manoeuvred the ship towards the harbour entrance and into the safe channel between the two concrete beacons at its mouth. Bystanders waving farewell lined the harbour shores while sloops and other smaller vessels accompanied the steamer to calls of *Au Revoir*, *Merci* and *Bon Voyage*.

Long shadows began stretching from the corner towers of the imposing 19th-century train station as its glazed arches glittered brilliantly in the afternoon sunlight. Nearby, elegantly dressed crowds promenaded the quayside while others casually strolled out to the three-tier Semaphore building near the harbour entrance. They were here to farewell the khaki troops, those courageous men who had fought alongside them for what seemed a lifetime of unfathomable fear and grief. Their own personal sacrifices were not forgotten.

For the waving troops onboard, Le Havre never felt so distant than at this moment as they watched the familiar port retreating further into the distance. This sweeping vista would almost certainly be their last glimpse of the French shoreline, their last contact with the land where brothers and mates lay forever.

In the beckoning calm of the English Channel ahead of them, the *St George* could clearly be seen nearing the horizon as the *Lorina* steadied her course for Southampton, 9 ½ hours away.

Compelled by some unseen force, the departing soldiers remained at their viewpoints in a deep sense of quiet reverie as the once unfamiliar shoreline, the very place Jim originally glimpsed under the duress of an inflamed inner ear, grew steadily distant. After a while, the rhythmic blinking of the beacons at the harbour entrance, showing them the way back, was the only indication of Le Havre.

Two and a half hours later, they were fully fed and apprised of their disembarkation details. Afterwards, a lively and humorous show performed by a Concert Troop kept the men amused, adding to the light-hearted atmosphere.

Draft 98, with its three officers, 73 other ranks and one Y.M.C.A. officer, would arrive at Southampton at 0200 hours for disembarkation onto another train to their respective Sutton Veny or Codford camps. In the meantime, soldiers slept on deck wherever they could, making a bivouac for themselves or in hammocks down below. Most found the clear night inviting enough to stay on deck, a preference they had developed during anxious voyages fraught with U-boat attacks. For others, it was as if a sense of freedom was drawing them to the open space of the deck rather than being confined below.

On arriving in England in the early hours, Jim's Draft 98 was met by the General Combatant Commander (G.C.C.) and the Group Staff Captain (G.S.C.), with their Standing Orders and General Instructions for issuing to the Quota Adjutant. Now, the troops were checked off against the Nominal Roll as they disembarked to board a train for the 6-hour journey to Sutton Veny, with sleep quickly taking over the tired soldiers. In four days, they would be settling into their 14-day Embarkation Leave, their last of any description, before departing for home. Subsequently, leave would not be extended, and any absence beyond that would be considered A.W.L.

By around 0800 hours, Jim and the rest of his draft had left the train for processing and to be issued with equipment, kitbag, pay, leave arrangements and any special applications, including those for Family Ship and Marriage Leave, if required. Jim hoped that his old schoolmates would be waiting in Codford, but only time would tell.

For the moment, though, the men could enjoy the opulent Greenfield House manor, the Headquarters of the Y.M.C.A., where they could relax comfortably and indulge in its flavoursome meals. Photographers recorded the soldiers' comings and goings throughout the manor's grounds with their dazzling flower borders and lush lawns.

After a few days, they boarded a train for Codford, the railway line passing through Fovant, where the men admired the familiar military insignias etched deeply into the chalk hillside by the troops of 1916. The impressive A.I.F. Rising Sun Badge was the largest, measuring 175 ft wide by 150 ft high alongside the Y.M.C.A. insignia, a kangaroo and other foreign regimental crests.

On another nearby hillside, a chalk map of Australia stood 150 ft across overlooking Hurdcott, although the New Zealanders, not to be outdone, had carved out an immense kiwi covering two acres at Bulford, a neighbouring camp. Sculpting the emblems and maintaining them regularly was a well-known punishment for those on disciplinary charges at Salisbury Plain. Not an unpopular task, depending on the contrary weather conditions.

Codford's recognisable huts came into view, the place where it had all started for them. Segmented groups of 40 huts belonging to each of its 15 training camps were regimentally lined up in rows of five across and eight long. Each camp had a kitchen, mess hall, store, library, showers, laundry, games room and a recreation hall with cinema facilities, all conveniently located on either side of the flag area where they paraded. There was even a billiards room for the officers.

Within the hour, they were all detrained, paraded, and appointed their billets. Depositing their kits, they made their way to the mess hall, where a hot lunch of stew and potatoes waited for them, followed by stewed fruit and steaming tea. Their mail had also been sorted, and they were to front to the Post Office Hut for collection.

Their final leave had begun, time they would not only spend enjoying with mates they would soon part with, but also idly thinking of home and the future.

Demobilisation Movement Card

A.I.F. Form 541

Unit *Aust Corps Central School (41st Bn)*
Surname (in block letters) *RAINEY*
Other Names in full *James Henry*
Reg. No. *3653* Rank *Pte*
Where to report in U.K. *2 group Sutton Veny*
Proceeding to U.K. for reasons [*C*] set out below.

(A) Early Repatriation.
(B) Early Repatriation with wife.
(C) Ordinary Repatriation.
(D) Extended leave _____ months.
(E) Discharge elsewhere than in Australia.
(F) Educational or Industrial Employment.
(G) Any other purpose not mentioned above

Reference letters

The reference letter designating the reasons will be marked in the square above.

Date *5 MAY* Signature _____
O.C. Unit _____

EMBARKATION QUOTA No. ___ (To be filled in by Unit and ONLY when the individual is a member of the Quota).

DRAFT No. *98* (To be filled in at Base, HAVRE)

Jim's Demobilisation Card. Note Unit as Australian Corps Central School (41st Btn) From personal collection.

1919. Sutton Veny, England. Australian soldiers at the front of the Y.M.C.A. Headquarters at Greenhill House. AWM H01729.

The famous chalk badges of Fovant. Note the Australian Rising Sun insignia on the right. AWM P05845.046.

CHAPTER 14

Last Weeks at Codford

Huts stood forlornly empty, with that same haunting quiet permeating every corner of the camp like an oppressive fog.

A typical 1914-1918 hut. Note the Australian humour... 'Ye olde coal hole' and 'Down pan'. Photograph courtesy of Australian War Memorial.

AS HOPED, HIS OLD MATES were waiting for him. Well, some of them, at least.

On his arrival at Codford, Jim discovered that Harry had been transferred home on the *Demosthenes* on 16 January, news that was not entirely surprising, only that he had not heard it until now. Nonetheless, he was relieved for his wounded mate.

Finally reunited with Bill, Ted and Ernie, more news greeted him that three of them would be attending a wedding...in *Scotland*. Using the last week of their Embarkation Leave to get there, Jim, Bill and Ted knew they would be A.W.L., in all likelihood, by the time they returned.

Parental consent was needed for a couple to marry in England, a situation that led to many English couples, especially copious numbers of soldier brides, escaping across the border to be married. This was not the case in Scotland. As long as the bride was over 18 years old, she could marry there legally and freely of her own volition.

For this wedding, though, the boys were travelling to Campbeltown, a seaside village on the Kintyre Peninsula. The occasion proved a happy time for Jim, adding up to a dozen names and addresses of Scottish lasses in his address book...or, more precisely, the girls added them.

On their return journey, the jovial trio hoped their travels would go unnoticed, a hope that was short-lived as the train pulled into Glasgow Central Station. The three men quickly spotted two 'provos', the Australian Army Provost Corps (Military Police), watching the train as it ground to a lurching halt in a hiss of steam. Their luck was entirely out.

Lieuts. J. Row and H.L. Wheeler of the Provost Corps entered the train looking for identification. On presenting their paybooks and Demobilisation Cards, the absconders soon found themselves escorted from the train and along the grand platform they had admired only days before. Fined six days' pay, the boys received a sound admonishing for good measure.

Statistics showed that by 1919, one in 14 Australians in the A.I.F. were imprisoned under a Court Martial, as against one in 50 New Zealanders in the New Zealand Corps, evidence that the Australian troops lived up to their reputation as reckless and headstrong, matching their reputation as warriors in battle.

June 10 saw Quota 48 had returned from Embarkation Leave unless they had been A.W.L. like Jim and his mates. Those who had returned from leave, including Charlie, Ed and Tommy, had been organised into their respective school's classwork, so Jim soon settled into his studies and Embarkation Drills alongside them.

Further away in the camp, Ted and Bill had returned to A.I.B.D., Codford, to recommence their other duties. It was the English Summer, and everyone sported an unapologetically carefree attitude towards the world. A.W.L. was the least of anyone's concerns - their first and last thoughts were of embarkation and home.

Quota 48 had now re-established its solid Debate Class which was summarily beaten by Quota 42's team in the Inter Quota Debates conducted by No. 3 Group. The helpful event enabled the men to voice candid and robust opinions in demonstrated belief, or non-belief, of a topic. It was an opportunity to develop skills such as confident vocal projection, critical thinking, and logical arguments with newfound, expressive energy.

On the learning front, though, textbooks were simply non-existent, meaning Rue and Jeumont Schools could not offer any operational classes during the third week of June. Two hundred pounds worth of textbooks and materials were slated for the trip back to Australia, suggesting the men would either have to wait, or classes would recommence onboard during their long journey home.

Either way, there were high expectations of Jim's quota, but with few or no books available, or any other material for that matter, Quota 48 was left entirely unequipped to study. Instead, the troops were kept occupied with lectures on varying subjects, drills and parades to prepare for the forthcoming Peace Day Parade, along with undertaking any maintenance or demolition to keep the men busy and boost morale.

Just under 5,000 men had sailed for Australia in this past week, and an eerie quiet pervaded the camp. The deserted huts were dismantled by working parties to which Jim and Tommy had been assigned when Charlie and Ed, both highly amused, arrived from Guard Duty with a rumour they had heard and believed on good authority to be true.

The story went that some weeks earlier, when two men were carrying out Changing of the Guard, two in the Guard had performed a mock 'change over' involving slapstick theatrics, reducing the incoming guards to helpless laughter. The officers, however, were not amused, and the two men narrowly avoided charges of Dereliction of Duty.

Told and enjoyed many times, the humorous account boosted the men's spirits in their final weeks. There was a good chance of someone else trying on the same lark, regardless of the tighter protocols the Brass was determined to inflict on them concerning unruly behaviour.

Private Frank Blake, previously of the A.N.Z.A.C. Mounted Division, wrote in his diary only two months earlier:

Wednesday April 18th

Guard duty to day our S.M [Sergeant Major] is considered a Military crank. Very amusing. Going through procedure changing guard. Everybody fed up. S.M at his word. Jim B supposed to be on duty at Guard room. Your humble expected to march up with guard, halt & proceed with Military manoeuvres. Jim B. supposed to challenge & call out guard. This is what happened. Marched up to Guard room. Jim B. instead of challenging said in a dramatic voice (Who are these people) Little Ernie a Corporal appeared from nowhere & said I'm _____ if I know. Result collapse of Guard with laughter. SM. went mad & dismissed us with disgust.

On a more grounded level, the Group Education Officer and Rue School established a well-considered lecture syllabus rostered to allotted huts in the coming days, regardless of the ongoing lack of textbooks. Jim's syllabus had him in the Senior Arts Hut from 0930 till 1230 hours, covering English, history and mathematics.

Lunch and Embarkation Drills filled the afternoon until classes resumed beginning with French from 1600 to 1645 hours and finished with Geography at 1800 - 1845 hours after tea. There was hardly any spare time. Up to the last week in June, Jim's Quota 48 for both Rue and Jeumont Schools were still unable to commence classwork, not that it concerned most in either school greatly, but the hierarchy's considered opinion was that Quota 48 had not yet settled down to work despite having been in camp for some weeks.

Enrolments from all schools now totalled 1,064, including Rue and Jeumont, averaging an attendance of 121 at lectures but gradually rising. Jim was eager to begin the upcoming classes, reading up on topics in his spare time. He used the opportunity to explore the additional 31 reference books available at the Library, believing there was no more satisfying resource than reading to broaden the inquiring mind. Evening debates continued to broaden the mind also, developing competitive confidence and speaking skills. Two recent debates were, *Is* the *White Australia Policy possible with the League of Nations?*, resulting in Quota 48 defeating Quota 42, and *Should the White Australia Policy be Modified?* with a loss to the team after compelling arguments from both sides.

The free evening of 2 July brought Jim a surprise visit from his three mates, Ted, Bill and Ernie, who were due for embarkation; Ted and Bill the next day on the *Prince Herbetus*, and Ernie on the 8th having been allocated to the *Fredricksruh*. The four re-lived old times and shared their favourite amusing stories until well after lights out.

Joined by Charlie, Ed and Tommy, drinks were customarily handed around for good mates, good times and good luck, knowing that the four schoolmates would next meet in Brisbane around September following Jim's return. More immediately, though, his embarkation date remained unscheduled.

Jim, Charlie, Tommy and Ed farewelled Ted, Bill and their other mates before dawn on 3 July. Some, like Harry and Steve, wounded during the September end of the Hindenburg Campaign, were either sent home earlier or approved for early release. Tommy had been gassed but was staying longer with Jim and Charlie. Two of the 9th Reos, Bill Rowland and Harry Colsell, had applied to stay permanently with family in the U.K., while another 13 remained for some months before finally returning to Australia.

FALL IN! was the order resonating in the crisp pre-dawn air, followed promptly by that old familiar scuffling of heavy boots on the Parade Ground. This would be the last vision of these gallant men parading in columns as they had been trained throughout their Embarkation Parades over the past weeks, now preparing to march into the dark for the train to take them to Devonport Harbour. Only this time, they were returning home to peace, the final antithesis.

Huts stood forlornly empty, with that same haunting quiet permeating every corner of the camp like an oppressive fog. Mates, once familiarly connected at a glance across the Parade Ground, in a distant work party, or simply marching past, had now disappeared into the ether of a

15,000-mile journey, under promises to keep in touch, although many would not see each other again.

Five further quotas marching out brought a noticeable decrease in enrolments throughout the following week of 5 - 11 July. An increased class attendance ensued, though, due to the enthusiastic educational personnel's dedication and popular activities.

At this stage, Quota 48 and an Adhoc Quota 'Valencia' were the two remaining quotas in No. 3 Group at Codford. 'Valencia' consisted of remnants of other details totalling 116 men, each enrolling in classes of their choice under four new instructors. This new quota would eventually sail on the *H.M.A.T. Valencia* and the *Main*.

Jim's birthday, Monday, 7 July, had come and gone relatively uneventfully: attending parade, going to classes, studying, and re-reading the birthday letters that had arrived the week earlier from home. Additionally, his mother's parcel was full of cards and letters, Anzac biscuits, a pair of socks knitted by Mrs Hackett (the family's adored neighbour), a book, writing paper, a native paper daisy from down near the dam, as well as a clip of Cobber's mane.

Jim had recently made arrangements with H.Q. for parcels arriving for him after his embarkation to be shared among the Red Cross nurses in appreciation for their tireless dedication. Patching up those who could be and easing the pain of those who could not was a stressful job that they conducted with grace and kindness.

He had since written home on some Y.M.C.A. paper advising the family of his confirmed embarkation date of 23 July, having already advised everyone to withhold writing any further letters. Thoughts of his mates, Steve, Emmel and Harry, who were already home, came back to him, and he looked forward to seeing them again.

Steve had been mistakenly reported as Killed in Action on 6 September in the 42nd Battalion's fighting around Peronne. This was soon corrected to Wounded in Action, with his shattered left shoulder requiring extensive surgical work. Steve's swift evacuation resulted in his arrival at Bristol's 2nd Southern Military Hospital before Jim had the chance to see him. Word finally came of Steve's embarkation on the hospital ship *H.T. Saxon* in mid-December, to Ciss's enormous relief.

There would be a lifetime's worth of news waiting for them on their arrival home. All the Ceremonial Parades, the 19th's Peace Day Parade, their classes, debates, concerts and cinema nights would soon become long-distant memories.

Rue School's resumed classes brought the students in line with all quotas undergoing their own lessons at other camps, except for Jeumont's Quota 48 and Quota 'Valencia', the latter being prepared for embarkation. Instructors continued delivering lectures throughout the schools, amounting to 38 during the past week, with an average attendance of 194.

Increased attendance at lectures exemplified the men's determination to use each remaining day productively. Every measure was taken to increase the soldiers' awareness that Civilian life was almost upon them, a reality foremost in all their minds.

The 2,004 men of No. 3 Group attended a total of 5,200 lectures, reflecting the importance the men gave to the opportunities provided by the Education Service and applying their waiting time to their best advantage. The well-structured lectures were of a standard to interest all thinking men and broaden their outlook. Rue School students settled down to serious classwork and focused on their impending exams, while Jeumont preferred to postpone their classwork until embarkation.

No. 3 Group was indebted to Reverend Lawton for his assistance with lectures. He was their mainstay, an influential educationalist who taught the men that they belonged to the finest country in the world for opportunities. The power was in their hands to make it or mar it. That week, Rev. Lawton delivered another of his inspiring subjects, 'Ideals for Australia and Reconstruction'.

Another recently introduced activity similar to the Debate Teams, the 'Diggers Parliament', stimulated discussion over the proposed 'Government' introduction of a 'Bill' to provide State allowances for wives and children. Subsequently, the 'floor' was a source of great entertainment with theatrics conducted in typical Australian expressions. The resulting landslide defeat arose between fits of good-humoured laughter.

Later on Thursday evening, the Debating Society also held its weekly debate. This week's subject was 'Should Bachelors be Taxed?', a revived debate that was ultimately decided in the negative after yet another entertaining presentation of plausible arguments. Among the student audience, the newly married men of the 41st Battalion had a special interest, being firmly entrenched in the 'for' side. Those 'against' conceded defeat after an hour's debating, leaving those on the bachelors' side to reluctantly settle any ensuing bets.

Listening to the debate with great interest, Rev. Lawton was overcome by a sudden surge of great pride. Never before had he encountered such inspiration from men who had not previously spoken publicly to take the floor and speak with such confidence. These remarkable men were reinventing themselves before his eyes.

Rue School continued to engage actively in classwork, with all instructors kept busy managing the increasing daily attendance. Essentially, all Rue students had studied privately in their huts instead of classrooms, although Jeumont School had received a grant to obtain the necessary trade textbooks.

In the meantime, the Peace Day Parade in London had been confirmed for 19 July, and the day was swiftly upon the men. Their recent weeks of ongoing parades prepared them well, and the celebrations were spectacular with crowds numbering as many as 5 million lining the route of the march through central London. The immense pageantry of troops from Belgium, China, Czechoslovakia, Greece, Italy, Japan, Poland, Portugal, Romania, Serbia and Siam was applauded fervently.

Allies, troops of the Commonwealth, including France, the U.S. admiralty, sailors of all ranks and the naval nurses (W.R.E.N.s) followed, the curtain-raiser ahead of their artillery crews, engineers, infantry and machine gunners. Only then did the Commonwealth's dominions come into view, to the crowd's great delight. Australian troops marching in full ceremonial dress with fixed bayonets led the New Zealand and South African contingents, Women's Legion, doctors, nurses,

Voluntary Aid Detachment, chaplains and the W.A.A.C.s, followed lastly by the new Royal Air Force, Britain's most recent addition to her Forces. Previously the Royal Flying Corps, this proven Army air division had merged with the Royal Naval Air Service last year, coming of age as its own rightful Force.

Jim absorbed the jubilant atmosphere of the ecstatic crowds and the buildings along their wide streets festooned with bunting high overhead and colourful garlands, all heralding the dawn of a long-awaited peaceful future. Every viewpoint was taken: all obliging wrought iron lamp posts with scalable fretwork, casements, balconies, canopies, and rooftops. Everywhere he looked, Jim saw elegant drapery and flags of all nations. Some almost appeared to hover unrestrained as they hung suspended from the ornate lamp posts along Oxford Street, across every street and street corner, and adorning monuments and grand hotels.

Extending for 7 miles from Knightsbridge, through Central London to Westminster, the magnificent parade took over 2 hours to complete. As they passed through Admiralty Arch leading to Buckingham Palace, the men were filled with an electric surge of adrenaline. If there was ever a time the men felt their fallen mates near, it was now when the contingent turned their eyes right to salute the immense plaster cenotaph in honour of them all at rest in battlefields and cemeteries across numerous foreign lands.

Temporarily built within 11 hasty days, plans were already in place for the plaster and timber-framed structure's permanent replacement in marble for the following year's Remembrance Day, a reflection of the vision it currently presented.

Threading twice across the Thames River, the mighty procession passed navy ships gloriously bedecked in bunting and flags until reaching Victoria Memorial, where the troops were saluted by King George V with Queen Mary by his side. Buckingham Palace itself was decorated in victorious colours and draperies, a majestic backdrop for the euphoric spectators watching the approaching procession in the royal couple's presence. The thrilling day was even more splendid than they had possibly imagined.

Festivities continued in London's parks with dancing, singing and general entertainment, followed some hours later by a fireworks display illuminating the night sky. Jubilation was mixed with sorrow, however, as an undercurrent eroded the victory celebrations. Freedom was going to take some rebuilding.

In Luton, a town just north of London, the high cost of the celebrations had triggered a resentful and bitter protest at the continuing lack of support and disregard for their veterans' welfare. The bitterness turned ugly when the town hall was set alight and firefighters hospitalised. The wave of violent riots spread to London, and among the scenes of vandalism and looting, over 100 casualties were reported.

Embedded in the carnage was the message for politicians, if they were willing to hear it: *lavishly funded victory celebrations were not good enough*. Much more needed to be done to support the broken soldiers returned from the Great War, a war fought protecting a nation that seemed to have forgotten them already.

Meanwhile, the dismissed columns of soldiers filtered throughout London on a brief leave. Aside from the popular 'War Chest', the 'Connaught Club' at Marble Arch was a lively meeting place for the retiring Australian troops, W.A.A.C.s and nurses. Jim and Charlie caught up with friends there, including Kay Baker (Regimental No. 35949) of the 2 W.A.A.C.s, while Ed met with old friends at another venue.

Newlywed soldiers and their brides were also making their arrangements in preparation for their journey to Australia. Some would be on the *Main*, although others from the various surrounding camps would sail on the *H.M.A.T. Bakara* and the *S.S. Bahia Castillo*. All three ships were due to sail on the 23rd, a mere four days away.

No. 3 Codford midday meal being brought in from the cook house.
AWM P0002.006.

Australian soldiers playing Two-Up at Hurdcott. Note the chalk map
of Australia on the hillside. AWM P11848.002.

1914-1918 Fovant Military Station. Photograph courtesy of Rupert Williamson - Fovant History Interest Group.

Glasgow Central Station where Jim and his mates were arrested for being A.W.L. Photograph courtesy of Network Rail, UK.

19 July 1919. Peace Day Celebration Parade through Admiralty Arch.
Photograph courtesy of the Imperial War Museum.

William (Bill) Mitchell 3643. Fovant 1918.

CHAPTER 15

H.M.A.T. Main

The tug kept her position from the Main as it drew her bow away, leading her past the cheering crews of the Centurion and the many other nearby vessels as her wake washed against the British cruiser.

1919. Exeter, England. Australian troops travelling by train to Devonport. AWM H01851.

THE TRANSPORT *MAIN* WAS ALLOTTED to Quota 48 12 days before sailing, so on 16 July, the men were medically examined for venereal disease and scabies. The results were subsequently submitted to London, and those passing their medicals would be granted their entire Voyage Pay the following day.

Marching past the medical officer the day before embarkation, Jim, his mates and the rest of the troops were checked off against the London Roll, presenting their kits for inspection by the General Officer's Command (G.O.C.) for any contravening items or indecent literature.

189

It was 0300 hours, and this had been their last breakfast at Codford on Salisbury Plain. The quota finally cleared up its camp, ready for assessment by the Officer in Charge before marching out to board the two awaiting troop trains from Warminster to Devonport at 0400 hours, the early hour incurring the least congestion on the main lines. Men leaned from their windows in threes and fours, heckling their mates still making their way in groups of eight through the station yard, while others sat relaxed rolling smokes and quietly muttering to each other in easy conversation.

A railway traffic officer and his two assistants diligently worked through each group, counting the growing numbers boarding the train. Cohort by cohort, the troops proceeded to the second idling train; the first, with Tommy already onboard, was ready to pull out. Some were still under the influence from the previous night's celebration, their last in Blighty, and struggled under the weight of their kits.

Along the banks of the road leading to the troops' temporary railway platform, the last 50 of the draft were distinguished by the glow of their cigarettes and muffled voices as they picked up their kits, shuffling closer towards the gate.

Tommy's train, loaded with its rowdy wayfarers, had blown her haunting whistle on leaving Warminster Station and could be heard rolling through the village half a mile away to the risqué strains of *Mademoiselle from Armentieres*. Meanwhile, currently at Jim's platform, two Y.M.C.A. ladies and the group padre passed from carriage to carriage with the troops' 'buckshee' rations of morning snacks and cigarettes. Everyone was now onboard, and cheers resonated through the cool morning air as the train finally left the station.

In the ensuing hours, the troops were in various states of mind, immersed deep in thought watching the passing countryside, anticipating their next strategic trick in a card game or just simply asleep. Jim was one of those who chose to sleep as the rocking of the train lulled him deeper into slumber. Soon, they were pulling into Exeter Station with its floor-to-roof columns and arched windows for the last time. Piling out of the train onto the lengthy covered platform, the troops stretched out, leaving their carriage doors wide open as the speaker hailed them with the announcement that tea and refreshments were available, generously provided by a party of women from Exeter.

As Jim and the other men gratefully enjoyed the sustenance, they considered the forthcoming stations to Devonport, where their ship waited to sail. Wives and children would be on another train arriving at the Devonport Dock later that morning, so expectations for a sociable afternoon were high.

The troops, including Jim, Ed and Charlie, stood smoking in gathered groups, some taking a long-lasting look at the Exeter farmhouses nearby while those among them compared the difference in themselves since they had first arrived from Australia. They were relaxed and happy, a noisily cheery lot, directing typically good-natured Australian wit at each other in their usual boyish humour. They were going home.

With the train resuming its journey, their route took them along the coast within 20 feet of the waterline, where a rock wall and concrete barrier protected the train from heavy waves. Workers maintaining the seafront, along with those simply out fishing or meandering to take in the fresh sea air on a calm summer's day, responded enthusiastically to the cheery greetings from the homeward-bound soldiers.

An hour later, the stone facade of the Devonport Naval Base rose ahead, looming ever nearer with its magnificent brick towers on either side of the vast arched gateway, adorned with four decorative casements. The primary pedestrian entrance on its circuit to the docks beyond led the way to the *Main* waiting dockside for her khaki-clad homecomers, her flags and pennants dancing erratically in the harbour breezes.

A few hundred yards inside Devonport Station, the powerful engine was replaced by two small dock engines before resuming the winding route amongst workshops and dismantled guns, taking them past an immense view of the harbour, where masts of cruisers and battleships rose above the dockyard buildings, obscuring the ships from view.

More cargo ships and smaller craft lay at anchor in the harbour out past the jetty, with fishing boats dotting the anchorage in front of the boatsheds. The dock's surrounding yards, once maximised to their brimming capacity during the height of the war for storing heavy armament and accommodating makeshift camps, were now a transfer station for obsolete camp materials awaiting loading.

Devonport's docks, themselves, bristled with British warships at rest, including two revolutionary Dreadnoughts, whose distracted crew were contentedly watching as Jim's train pulled in alongside the *Main*. The naval ships were still decked out in flagged bunting from the Peace Day celebrations, and a crane towered above a recently unloaded cruiser on the far dock crisscrossed with train lines.

Strategically dumped wooden drums the size of the wheels on Jim's father's spring cart stood in place with a further 20 cooperage barrels sectioned neatly behind a stack of timber and broken crates. In the distance, another stationary crane stood silhouetted against the cloud-free skyline. The crane's immense bulk now waited for the next cargo ship to replace the one currently bunkering with coal after having unloaded earlier that morning.

Closer at hand, passengers, soldiers and naval crew milled near the docked vessels, either taking in the view or attending to nearby battleships, while others assisted in relocating unhitched limbers. Everywhere, something was going on.

It was time, and the troops prepared to detrain. Retrieving their gear from the decorative iron compartments above them, they would queue alongside the train to board the *Main's* gangway directly ahead. Each soldier and officer had been fully immunised for the return trip and held their Demobilisation Card with their draft number, paybook and tags ready to present on embarking.

The embarkation staff sergeant proceeded to call out the drafts in unit order as they appeared on the roll, and the first of the drafts filed onboard: kits over their shoulders, identification in their hands and triumphant smiles on their faces. Finally boarded, the exultant men could dare to believe they were actually going home, and under the jurisdiction of C.O., Lieut. Col. A.T. Paterson, the newly promoted major from Warlus.

Captained by Hugh W.N. Evans, the *Main* was a black and white steamer commandeered by the British earlier in May for troop-carrying. For the next two and a half unpredictable months, she would be home to around 2,000 soldiers, wives and children, with three extras being born at sea the week before reaching Fremantle. Her four varnished masts were trimmed with rigging splayed on booms like taut spider webs. There were no guns or dazzle camouflage, but her sea-spray-stained hull, one smoking funnel and two flags - the Australian and Armistice Flags - beheld a sight for sore eyes.

Kit bags were slung over broad shoulders or rested upright against the respective soldier's leg, ready to be tucked under his arm when he moved off. Occasionally, soldiers bent down to check in it or put something away, often holding the opening in their teeth to free their hands for retying the drawstring.

They no longer laboured under the 62lb weight of supplies they once carried. Nor would they ever again need the supply of ammo, gun oil, bayonet, gas mask, binoculars, entrenching tool, wire cutters or helmet. Nevertheless, they still depended upon their regulation kit, including boot polish, watch, razor and comb. Additionally, they carried foot powder, photographs and lucky charms, not to mention any other incidentals considered necessary or otherwise. Jim's kit included his own pair of binoculars, souvenired from the battlefield and convenient for spotting the longed-for Western Australia coast.

Like well-oiled clockwork, the line progressed in proficient army fashion towards the gangway, with each soldier presenting their Demobilisation Card displaying their quota and draft. There would be an Emergency Drill when everyone was onboard, but right now, the jazzy strains of the 48 Quota Band filtered throughout the ship from their dutifully staged position on the main deck.

Within shouting distance, the British C-Class Cruiser bedecked in her festive bunting from the celebrations four days earlier, lay serenely at dock with her sailors lining the rails waiting to bid the *Main* and her departing travellers' safe passage home. She was the *H.M.S. Centurion,* and her guns lay peacefully covered while her whole appearance gave her the character of a sleeping lion readily woken. But this was peacetime...and the lion continued to sleep.

More laid-back troops arrived in unabating numbers for processing, moving on gladly in their semi-orderly fashion. They had all done this many times before, but today was steeped in consummate complacency dotted with outbursts of raucous laughter.

Two hours later, with the last arrivals now onboard, the 10-minute Life Jacket Drill was completed ahead of the *Main's* departure, closing with the Captain's statement that further Abandon Ship and Man Overboard Drills would be held intermittently at sea.

Out low in the water to starboard, remarkably diminutive against the steamer's dark mass, the tug hovering in readiness was at last engaged, her tow line securely in place to the *Main*'s deck fittings. Along the ship's lower rails, the departing soldiers sat happily dangling their legs over the side while others leaned against the railings above them. Many made eager use of portholes or climbed the rigging for better vantage points, all yahooing to those waving below from the dock.

Quota 48 Band played *Good-bye-ee* on the midship deck as the *Main's* engines roared into reverberating life, ready for the lines securing her to be cast from the bollards. Ever slowly, her propellers created an agitated swirl of water, gradually increasing as the ship cleared the dock.

Keeping her position from the *Main*, the tug drew her bow away, leading her past the cheering crews of the *Centurion* and the many other nearby vessels as her wake washed against the British cruiser. Only then did the second tug come into sight, nosing the *Main*'s stern steadily into position as the three vessels aligned, clearing the harbour before reaching the open channel beyond the hearty cheers and farewells.

The *Main* was Australia-bound.

* * *

Sleek and clean, the *Main* was a German ocean liner. Built in 1900, she had a capacity of over 3,450 passengers plus crew and had been reconditioned following the tragic New York dock fire of 30 June 1900.

A newspaper article in the *New York Times* almost 20 years earlier spoke of untold horrors witnessed when the *Main* and three other vessels caught fire at the dock in Hoboken Pier, New Jersey, on 30 June 1900:

FIRE STILL HOLDS THE LINER MAIN. SEARCH MADE FOR BODIES.

Only piles of ashes found – intense heat that ravaged the Main.

Around 4.00 pm on Saturday, 30th June, 1900 fire broke out at Hoboken, in New York. Kaiser Wilhelm der Grosse and Main were at Pier 2, Bremen and Saale were at Pier 3. They were surrounded by coal barges, lighters and canal boats, laden with bales of cotton and drums of oil and petroleum products, including turpentine.

An explosion amongst cargo on Pier 3 set stacked bales of cotton on fire: the flames spread rapidly. The fire spread fast on the dry, wooden piers; 40 dockers died before they could run to safety. The flames jumped across adjacent piers before spreading ashore, destroying many buildings. Local fire crews responded but had little effect.

Two city fireboats, Van Wyck and New Yorker, arrived and played their firehoses on the burning Liners, in a hopeless attempt to quell the fires. The Main is simply a great mass of twisted iron, there is not a particle of woodwork to be seen anywhere and no single portion of the once beautiful vessel has retained its shape.

Eye witness accounts were devastating to read, let alone the fact they, themselves, were driven mad from being unable to save those who burnt alive in front of them:

Then the real horror began. Faces and arms appeared at the eleven-inch portholes of the Saale, Bremen and Main, portholes too pitiably small to permit the passage of any adult body. A woman appeared at a porthole on the Main. She looked down at a half-dozen tugs and 100 men unable to help her.

The young woman, a stewardess, began praying loudly. Smoke drifted past her head and flames could be seen behind her. Hoping to save her, one man grabbed a rope, clung to the red-hot side of the Main and with a hose climbed to an adjacent porthole, through which he sprayed water on the creeping flames. He fell. Flames and smoke began to envelop the woman. Purple fire pulled over her face and with a quick shriek she was gone.

Below decks on the Main dozens of stokers, engineers and stewards died miserably, waiting for death as ten feet of flames roared over their heads and ate downward to them.

When time allowed for the wreckage to cool enough to begin the futile search for survivors, an eyewitness account reported:

In looking down into the fireroom hatch, the fully-dressed body of a man was seen lying in a water tank used in the fireroom for cooling furnace tools. The body appeared as if the man, driven mad by the heat, had plunged into this tank and died there. The place was too hot to reach the body on Sunday and yesterday the place had been flooded.

In the aftermath of the horrific tragedy and the loss of over 250 souls, 44 on the *Main* alone, an inquest later proclaimed portholes were to be re-designed large enough to enable an adult to escape to safety. This entire notion could not have been further from the minds of the blissfully unaware troops aboard her today.

S.S. Bremen (left) and S.S. Main (right) during the Hoboken Pier, New Jersey, disaster 30 June 1900. Photograph courtesy of the Hoboken Historical Museum.

Damage to S.S. Main from the fire disaster at Hoboken Pier, New Jersey, 30 June 1900. Photograph courtesy of the Hoboken Historical Museum.

Devonport, England, 1919. Australian troops leaving the train prior to embarking on H.M.A.T. Takada for Australia. AWM H01840.

Devonport, England, 1919. Australian troops embarking on H.M.A.T. Takada for their journey home. AWM H01809.

CHAPTER 16

On Their Way

Here, above the southeast horizon, lay the bright five-star constellation the troops had been waiting to see for the longest time...the 'Southern Cross'.

Freetown, Sierra Leone. Photograph courtesy of Lisk-Carew Brothers.

EXCITEMENT FOR THE ENSUING voyage was short-lived.

Those who were oblivious to it, or simply disregarded the sudden shift in the vessel's motion and its altered tone, would have been forgiven in their confusion for waking bizarrely back in Devonport the following day.

The *Main* had steadied her course out of the English Channel bound for Cape Town, South Africa, but 12 hours into the voyage, her auxiliary engines failed and, with little in the way of choices, laboured her way back to Devonport for repairs. Though, if the men thought they would be resting on their laurels, they were sadly mistaken. Education still ranked a high priority on the Demobilisation and Repatriation agenda, so classes continued as planned, with many beleaguered soldiers welcoming the productive focus.

Five restless days later, with repairs finally accomplished, the *Main* returned to the open water, once again resuming her interrupted journey in choppy seas towards the Portuguese coast.

On this leg's third day, Jim, Charlie and Ed caught up with Tommy on deck, enjoying the open spaces and some welcome sunshine as they took in the northwestern Spanish coastline, their educational classes now finished for the day.

Suddenly, a cry of *Man overboard!* was heard as one of the soldiers on deck swiftly launched a lifebuoy in the direction of the stricken man in the white water behind the boat. Triggered instinctively by the urgency, a crewman swiftly alerted the Bridge by sounding the Man Overboard alarm bell situated on the deck.

This was no drill!

As the bell's urgent tolling rang through the ship, the engines' revs instantly dropped, and the crew readied a lifeboat as the vessel slowed to a stop before pivoting into her rear-manoeuvre turn. All eyes remained fixed on the area where the man was last seen hitting the water, but the rough waves were yielding no sign of him.

Working together in pure synchronisation, the cohesive team of crewmen lowered the lifeboat to the water in record time to undertake a thorough 'Expanding Square' search: a lifeboat search with a doctor, third officer and four of the ship's crew.

In a demonstration of careful coordination, the lifeboat steered outwards, radiating in increasing squares like a ripple effect while the *Main* carried out a simultaneous elliptical search of the area for 2 hours. After finding nothing except the empty lifebuoy, the unsuccessful search was called off following the decision to sail on without him.

As the returning lifeboat and its crew pulled closer to the ship, the crew onboard the *Main* prepared to raise the small craft from the water, returning the dedicated searchers and boat to their respective safe havens. Those on deck applauded the courageous team as the crew made their way past to the Bridge with their report for the waiting captain.

In the wake of the sobering event, the afternoon was spent mainly in sizeable groups playing Two-Up on the open deck near the funnel, most placing their bets while others idled their time away casually. For Jim and his three mates, this was one serious game of Two-Up requiring their solid attention. The game was addictive and had been a traditional Australian pastime since the mid-1800s, regardless of its notoriously unconstrained gambling, causing the game to be arbitrarily banned at home. Here, though, on an Australian troopship laden with returning troops, no holds were barred, and bets were on.

Regardless of whichever way Two-Up is played, bets or no bets, the atmosphere promises light-hearted camaraderie and anticipation, the perfect drawcard for returning troops on an unhurried afternoon at sea up on the top deck. Slouch hats had been dropped to the full brim by removing their Rising Sun badge, aiding the necessary protection from the sun as they neared the North West African coast, now visible in the hazy distance. Everyone would need to move their watches forward an hour that night, a rule of thumb for them every couple of days, depending on the ship's unreliable speed.

The *Main* was still a significant way off the Equator, with the next port expected to be Cape Town, when, once again, the engines faltered into grinding revs. This mechanical problem was inherent and not going away readily.

Gradually, the *Main* again limped her way to sanctuary. This time, it was the port of Freetown, the capital of Sierra Leone, on West Africa's Atlantic-swept coast. The dire condition of the engines and lack of water onboard had become critical, making the haven's much-anticipated appearance one of utter relief.

Well-positioned as a river port, Freetown was strategically pivotal for trade and critical to the British war effort as a base and distribution point for providing fuel and supplies. Located along the Cape route, the port lay midway between the United Kingdom and Simons Town Naval Base in Cape Town.

Subsequently, Freetown was also an ideal and welcome port for a returning troopship's urgent repairs to its failing engines, amongst other necessary repairs fleets of naval vessels may incur, especially if the Suez Canal was inconveniently blocked.

Signing the Peace Treaty revealed that Germany's sights had been squarely set on the prized Sierra Leone harbours of Freetown and Bonthe to seize the West African ports and effectively crush British shipping. Germans living in Sierra Leone were expelled from the country, and any captives were imprisoned.

Aside from any port strikes Freetown had been experiencing, it also meant that while the threat of Spanish Influenza was rife along the West African Coast, the troops would be required to stay onboard during their interim stay. Between classes, they entertained themselves by watching water and supplies being loaded and engineers being ferried to and fro, returning the broken ship to order.

There would be better prospects ahead for sightseeing in Cape Town on South Africa's southern tip, then Durban along the East Coast shortly afterwards, as long as they managed to get there. For now, though, the broad mid-river anchorage remained tranquil as a lighter was engaged for the ship's mechanics to source components onshore for the *Main's* repairs.

The city was built on the estuary of the Sierra Leone River, making its deep water perfect for a safe harbour and a well-rounded industry, including the convenience of repairing the *Main's* engines, which progressed gradually over the next three days.

Problems onboard the *Main* did not stop at engine failure, though. Married men had now risen in disagreement about conditions in the married quarters, leading to a meeting held on 4 August. It had been essential to appoint a committee of some married men to represent the married sector and the women and children who travelled with them.

There was a growing disquiet regarding the quality of food, inadequate sanitary conditions, cots for babies and even the essentials for their diet, and something needed to be done. Some of the matters would be resolved during the next two weeks, with an impending meeting proposed later in Cape Town.

It would prove to be the start of numerous grievances, many of which were being similarly experienced on the *Bahia Castillo*. There, the O.C. deemed it suitable to sail without the protesting passengers who refused to return to the ship in Fremantle.

Later, on 29 September 1919, Perth's *Daily News* published an article relating to the Committee and the issues in question:

> *A meeting of all the married diggers (sic) was held at sea on No. 5 upper deck of the H.M.A.T. Main on August 4, 1919.*
>
> *It was decided that a welfare committee of third-class married men be appointed to look after the interests of the third-class married men and their womenfolk and children on the voyage to Australia. The following were appointed as the Committee: Driver S. C. Peebles (chairman and spokesman), Corporals Cottie, Petch, Pearce and Farrell, and Gunner Lawrence, the latter being of Fremantle.*
>
> *It was stated that the officer commanding the ship had agreed to recognise the Committee as the representatives of the third-class married men. We gather that the formation of this Committee was held to be absolutely necessary. The passengers held that they had a large number of complaints.*
>
> *They allege the food was indifferent, the sanitary arrangements bad, that no cots were provided for the children, no sanitary arrangements for the little ones, neither was there a special diet for them. The men's latrines were placed on top of the ladies' quarters; men were not allowed to go down to their wives' cabins when the latter were sick and there were many other minor complaints.*
>
> *On the way to Capetown (sic), many of these matters were remedied, but at Capetown, on August 24, the committee held a meeting, and the question of performing guards and pickets was discussed, and on it being stated by several present that in the terms of the A.I.F. orders all married men were exempt from these duties while travelling to Australia with their wives, a vote was taken, and it was unanimously resolved that neither of these duties be performed by married men while in Port.*

In the wake of the married quarter's issues, interests turned to one of many sports held onboard to ease the monotony; a 'Bun and Treacle' fight involving four buns smothered in treacle and hung in a row. When given the order to *Start*, the first of the four contestants to eat their bun wins. This was one of the more popular games, providing great amusement as the men passed their time after classes while stranded during repairs.

Finally back at sea, the troops maintained their regular Guard Duties and classes, later collecting on deck ready for bets or any reason to let off steam and be boys again. For the moment, there was nothing better.

Buffets were set up in the dining rooms laid out with sufficient organised seating to cater for the continuous lines of hungry repatriates and migrating wives with and without children. For the soldiers, anything was edible for the most part, having been used to army cooks resorting to whatever weeds and tricks the cooks could muster to provide sustenance for those in the trenches.

Horsemeat was not uncommon to be found in stews cooked over the rear fires of the battle lines, and whatever water that was acquired for boiling any scavenged vegetables was subsequently used to make tea. Invariably the soldiers' hot tea tasted more like turnips or some other unfortunately flavoured vegetable, enough in itself to become the subject of amusing bets.

However, the mistake of using oleander branches for stirring porridge had been learnt the hard way in the trenches as hundreds of men had suffered and died from the poisonous sap leaching into their food. Although conveniently available for stirring tea and porridge, it was soon realized the sap was lethal to adults, and the unassuming plant was left decidedly well alone.

Those of the wives who had finally overcome their seasickness could now cope better with the foreign food they had found themselves reluctantly introduced to, although encouraged by the promise of more adequate alternatives available in Cape Town. This came as a result of the meeting the married men held at sea with the O.C., raising objections on behalf of their wives struggling to sustain children in the raw military environment of a troopship.

After dinner, concerts were conducted by the Quota 48 Band and a group of onboard comedians, the perfect prelude to late-night stargazing, now the *Main* had arrived in the deeper south. Here, above the southeast horizon, lay the bright five-star constellation the troops had been waiting to see for the longest time...the 'Southern Cross'.

Jim and scores of others lined the rails almost two long years after the Australian icon had slipped from view beyond the southern horizon on their way to Suez. Ahead of them now, low in the night sky, the revered group of stars glittered amongst the bright, starry void, transfixing all who gazed upon its oblique wonder.

Into the night, the deck lay typically strewn with soldiers bunked down wherever they felt like, some snoring, some listless, but however arranged, they did it knowing they were ever closer to reaching that homeward run to Fremantle.

April 1919. Australian soldiers relaxing onboard S.S. Shropshire on their way home to Australia. Donor W.J. Deane. AWM H04170.

1919. Troops returning to Australia onboard the S.S. Orca playing Two-Up on deck. Donor Mr J. Lee. AWM J02913.

RETURNED WITH A CREED — 207

February 1919. Troops lined up on the deck of the H.M.A.T Derbyshire on Thermometer Parade. AWM P01425.015.

Church Parade onboard Troopship Argyllshire (A8). AWM H02398. Donor Mrs Mercer.

Lectures and drills on deck of S.S. Euripides. Photograph courtesy of the Royal Australian Navy.

CHAPTER 17

South African Shores

"Cape Town is quite dead since you Aussies left."

Cape Town Pier, 1919. Photograph courtesy of Cape Town History.

AUGUST IN CAPE TOWN WAS a beautiful sight; there was really nothing quite like it. A mild to cool 15 degrees Celsius made it one of the best times of the year for a troopship loaded with eager soldiers to visit.

It was 22 August, and the magic the troops woke to filled them with vast expectations.

In the early morning calm, low clouds appeared to roll over the weather-beaten tors of Table Mountain, which stood as a monolithic backdrop to the inviting city sprawling in hazy welcome beyond the safety of the opulent harbour.

Ahead of them, the recently built Cape Town Pier with its ornate steepled beacon, reached out spectacularly 300 yards into Table Bay, its scalloped balustrade providing convenient viewpoints and seating for sightseers along the boardwalk. Minarets festooned the pier's recreational pavilion, where dances were regularly staged, and crowds of visitors could wander contentedly out to the domed bandstand to take in the vibe of the passing day.

Rising splendidly above Table Bay, the grand, Turkish-style beacon's reflection gently rippled in the morning's millpond waters. The sensational vision against the curtain of clouds cascading like mist over Table Mountain's craggy face was a sight none of the soldiers would ever forget. Similarly themed buildings garlanding this favourite waterfront venue provided spacious shelter, and gas lamps lit the pier gloriously at night.

From portside, the dock joined the full width of the wooden pier, leading directly towards Cape Town's expansive shoreline and seafront boulevard mantled with widely varied customs houses, government buildings, hotels, business houses and residences.

While the *Main* waited for clearance and a clean bill of health to dock, the assigned men found themselves posted to their Picquet and Guard Duties. Assisted by harbour jibs, cargo ships ahead of them unloaded their vast supplies before filling their depleted coal bunkers.

Troopships and cargo carriers at anchor surrounded them out in the bay, a superb sight that never failed to fill Jim with awe, although there was no sign of the *Bakara* or the *Bahia Castille*. They had left for Durban during the *Main's* extended stopover in Freetown.

Coaling was again becoming increasingly arduous due to the coal shortage, threatening to delay their departure from Cape Town even further. The distinct lack of coal did promise eagerly anticipated opportunities, though, considering they would have an entire week to enjoy the South African city.

When the *Main* finally made her way into her allotted berth, the disembarking troops found the dock lined with hospitable Dutch South African locals who had come to welcome the new arrivals. Jim noticed some men working or tending to their fishing boats or cargo were dark-skinned, and the unsettling realisation came to him that this was clearly a divided country, significantly different from the culture he experienced in Suez.

This morning would start with a route march around Cape Town to keep regimental precision and maintain troop discipline. Renowned for its indisputable morale-building, the opportunity was relished by the troops, as onboard drills and callisthenics could only manage so much. They were itching to get off the ship, where they had just spent the past four monotonous weeks with precisely zero Shore Leave of any description. And now, here was Cape Town, alive and vibrant, celebrating the returning soldiers everywhere.

A fervour coursed through the troops as they assembled for parade at the beachside camp. Throughout the next hour's march around the city, especially down the main street, Table Mountain seemed to hover eerily above, permeating their senses with its intriguing presence.

Plenty of leave was given for the men to roam freely, taking in the sights and restaurants as they patronised the free trams rattling their way throughout the city, a privilege Jim and Charlie spent much of their time enjoying while Ed and Tommy were on other duties. The locals were accommodating and exceptionally helpful, offering directions and advice on the best places to visit, most of which were free to the returning soldiers.

Abundant with Boer War artifacts and maritime history, the museum displayed a massive whale skeleton filling an entire section of the grounds. Completely captivated, the men would walk beneath this once magnificent marine creature's bleached backbone just to gauge the pure power of its size.

Exploring the promenade, Jim and Charlie wandered out to the two-level conservatory built at the end of the pier to marvel at its upper storey's glass-panelled shelter topped with a bell-shaped roof. The lower level formed an open area below with a concrete path leading down to the pontoon, where Jim could see locals fishing. Discovering there were steps inside the minaret-style beacon close by, the two mates raced to the upper landing like a pair of teenagers for a better view, overlooking the cosmopolitan Cape Town.

It was on this landing that a stylish young woman, Susie van Rensburgh, surprised the two mates, immediately capturing Jim's attention as she sat quietly on her own. Susie was intrigued by the two friends, especially Jim, and after some engaging conversation, offered to show them around Cape Town while the *Main* was in port.

Some of the scenic attractions Susie introduced them to included the Botanical Gardens with its sundial amid countless cycads and palms before they moved on to the Round Church at Sea Point. The church was as curious as it was unique, built circular in stone with a spire and thatched roof; Cape Town just kept on surprising.

By now, though, Charlie felt he should leave the couple together for a few days, as there was a definite chemistry brewing between them. So, under a plausible guise, he made his escape to meet up with Ed and Tommy now that they were off Picquet Duty.

Finding room on one of the trams, Susie took Jim out to the outstanding beauty of Camps Bay, a popular beach overlooked by the monoliths of the Twelve Apostles. Here, visitors and locals braving the cool of late August were diving off some of the bay's granite boulders. Infectious shouts and laughter rang out along the beach, immersing the beach-goers in an easy holiday atmosphere.

A half-hour amble on the road back to Cape Town took the couple through the neck between Table Mountain and Lions Head before catching another crowded tram to Mowbray. Here, Susie ushered Jim up the hillside steeped surprisingly in eucalypts and wattle, where he briefly stopped to absorb the desperately missed scent of the gums, another of those reverent moments similar to the sighting of home's 'Southern Cross'.

When he was ready to move on, she led him past the crowded drinks hut and on to the magnificent Rhodes Memorial commemorating Cecil Rhodes, the mining magnate and former Prime Minister of South Africa's Cape Colony, set perfectly against the breathtaking Devils Peak. In its towering might, the bronze statue of Rhodes on his horse stood on a stone column at the head of five levels of its 49 vast steps, each level lined with resting lions 'guarding' the shrine.

Before them, the stunning panorama of Cape Town, cradled by the Atlantic Ocean, stretched out unforgettably to meet the Indian Ocean at Cape Argulus. Soldiers in their scores would sit for group photos on these granite steps, keepsakes of better times that would bring reminiscent smiles for many years.

Apart from the other two days Jim and Suzie shared together, their last day was filled with promises to write and the memories between them as Jim's departure loomed closer.

Susie had invited Jim and Charlie to a Sunday birthday party where Susie's friend, Tena, was keenly interested in meeting Charlie. With the *Main* leaving the following morning, though, the men would have to attend to their various duties first, including washing. Charlie delivered the message they would not be there to share the festivities, a tremendous disappointment to the two girls, especially Susie.

As scheduled, the *Main* pulled away from the dock at 1030 hours the next morning, her bunkers full of coal and her engines again maintained. But Susie would not be there to wave Jim off. Instead, she was already selecting a card to write to him, as she had promised:

Dear Jim,

Please don't think it forward of me in writing to you first but I told you I am going to write so I am fulfilling my promise. I was ever so sorry that you could not have come out to our place. I intended to invite you and your friend that Sunday because we had a birthday party but he told me you expected to leave early the next morning. Right enough, I was thinking of you at half past 10. Did you do your washing? I expect to leave early next month so am sorry my holiday's all over. Please write to enclosed address. Remember me to your friend Charlie. Sincerely hope to hear very soon from you. Do send me a photo of yourself in 'civvie' clothes.

Love and regards from your friend Susie.

While Susie busied herself with her writing, well-wishers down the hill waved their farewells amid the sporadic blasts of foghorns and ships' whistles from the tri-masted sailing ships and steamers witnessing the *Main* creep her way towards open water. And as Cape Town faded from view, the lighthouse on Da Gama Peak, the summit of Cape Point, rose as a sentinel above the rugged South African coastline. Here at the foot of the Cape, the force of the Atlantic waves crashing against the shoreline's lethal rocks seemed to blur into the distance, spraying their combusting rollers upwards into the heights of the craggy cliffs.

Originally built in 1869 lighthouse, frequently rendered invisible in low clouds and dense fog, was supplemented by a second lighthouse constructed in 1914, closer to the waterline 165 yards below, where it proved significantly more visible in adverse conditions.

In proper ceremony after passing the Cape of Good Hope, the *Main* cruised past the most southerly point of the South African mainland, Cape Agulhas, all onboard lining the rails to watch for the red and white lighthouse positioned on a flatter stretch of coastline.

Craning their necks, the onlookers peered through the misty haze to glimpse the lighthouse, an indication they were passing the iconic southern tip of Africa. This was a moment in time to treasure, as not many among them ever intended to pass this way again.

A respectful pause descended upon the transport to honour the 211 passengers and crew lost on the *S.S. Waratah,* which disappeared in this vicinity ten years earlier on 26 July 1909. The steamer had vanished without a trace or distress call after leaving Durban bound for Cape Town, possibly falling victim to a rogue wave or mechanical failure in the most turbulent fusion of two great oceans, the Indian and Atlantic.

True to her reputation, the *Main* barely held up under her ill-equipped engines for this leg of the journey between Cape Agulhas and Durban. They would coal up again at Durban and undergo further engine repairs for the final crossing of the Indian Ocean on their way to Fremantle...their first touch of Australian soil after so very long.

Durban would take just days compared to the arduous voyage to Cape Town, and an atmosphere of boyish recklessness filled the ship...no one could take anything seriously. There was nothing geographically between them and Australia now.

Their last South African stop was still 840 nautical miles away, where they would top up the bunkers, even though the ongoing coal shortage and engine repairs could see them delayed in Durban's Port Natal for over a week. Six weeks would see Jim back home in Brisbane...if the faltering engines did not continue to break down.

As they passed Port Elizabeth's lighthouse midway between Cape Town and Durban, Jim, Charlie, Ed and Tommy were at the rail with so many others taking in the flashing landmark. Gradually, behind them in the turbulent waters of the *Main*'s wake, phosphorescence began to boil like luminous clouds under the water for 150 yards out from the stern, captivating everyone's attention with its magical sight. Jim and his mates stood confounded, perfectly mesmerised by the glowing spectacle. The waxing moon overhead revealed the slight ghost of its barely visible half as the phosphorescence continued its eerie dance.

Three nights later, on Thursday evening, as the *Main* was a mere 24 hours out from Durban, Susie and Tena had wandered into downtown Cape Town where the two girls had a chance encounter with a couple of Australian soldiers, prompting Susie to write to Jim again:

Dear Jim,

I was ever so sorry that you did not come out to our place. I should have liked you and your friend to have come out to us and spend the day with us. You know I've told you about the B.d. party we're going to have that Sunday afternoon. Really man we had some fun. Tena my friend has been here as well. I told her about the good time she was going to give Charlie that Sunday. After I told her she could only laugh. Cape Town is quite dead since you Aussies left. We quite miss you boys, especially you good boys. I met two Aussies in town on Thursday evening. They absolutely looked like lost sheep. I believe they missed their boat. They did say your boat the Main. Remember me to your friend Charlie.

Regards from your friend Susie.

On cue, Ethel Campbell burnished like a beacon as the Main approached the dock in Durban's busy port. Dressed in white and sporting a white broad-brimmed hat, she worked her semaphore flags to welcome the cheering troops from where she stood on a wooden crate. Her reputation preceded her, propelling her into an almost legendary status.

Known as the 'Angel of Durban', Ethel was a vibrant young woman who greeted every arriving troopship in semaphore from the dock. Not only did she relay her warm welcome, but she also dispatched helpful information about refreshments and entertainment available at the Y.M.C.A. and the free tram service around the bustling city. Ethel continued her generous reception by throwing fruit up to the grateful troops onboard as they waited for clearance to disembark. She was the perfect morale booster.

The men had experienced some of the most congenial hospitality throughout their service abroad, but Ethel's dedicated introduction to Durban made their arrival even more memorable. For now, they would bide their time waiting for clearance by lining the rails with their feet dangling over the side, enjoying the view of the people below them and calling out any questions to the Angel herself. Beside her, the barefoot native boy of perhaps 13 years old continued to hand her fruit from a box for her to throw to the waiting men above.

Once cleared to disembark, soldiers soon gathered in a considerable group around Ethel, remaining politely quiet as she explained the city's tram routes and distributed leaflets with information, including the sights of Durban.

Others still onboard were not suffering the agonisingly slow disembarkation routine down the crowded gangway a minute longer. Instead, one soldier with a smoke in the corner of his mouth, muscled his way through the line on a mission to reach the ship's 'Jacob's Ladder' that was fastened to the rail.

Unbuckling the neatly tied rope ladder with its wooden rungs, the soldier slung the free end over the rail, scaling down the side of the ship effortlessly. One after the other, an exodus of eager men disappeared over the side, bailing out of the slow-moving line to freedom.

As more troops quickly gathered, they were even more encouraged to see Ethel freely handing out newspapers as some walked away with heads bent down over their chosen issue of English, Australian or Durban news. Today was 4 September 1919, and they had expected to have arrived back in Australia by now.

In the interest of pride and polish, the troops were rallied to march to the town hall for a reception by the mayor before being dismissed an hour later to enjoy the welcoming atmosphere and the hospitality Durban offered. At this point, Jim, Charlie, Ed and Tommy ventured off among the crowd of khaki to explore their host city.

Rickshaws, they discovered, were a novel form of transport throughout Durban, with their colourfully painted native drivers dressed in a loincloth and their feathered headdresses charging a fare of sixpence.

The men had not seen rickshaws in Cape Town, nor were there even quite so many natives, but the city's unmistakable division of people was perfectly obvious. Here in Durban, black South Africans were a significant proportion of the population tasked with heavy manual labour such as coaling steamers. This was an exhausting job borne with great endurance as an endless line of African men carried one coal-laden basket after another aboard until the bunkers were full.

Heavily restricted by law, the indigenous locals were only permitted to walk on the streets, never the footpaths, except in certain restricted areas of the city. Likewise, they were only allowed to travel in the four back seats of trams, with their admission prohibited to venues everywhere, clearly stipulated by signage, "Europeans Only Admitted". Like Cape Town, apartheid squarely divided Durban.

During their extended stay, the soldiers were generously granted free access to many venues and transports in the city, including the convenient motorised trams that replaced their horse-drawn predecessors in 1903. Everywhere the soldiers went, the people of Durban would invite them into their homes in welcoming hospitality, along with cafes and restaurants offering free meals and refreshments, privileges as unforgettable as the memories.

A cenotaph had recently been erected in Gardiner Street in dedication to those lost in the great conflict of 1914-1918, drawing the attention of passing Australian soldiers during their exploits throughout the vast city. An increasing number of cenotaphs were appearing in cities everywhere, but Jim did not imagine there would be one at Chermside, being such a small suburb. Perhaps an Honour Roll, though.

The Y.M.C.A. was on the corner of Field Street and the Embankment, with outstanding views across the Esplanade out to the golden surf beaches of the Bay, exactly where Ethel had directed. Here, the soldiers rendezvoused for supplies and any military information relevant to their status during their week-long stay in Durban. On the opposite corner stood the white three-storey Criterion Theatre, which not only provided a prominent landmark for the men but also an inviting tea room on the upper level for their enjoyment.

For the troops, it was nothing short of a holiday atmosphere, regardless of the continuing Guard Duty issues while the *Main* was in port. Even the concrete pier where she lay docked was unique, backing onto the treed shoreline where the hill met the Bay.

Durban's modern edge filled the air with a confidence that embraced the homeward-bound men. It was soon discovered that the people of Durban had recently recovered from an outbreak of Spanish Influenza, resiliently bouncing back with the promise of new and compelling times ahead.

Built in 1909, the Electric Theatre was esteemed as Durban's first permanent cinema offering free admission, along with Mitchell Park Zoo on the long list of attractions. Single-handedly, the zoo enjoyed the reputation of being the best in the world, just as Ethel Campbell had enthusiastically described, drawing many of the soldiers back to its fascinating collection.

Originally an ostrich farm, a recent refurbishment had cleverly transformed the enterprising zoo into a collection of the country's finest animals and birds. The ostriches were now accompanied by magnificent lions, leopards, cheetahs, elephants, zebras, giraffes, crocodiles, monkeys and exotic birds, a true splendour for the young Australians.

Stone and mortar buildings with steel bars housed chimpanzees, sloths and lemurs, surrounded by high-fenced enclosures with gate access. Jim, Charlie, Ed and Tommy had seen London Zoo's array of lions, tigers, giraffes, gazelle and wildebeest, but this was Africa, their home.

Peacocks strolled aimlessly throughout the grounds, entertaining the crowds with displays of their iridescent colours while they reverberated their fanned plumage to the passing peahens in its vicinity. For some, this was the first sight of the exotic birds, apart from the familiar peacock feathers adorning wealthy establishments in France and London.

Ultimately, the coal shortage dragged on for days, so Jim and his mates found themselves on one of the many free tram cars rattling their way down West Street, watching the locals go about their business and waving back to passers-by. Their excursions took them to Durban's historic Old Fort and Warriors' Gate, now rejuvenated into a memorial garden courtyard with the stone ammunition storage (the magazine) converted cleverly into a chapel. Others on their list were the art gallery and museum, Zulu dancers and the Indian and native markets. They were even in time for the local horse race meeting at the Durban Turf Club, Greyville.

While exploring the wide back roads dotted with stores and occasional eateries during the next few days, they discovered bullock drays had arrived loaded with sacks of tea, flour, sugar and stockfeed. One had already been unloaded, so in the interest of repaying the favour in their host city, Jim and Charlie, who were on their own again, stopped during their wanderings to help the two drivers unload supplies. One of the drivers was Walter B. Southwood. Walter would later write his address, 185 Bulwer Road, Durban, in Jim's book before shaking hands and wishing both young soldiers well for the future.

Finally, returning to the *Main* several hours later, the welcome news came that they would be pulling out of Durban in two days' time, so everyone must be onboard by 1700 hours the night before sailing. Jim had pulled Guard Duty for the next day, deciding in all perspectives to organise himself first before endeavouring one last venture along the seafront. They were heading into 15 days at sea, so all land time was enjoyed to the fullest extent.

It was around this time, after much concern over the *Main's* delayed return, Perth's *Sunday Times* released the following article on 7 September 1919:

> THE TROOPSHIP MAIN still in South Africa
>
> *A good deal of mystery has enshrouded the movements of the troopship Main ever since she sailed from England. Inquiries at the Navy and Military Departments yesterday morning could not throw definite light on her whereabouts. There are four officers and 286 other ranks aboard for this State.*
>
> *Last night a wire came from Melbourne "News" had reached the Defence Department that the Transport Main left Capetown for Durban on August 29 to fill her bunkers with coal. Some delay was caused by engine trouble. The Bakara and the Bahia Castello left Durban for Australia on September 4. Some concern has been felt by relatives of the Troops, on the Main, for a rumour gained currency that a mishap had occurred.*
>
> *The agents, Messrs. George Wills and Co. inform us their advice (sic) are to the effect that the Main is still in Durban undergoing repairs to her engines. This differs somewhat from the Melbourne version, but the fact remains that the vessel is safe and that is the main thing.*

Dawn had already broken as the *Main* pulled away from the dock, aided by a tug, making her way out of Port Natal as she was heralded by the horns of steamers lying at anchor nearby.

Many townsfolk had gathered to see the homeward-bound troopship embarking on her journey, with calls of farewell ringing out above the roar of her refurbished engines and the *Main's* foghorn.

Even the Criterion Theatre's upper level, with its second-storey tea room and French doors leading out onto the front façade's balcony, was full of waving patrons. Some would linger, staying to enjoy their coffee on the curved terrace, decked with green cafe tables and chairs, watching as the *Main* gradually diminished into the distant horizon of the Indian Ocean.

Troopships at anchor in Cape Town Harbour. Photograph courtesy of Cape Town History.

H.M.A.T. Main, Cape Town, 22 August 1919. Photograph courtesy of unknown donor.

RETURNED WITH A CREED — 223

Durban, 1919. Informal portrait of Miss Ethel Campbell, known as the Angel of Durban. AWM P08129.002.

1919. Miss Ethel Campbell, known as the 'Angel of Durban' distributes newspapers to Australian troops at Durban Port. AWM P08129.005.

1919. The Criterion Theatre, Durban. Illustration courtesy of 432 Postcards. (Monissa.com).

CHAPTER 18

Into the Blue

And now, there she was, still distant, but out in front of them, at last...Australia.

April 1919. Members of the 1st Wireless Signal Squadron catch their first glimpse of Australia on the return trip home. AWM P00562.158.

BY THE TIME THE LAST glimpse of land had slipped from view, the troops had settled into their evacuation drills and various other duties delegated to the men.

Four tiresome days, nautical mile after nautical mile, were broken by the furore during the follow-up meeting the married men held in Durban. The word now was that charges were going to be laid against any married men who did not perform Guard Duty.

Thirteen men determined not to comply attempted to leave, taking their wives off the ship in Durban, only to be forcibly stopped and reported. Events became quite heated, culminating in the committee requesting that the O.C. withdraw the charges as long as the men carried out their Guard Duties.

Unsurprisingly, this proposal was met with resistance, so a vote was held to decide the outcome. The vote carried 76 for married men to perform their Guard Duty, 36 against and 40 no votes. Fifteen married men and their single male counterparts remained on charges while awaiting Court Martial during the voyage home.

Perth's newspaper, *The Daily News*, on 29 September 1919, would later explain the contrary situation onboard the *Main*:

On August 24, the Committee held a meeting, and the question of performing guards and pickets was discussed, and on it being stated by several present that in the terms of the A.I.F. orders all married men were exempt from these duties while travelling to Australia with their wives, a vote was taken, and it was unanimously resolved: 'That neither of these duties be performed by married men while in Port.'

At Durban, on the 2nd inst., thirteen married men having been detailed for guard while in Port, a meeting of all married men was held and it was resolved: 'That these men be instructed not to perform guard duty, and that the rest of the men support them in this refusal. It was further decided: 'That the O.C. of the ship be approached with a view to releasing these men from this duty, and that in order to assist in the good conduct and management of the ship, the married men should perform all fatigues onboard the ship from 8 a.m. to 10 a.m. each day while in Port, and that for any duties missed or not performed by married men while in Port, double duty should be performed by them while the ship was at sea.' Colonel Patterson would not accept this proposal, as he maintained it would split the ship.

A meeting was held next day, and the company O.C. attended, and explained that Colonel Patterson had stated if the men did their guard duty, they would have facilities for leave in the same manner as the other classes, and no charge would be laid against the 13 men. The meeting resolved: 'That the married men do not perform guard duty.' It was stated there was rather a rough crowd ashore, and the women from the ship were not physically fit to go about on shore unescorted. The married men, we are informed, endeavoured to go ashore in the afternoon, and were stopped by the officers. The passengers allege that some of the officers used violence both against women and men.

The Committee held a meeting a little later, and decided that: 'The committee endeavours to pacify the married men, as matters are assuming a serious aspect.' It was decided to hold a secret ballot so as to ascertain whether the married men should perform the guard duty or not. Later, the Committee approached the O.C. of the ship, suggesting that he should withdraw all charges against the men conditional upon them doing their guard duty. He would not agree to this and stated that the matter would have to be referred to a Court-martial.

A general meeting was held the same evening when 76 voted for the married men to perform their duty, 51 being against, and 40 not voting. The meeting decided that it be placed on record that all the third-class married men are equally to blame, with the 13 men who were detailed for guard for the non-performance of, or delay in, performing that duty, as it was on the instructions of all the married men that such guard duty was not performed or delayed.

On the way out, we understand 15 married men in all were Court-martialled, 14 were adjudged guilty and fines amounting to 60 odd pounds were imposed.

It would not end there. The matter would be brought before the authorities on the ship's arrival in Fremantle.

Under blue skies a couple of mornings later on Deck Parade, the announcement was made of a baby's tragic death, requiring the fundamental Burial at Sea. For this reason, the ship would stop at 1000 hours for the Burial Service; there would be no classes today.

Precisely at 0945 hours, the troops took up their positions. Respectively, wives stood with their soldier husbands alongside the mourning parents as the ship's engines slowed, bringing the Main to an idling halt.

The chaplain presided in his solemn voice over the tiny bundle wrapped in its canvas shroud adorned with flowers while twine secured the neck and feet. Weights were wrapped with the infant's body lying on the smooth timber board, ready for internment to the sea.

After all the death and physical destruction the men had been subjected to, the tiny lifeless form before them left their hearts forlorn with loss. The sea breeze lifted the rigging above the congregation as if in reply to their connected thoughts for the salvation and gentle rescue of a life never lived.

As the chaplain concluded the prayers, 2,000 voices recited the Lord's Prayer while the near end of the board was lifted upwards, surprising the attending soldier at its lightness, and the lost child plunged to the waves below. The silence that followed was broken by the anguished sobs of the grief-stricken mother as the baby's wrapped body rapidly receded into the dark blue depths.

With the ceremony over, the *Main's* engines roared back into life as the ship recommenced its sombre journey. Occasionally, watchful seabirds would accompany the ship, looking for scraps thrown overboard or ejected from the kitchens, ever ready to swoop on the flying fish that streamed in silver flashes above the water on either side of the bow, sometimes for 50 yards or more.

Across the ship, everyone was endeavouring to distract themselves by whatever means available: reading, watching for flying fish, an island, or a lucky hand of cards.

For days on end, the trip's tedium was peppered by stories of home and the expectations of who would spot the Western Australia coast first; the bets just kept coming. Friday sports days always brought the welcome relief of games and amusing deck races of all sorts, particularly sack races on a rough day. Some were known to break the occasional arm or dislocate a shoulder, but generally, it was outright good fun.

Jim instinctively sensed changes in the air, their lingering pull reaching deep into his symmetry. So, had he known of Pte Geoffrey Rose's notes written three weeks earlier after leaving Cape Town on the *H.M.A.T. Port Melbourne*, his words would have come as no surprise:

29 July.

We ran into frequent fogs for four days & nights. The whistle was kept continually booming out a warning. I heard another boat once, answering, but the fog was too dense to see anything. It must have been very hard work for the officers & crew keeping watch through it. The water was fairly calm but this heavy blanket of fog made things very miserable. No Sun – nothing to be seen, & a continual clammy feeling.

6 August.

It was very cold & a terrific wind was blowing coming almost head on. From the feel of it, it seemed to blowing straight from the South Pole, bringing with it sleet & snow. The spray from the waves was turned to ice before it reached the decks. Ice was hanging from the masts & the wireless aerial broke away. I got caught in a gust of wind blowing through an alleyway, which was so strong that I was blown against the rail.

11 August.

There was a big swell on this day. I was sitting just below the open porthole reading, when the boat rolled, & a wave, or a good part of one came through the open porthole drenching me & another man. It's rather queer to find the light from the porthole suddenly turn to light green, & a solid stream of salt water about a foot thick come falling on one.

While the troops were restless for home under the duress of storms, engine troubles and coal shortages delaying their progress, families and relatives back on home soil sensed more than just restlessness but increased alarm.

A frustrating lack of explanation enveloped the *Main*'s absence after it was anticipated that there should have been at least some contact by this stage. People wanted answers…had the *Main* sunk?

In the *Daily News* of 26 September 1919, a Letter to the Editor written by A.T. Wreford expresses his concerns:

TROOPSHIP MAIN

Sir,

Can anything be done to "shake up" the Navy Office or the Defence Department, to give definite information about the landing of Troops, ex Main? Three weeks ago they allowed to be published reports that the Steamer was due on September 7th, when as a matter of fact the vessel had not left Durban.

Today they publish the bare statement, which has been current for a fortnight, that the Main has left Durban and is due at Fremantle on September 27. The agents of the vessel very kindly add an intimation that the vessel is due at Fremantle on Saturday afternoon, which is somewhat more explicit than the Navy Office statement.

It is to be hoped that these statements are more trustworthy than those published three weeks ago. Seeing that the Main is reported as being in wireless communication with Applecross for several days past it should not be impossible for the Defence Department to know, within an hour, the time of the vessel's arrival, and publish the disembarkation time so that those interested can arrange to meet their soldier friends.

Three weeks ago the misleading information brought whole families hundreds of miles to Perth on a 'wild goose chase'. Now the same people are waiting for some information that they can rely on, and the people who should know all about it are apparently too tired to say a word.

Demobilisation has been going on for several months, should it not have commenced at Headquarters, where the simplest duty seems to be unperformed? If you can obtain any information and publish it today, it will be of considerable assistance to the people in the metropolitan area, although too late for those in the country.

Yours etc, (sic)
A.T. Wreford

Wreford's shared frustrations were finally allayed when, on 27 September 1919, the *Main* echoed with the shouts of *Land, land, land!* to a chorus of cheers and whistles ringing throughout the ship. For hours men had lined the rails, including Jim with his binoculars, to get their first glimpse of home. Someone even sported a telescope that they rested on their mate's shoulder for stability. And now, there she was, still distant but out in front of them at last...*Australia*.

Tommy, unfortunately, found himself admitted to the onboard hospital the day before as illness continued to catch up with him. He had not been the same since he was gassed. Those who could make it out on deck for this long-awaited view of home did so, while others vied for shared views from any available porthole throughout the ward. The very vision ahead of them brought colour to their faces and tears to their almost disbelieving eyes.

It was late Friday afternoon, and the sun behind them illuminated the distant Fremantle coast. This afternoon at 1700 hours, they would dock at Gage Roads after entering the 8-mile wide channel between Rottnest Island and the surrounding shoals. The following morning, 28 September 1919, the *Sunday Times* in Perth reported her grand arrival:

TROOPSHIP MAIN ARRIVES

The Troopship Main, which was delayed for a considerable time at Cape Town owing to engine trouble, arrived at Gage Roads yesterday afternoon at 5.30. Latest advices are to the effect that the ship is clean and that the Troops and their dependents numbering 225 will be landed at E shed at 10.30 today.

Below deck, unbeknown to anyone, cabin steward Thomas Williams, an amiable man who had become familiar to the soldiers and families during their long two months at sea, was re-reading the drying ink of his last Will and Testament.

In the past week, the steward had been at loggerheads with his desperate emotions, which he was incapable of shaking. Swirling miserably from one overwhelming adversity to the next, he was no longer thinking coherently. In his trapped rationale, there was only one possible escape from the bitter turmoil within him. He had found the right place and knew the equally right moment to regain his freedom.

It was 25 September 1919, and the correction he made to his Will bequeathed his worldly possessions to his friend, Jones, and the wages owed to him he bequeathed to his mother.

Locking the wooden door to the two-berth cabin, Williams moved a chair to the centre of the cabin, where he secured his towel through the 2-inch eyelet attached to the ceiling, knowing it would readily support his weight. The knot tied, Williams tightened the looped towel around his sinewy neck before closing his eyes. Oblivious to the ecstatic troops on deck viewing the lights of Fremantle, Williams dropped heavily from the chair below him, his moving legs kicking the chair backwards intentionally in the momentum.

In moments, he was incomprehensible. The ship's reverberations around him grew slower, ever slower, until diminishing forever as all life subsided from his suspended body.

The *Daily News* reported the tragedy on 29 September 1919 as follows:

Suicide on H.M.T. Main

At the Fremantle Courthouse this morning, an inquiry was conducted by the Acting Coroner, Captain J. H. Foxworthy, and a jury consisting of T. H. Ryan, Lee Wilson, and J. E, Munro, into the death of Thomas Williams, late steward on the S.S. Main now lying in Fremantle, which happened yesterday. John Arthur Marshall, a returned soldier onboard the S.S. Main, deposed that deceased was bedroom steward to the cabin occupied by witness' wife. Witness noticed that deceased seemed dazed and forgetful for a few days prior to reaching Port. Yesterday afternoon, witness' wife informed him she had found the door of her cabin locked. Witness looked through the grating and saw a body hanging from the ceiling, suspended by a towel. With third-class steward, Bunn, witness went into the cabin and took the body down. Dr. Henderson was sent for and artificial respiration was tried for two hours without success.

Corroborative evidence was given by E. H. Bunn and Dr. Henderson. P.C.C. Lambert stated that on searching deceased's clothes, he came across a piece of paper which had the following written on it:

S.S. Main, September 25. If I depart this life on the above named (sic) ship, I give and bequeath all my belongings to H. C. Jones, onboard this ship, except my Mother's will, which is in my notebook, but the money which is due to me, I give and bequeath to my Mother.

Signed, T. Williams.

21 July 1916. Heavy seas experienced aboard the H.M.A.T Bulla during her crossing of the Indian Ocean. Photograph taken by Private Arthur Harris, courtesy of Virtual War Memorial.

September 1919. Crowds greet H.M.A.T. Main docked in Fremantle. Photograph LH004708 courtesy of Fremantle City Library History Centre and State Library of Western Australia.

October 1919. Australian soldiers view Australia at last from the deck of the Barambah. AWM H16799.

1919. On board the 'family ship' H.M.A.T. Borda, similar to the H.M.A.T. Main. AWM D00935.

CHAPTER 19

Australia's Sons Come Home

Beaming Diggers rallied for parade in their drafts, each feeling 'home' reaching up into their bones as they marched in full uniform from the entrance of the dock to the town hall.

Sydney women awaiting the return of loved ones from the war. AWM H11576.

THROUGH THE CALM SPRING NIGHT, the spirited troops sang and cheered as they watched the lights of Fremantle grow closer. No one remained below deck except those in hospital and a lone, lifeless man in a cabin, so just finding room to stand was a mission in itself.

Dawn was just breaking as the *Main* entered the familiar outer harbour sea lanes of Gage Roads. She carried the officials who had boarded her with the pilot during the night to evaluate the ship's bill of health before clearing her for docking at 'E' Shed at 10:30 am *Australian* time.

Congregating joyfully on Victoria Quay, the lauding townsfolk of Fremantle and Perth had turned out in their thousands to welcome the *Main* and her euphoric troops presently clustered to every possible vantage point. Khaki figures filled every rail, both decks, the bridge, ropes, rigging, horizontal masts, and lifeboats. They were all loaded with waving, whistling, yahooing soldiers desperate to touch Australian soil, once again, after what felt like a doleful eternity. Never could any one of them remember cheering so loud for so long.

Today would see the final tally of 344 soldiers, as well as any wives and children sailing with them, depart from their fellow Diggers as Fremantle put on a welcoming tea at Fremantle Park, celebrating the returned men in true celebratory style.

Fremantle Park had mobilised into an Army camp within 24 hours of the declaration of war, complete with its massive recreational Y.M.C.A. Tent conveniently doubling as a writing shelter for departing soldiers to send any last messages home.

This morning, though, the Y.M.C.A. Hut would supply the gloriously returned veterans with hot meals, biscuits and tea, newspapers and writing utensils in an exhilaration that engulfed the entire town like a fire consuming parched tinder.

Their first steps back on Australian soil were hailed by solid stomps as each man strode fervently to reach the dock's dusty earthen yards. The cacophony filled the air around the ecstatic troops like music to their ears, bringing tears to the eyes of many while impatient calls sparked from the rear to *Hurry the bloody hell up!*

Beaming Diggers rallied for parade in their drafts, each feeling 'home' reaching up into their bones as they marched in full uniform from the entrance of the dock to the town hall. The resounding cheers surrounding them reverberated between the buildings lining High Street.

Welcomed by Mayor Fred McLaren, the freshly landed troops discovered the *Main* had indeed been a cause of particular anticipation due to the ship's mystifying whereabouts. No one had known where on earth she was, quite literally, and fair to say everyone was relieved to hear of her impending arrival when word had finally arrived. According to the trusted officials, *a more sociable shipload of Aussies and English brides had not yet been seen on any troopship.*

The troops happily took up the free 10-mile train rides to Perth, taking the opportunity to send telegrams, also at no charge, from either Fremantle or Perth Post Offices. This immensely assisted in reducing the mass congestion of soldiers 'bursting at the seams' to get word home of their arrival.

After a further 10 minutes of generous welcome and announcements, the parade right-turned with thunderous precision to continue its way to Fremantle Park through the endless, exultant crowds regaling and showering them with confetti. Here, the men dispersed quickly amid the bounty laid on for them by their gracious hosts, and the people of Fremantle embraced the returned Diggers as if they were their own.

Escaping the welcoming frenzy, their 'Westralian' mates found their wives, families, relatives and friends in an implosion of speechless emotion, the very sight instilling a profound longing in the remaining troops. This was the last their mates would see of the Western Australia boys, their last vision as they turned to give a quick wave before being led away by their families to disappear amid the throngs of teary, overjoyed onlookers.

The *Main* would leave at first light after coaling up overnight, so in the wake of the sumptuous reception and festivities, Jim managed to get a seat on the train to Perth for another look around the beautiful city by himself. He had been there before when the *Ormonde* had stopped at Fremantle on their way over to Suez and could not tire of the Swan River or Perth's neat layout. And besides, he was back in Australia…he'd go *wherever the bloody hell he liked*.

Finding the square façade of the sandstone Post Office in St George's Terrace, he penned a telegram to send home. He had a fair idea when he would expect to arrive in Brisbane but chose not to include that information, considering the *Main* could just as readily reduce their anticipation to abject misery.

Jim stood at the polished Blackwood bench along the Post Office wall, completing the telegram form as the words came effortlessly:

ARRIVED FREMANTLE TODAY. HOME SOON....JIM.

Joining the queue of 30 khaki-clad patrons and three civilians, Jim happily arrived at the counter to lodge his message home, then simply continued wandering freely on his own, just absorbing the surreal sensation of being back home.

Beyond the rippling river, cars could be heard blaring their horns in welcome through the aromatic air scented by the eucalypts dotting the city. Naturally, his instinct as a shooter was to look into the trees above for game, only now he was looking up into them out of simple satisfaction. In his reverie, the thought crossed his mind of those who had it all taken from them, left behind on battlefields far away, never to look above them into Australian trees again.

Their last vision of Australia had been right here in Fremantle and Perth, making it particularly appropriate that Jim, along with others under the same notion, should find the nearest pub to share a beer to honour their ghosts. Those currently engaging in such an enthusiastic agenda were clearly going to be worse for wear in the morning.

Jim lit a smoke and sat back, listening to their talk of old times and generally just taking in the surreal atmosphere. Twenty minutes later, with his beer finished and having bought the second round, he left to continue his solitary walk around the city. He was comfortable walking on his own along the river, watching for fish jumping in the dusk as he had as a boy, content to make his way slowly back to Fremantle on the late evening train.

Looking over his shoulder, as the alcohol's warm afterglow filled him, Jim's thoughts shifted as he noticed soldiers everywhere celebrating their first night back in Australia. Suddenly, he was reconsidering his evening's plans. He would find Charlie and Ed to carouse in the lively city's venues. Either way, he did not intend to end up back onboard the *Main* before midnight.

When Jim spotted Charlie and Ed, they were just walking out of a pub up the road, on the lookout for him with the same thoughts. They had heard of Thomas William's tragic death, so considered it appropriate to give him a send-off. There was no end of pubs in Perth to choose from, and the nearest one satisfactorily to hand was the Royal Hotel. It would do *very bloody nicely,* even if time were running a bit short. No doubt, there would have to be some convenient 'after-hours' available to the country's returned Diggers.

It had not escaped the group of mates that their final days together were fast running out, so it was time to revel in whatever opportunity they had left. Their onboard days were routinely free as of today, except for any essential duties, and classes were finished at last, so now, they could knock around happily unheeded. It was unsurprising that their efforts could hardly have been considered studious over the past two weeks, anyway.

Now safely in Perth, the men sought refuge in the memories of their enlistment where vast numbers of them had initially met, answering the call to arms. For Jim and Ed at the bar of the Royal Hotel this night, they remembered the round tents of Bell's Paddock in the new suburb of Enoggera where they had trained. This was where the 9th Reos of the 41st Battalion had assembled for their group photo, the same place in the studio tent where Jim had his official portrait taken in full uniform. He intended to have an enlarged copy of the photograph framed and embellished with the 41st Battalion's scrollwork as a coming-home gift for his parents.

On the other hand, Charlie told stories of the Sydney Showgrounds where he had enlisted, when the grounds had swarmed with training soldiers undergoing endless parades and drills.

Memories of their army-issued blue dungarees and white hats came back to them when they changed their civvie clothes for the Army's training kit; surely, it was a lifetime ago. The very thought took Jim back to the afternoon he, Bill, Ted, Harry and Ernie had arrived home on Home Leave before they had left Brisbane. The looks on their mothers' faces had said it all when each of the boys walked up their front steps in full khaki uniform for the first time, slouch hat, badges and all. Each mother looked like she had seen a ghost...and for good reason. Their service numbers had been so close together, too: Bill's 3643, Ted's 3644,

Jim's 3653, Ernie's 3656 and Harry's 3659. He had been glad to be a part of the war with such a great mob of blokes.

As much as they had shared such brutal times together as brothers-in-arms, being saluted by King George V (on three occasions for some of them) was as unforgettable as it gets: 2,000 of them marching past him as he sat on his white stallion large as life, the 41st Battalion's Guard of Honour outside London's Australia House, and then again at the superb Peace Day Parade.

And so, Jim, Charlie and Ed continued their laughter-filled banter for a while longer. Amongst many things, they relived memories of the gracious nurses who patched them up and saw them return to the lines in good health. They were the powerhouses who saw through their patients' bravado, working with them tenderly and digging deep for that inner strength to rescue their shattered minds and bodies.

They had heard the news that seven of the nurses from the Casualty Clearing Stations in France were awarded the Military Medal for acts of gallantry and devotion to duty under fire when their hospitals had been bombed: Sister in Charge Alicia Kelly, Sisters Dorothy Cawood, Clara Deacon, Pearl Corkhill and staff nurses Mary Derrer and Alice Ross-King. They also knew that these same nurses would quickly point out that each and every nurse, far and wide, was unshakable in her duty. The mention of hospitals reminded them of Tommy Edwards who remained in the *Main's* hospital ward on his first day back in Australia, and so a beer was raised to share the occasion with him from ashore.

Their conversation steered to the W.A.A.C.s in the U.K., having surged in numbers since the Women's Army's original intake of 3,000 in 1916. Thoughts of Kay Baker quickly followed and then, even more significantly, those of Susie. He would write to her after settling in again...at *home*.

Stories of Fovant resurfaced along with the leave they had taken, the weddings they had been to and A.W.L.; the memories just kept coming. The discussion then turned to the eucalypts they were surprised to see in Cape Town, and...ahh, that smell! Just to see them was a sight for sore eyes. And now they were finally filling their senses with their fragrance here at home; they could actually smell them from the ship before they had even docked.

Memories of 'The Sweeterie' in the white building on Plein Street with its Date and Walnut Creams and Everton Toffees brought back a maelstrom of sensations to their tastebuds. And with the thought of food, the men began thinking about just where they would get a hearty 'feed' before making their way back to Fremantle on the late train.

Finishing their drinks, the men stopped for beef stew and freshly baked bread at the nearby Y.M.C.A. Hut, completing the meal repletely with treacle sponge and custard. They gratefully thanked the ladies assisting for such generous helpings and good-humoured welcome before taking their seats at one of the long tables to enjoy their meals.

Literally, within minutes, their plates were empty and teas drunk, providing the cue to move on to the train station for their return to Fremantle and a late evening tour of the port city before boarding.

Dawn brought Fremantle's enthusiastic well-wishers to farewell the *Main* as she pulled away from the dock once again, with the men lining the rails and vantage spots, although noticeably less than usual. Some remained where they had fallen, inebriated, onto their bunks the night before, while others were 'holed-up' in some cranny on the boat, finally waking up disorientated and confused as to how they came to be there. Of course, there were those who had not made it back at all.

Ultimately, there were 344 fewer soldiers and families today, with an expected total of over a thousand having disembarked by the time they leave Melbourne. Their first stop from Fremantle would be Adelaide, the South Australian capital the *Ormonde* had bypassed after leaving Melbourne in March last year. This time, the interstate troops happily looked forward to exploring the southern city in the brief time available to them after the South Australian troops' imminent homecoming in a few days.

Entering the Great Australian Bight, the notorious waters appeared comparatively calm to their earlier experience with Spring winds up to 15-20 knots, the seasoned troops now having vanquished their challenge. Four days later, the residents of Kangaroo Island watched the lights of the *Main* as she passed like a dominant shadow, making her slow passage along the coast into the darkening twilight.

With her engines finally slowed, the *Main* dropped anchor out from The Semaphore's lights in the early morning hours, waiting for clearance to move into her allocation. The Semaphore was initially known as Lefevre's Peninsula until renamed in the 1850s in recognition of the signal station with its semaphore signal arms on the beachfront. In the true spirit of patronage, The Semaphore Hotel was soon built and 'The Semaphore' was cemented for posterity.

Many of the departing troops remained deep in thought at breakfast, generating a slight hush throughout the ship as she made her way into the outer harbour to await quarantine inspection. All onboard had moved their watches forward 45 minutes.

The *Main* docked by 9:00 am to the roar of the extraordinary crowds welcoming both their own returned and the rest of the beaming troops. Tall wire fences acted as barricades, keeping the masses some yards from the gangway to give the troops room to disembark. Only a few weeks earlier, the barriers had been breached here at the wharf, and families had swarmed the disembarking troops, resulting in some mothers accidentally kissing the wrong sons after their long absence.

Today, there would be none of that. Soldiers jogged over to the fences that separated them from their wives and young children (some of whom they had not met yet), mothers, fathers, brothers and sisters...all calling out or crying in pure joy.

Those leaving were given a send-off by their mates onboard and had their packs carried down the gangway before they all formed into columns to parade victoriously through the streets of their departing South Australian mates' capital city. Their glowing faces and beaming smiles of recognition when the rest saw their families and friends brought a joyous warmth but an entrenching keen sense of impatience and longing to those who were to return to the *Main* and bide their time, slowly making their way to their hometowns.

Before long, the troops marched down Hindley Street, which was adorned with flags of all nations. People lined the streets, hung out of windows and crowded the balconies everywhere to watch the soldiers pass the Theatre Royal on their way to the 'Cheer Up' Hut for their reception by the Mayor. 'Welcome Home' souvenirs were waiting to be distributed to the men by the Semaphore Cheer-Up Society before the parade dispersed for a tea in their honour.

Information containing Adelaide's many sights to visit was handed out freely among the new arrivals, with many, including Jim and his mates, taking the opportunity to explore the beautiful city. After two and a half months on a ship, no one needed to see the beach. Instead, they walked through the botanical gardens adorned with fountains and Australian birdlife before arriving at the city centre, where they admired the architecture of the magnificent churches. All too soon, their limited time found them heading back to the *Main* for the last two legs of their voyage.

It was soon noticed some were missing from among them during the voyage, those being Private G. Deer (6776), Private C. Forbes (3642) and Private J.H. Arnett (1619), presumably having overslept in Cape Town, Durban or Fremantle...it was only to be expected. Jim would later receive the greeting card from Susie telling him of her encounter with two soldiers who had missed sailing when the *Main* left Cape Town...just which two, he would never know.

Susie's words read:

> *I met two Aussies in Town on Thursday evening. They absolutely seemed like two lost sheep. I believe they did miss their boat. They did say your boat the Main.*

By this time, Tommy had gladly rejoined the trio and eventually, the mates made their way back to the ship, the thought of their disembarkation in Sydney never far from their minds. Punctually, at 8:00 am the following morning, the steamer sailed...Melbourne was next.

The sea remained calm for the next two days before they entered Port Philip Bay to drop anchor off Williamstown during the early morning hours. After quarantine clearance, the *Main's* 8:30 am arrival at the wharf was welcomed by the brass band and the familiar masses of extraordinary crowds. The Victorian and Tasmanian troops disembarked together, the Tasmanians having a waiting troopship on the other side of the dock ready for their onward embarkation to Hobart.

And so, without further waiting, the *Main* moved off at 1:30 pm on the last leg of her voyage to Sydney, where she arrived after midnight at Watsons Bay three days later, on 15 October. It was precisely two months and three weeks since they had left Devonport.

Moving into the outer harbour at daybreak flying her Armistice Flag, the sirens and whistles of the surrounding troopships and steamers resonated throughout Sydney Harbour and Woolloomooloo Bay as she positioned to drop anchor. The *Main's* pennants flew on all four masts, along with her two Peace Flags, which had remained in place on the rigging between the second mast and funnel throughout the entire journey. The Australian Flag and respective ensign both now flew from her stern.

Troops clung to anything and everything imaginable, negotiating rigging, tarps, beams, the Bridge, lifeboats…absolutely everything. This was the moment they had waited for, where it had all started; their home port. So many familiar ships were there: the *Takada*, *Chemnitz*, the *Demosthenes*, *Ulysses*, *Port Melbourne*, *Barambah* and the *Bakara*, just to name the ones they recognised, all of them sending welcoming messages in semaphore and blowing their whistles to mark the troops' momentous arrival. Ted and Bill's ship, the *Prince Herbetus*, must already have sailed for other duties elsewhere as she was noticeably absent.

Lagging several days behind the *Main*, the *Bahia Castillo* had been delayed in Albany, Western Australia, as she waited for her stranded protesting passengers to arrive by train from Fremantle.

An article in the Adelaide Newspaper, *The Register,* on 9 October 1919 read:

Bahia Castillo – Fremantle October 8

After having been stranded in Fremantle for more than a fortnight, the passengers of the Bahia Castillo joined special trains this afternoon to proceed to Albany, where the boat will be rejoined, and the voyage resumed. Delegates to make preparations for the proposed enquiry (Messrs. McCallum, Patterson and Martin) left by the transcontinental train.

In short time, the gangway was lowered alongside the *Main's* portside for the approaching cruiser carrying the Quarantine Doctor and any accompanying authorities to board, including Sgt. W.J. Stephens.

Soon after being cleared to dock, the *Main* moved into her berth at No. 1 Wharf, Woolloomooloo, where tens of thousands of veterans during the past months had departed for the final leg of their journey home; here at those same gates, where wreaths continued to be laid by grieving mothers.

Today, there would be no parade for Jim, Ed and Tommy who were leaving the ship for their waiting train. Sydney was Charlie's hometown where throngs of cheering crowds waited to welcome him and hundreds of others marching in the Homecoming Parade before dispersing among their families, speechless with emotion.

A lavish breakfast of sausages, eggs, bacon and damper with syrup was ready for the troops and accompanying families in the Anzac Buffet at 8:45 am. In true Australian style, a couple of gum leaves simmered in the cauldrons of billy tea; how the boys had missed that distinctive earthy tang.

Now, sharing their last couple of hours together, the newly arrived repatriates exchanged addresses in their notebooks, cementing those promises to meet up again down the track. Firm handshakes were seen everywhere as the hour to leave drew nearer, with others from country New South Wales drifting to their specific platforms as they waited for onward trains themselves.

Jim, Ed and Tommy now transferred to their waiting train a short distance away, scheduled to leave at 11:25 am for their return to Brisbane, the same way they had arrived. Anzac Buffets along the route would provide sizeable hot meals laid out on trestles at designated stations. The well-prepared, including Jim, produced a bottle of their favourite spirit for several farewell nips between mates along the way, generating relaxed laughter as the booze permeated warmly throughout their already ignited systems. Others were glancing through the 'Souvenir of *H.M.T. Main* and Quota 48' magazine, a compilation of witty stories and poems written during the voyage and printed for everyone's entertainment.

The New South Wales First Class train seats were as comfortable as those they had been used to in the U.K. or France, the ones the troops were *forbidden to occupy*, setting the perfect atmosphere for their long journey home.

Now, with Australia taking them back into her nurturing embrace as the countryside they had long pined for rolled past, the gentle rocking of the troop train lulled the soldiers into an easy quietness they had not experienced for the longest time.

RETURNED WITH A CREED — 249

28 September 1919. Returning soldiers welcomed outside the Town Hall, Fremantle. Photograph LH002058 courtesy of the Fremantle City Library History Centre.

15 October 1919. H.M.A.T. Main flying the Armistice Flag, Sydney, Australia. Note the gangway dropped alongside for the routine boarding of officials. Photograph courtesy of unknown donor.

October 1919. Cheer-Up Hut welcome for the returning Diggers, Adelaide, Australia. From personal collection.

Soldiers at a Sydney train station, possibly Liverpool. AWM H03422.

CHAPTER 20

The Homecoming

Jim's throat was tight with emotion, but his strangled voice managed just a few hoarse words; it was as tough a moment as he'd expected.

A returning soldier is greeted by his mother.
AWM H11575

THE PAIR OF SIZE 9 BROWN leather army boots, well-worn and covered up to the leggings in a layer of street dust, hit the grey, etched concrete pavement of the Central Railway Station platform in Brisbane.

Acrid steam and smoke from the coal-driven steam engine filled the air around the young soldier, as it had done the day he left here almost two years earlier. Much had changed since then; much had changed him.

No light spilled through a glass-panelled ceiling here, as grandly as Glasgow Central Station's concourse. Instead, the refracted light from either end of the station was muted by the smoke and shadowy stone walls while still illuminating the platforms sufficiently.

It was 20 October 1919, and surrounding Jim were the classic columns and brickwork of 'home'. Central Station was the hub for passenger trains, the nexus for the burgeoning city, and the place where he had left his family and friends, cheering and waving in the crowds.

He searched for the familiar face he knew could not possibly be waiting for him, let alone even aware of his arrival. Instinctively, Jim strained to hear the Irish voice above the hum of station noise, just the same. Hell, there was not even a good to fair chance his father would even be at the markets today, but it was worth a try to look for him after the parade.

Feeling an increased surge of adrenaline, Jim made his way slowly along the platform with the other troops towards the stairs leading to the massive block arches of the station's entrance. Forming up into columns in the shadow of the station's blockwork façade, the parade extended along Ann Street, which heaved with exultant crowds. Led by the 41st Battalion Band, they set off at a comfortable pace to the roar of the massive crowd, their hearts bursting with pride.

Some of the troops were not waiting. Having spotted their wives and families, they instantly Fell Out from the lines; who was going to stop them? The others remained on parade, all eagerly waiting for the conclusion of the address so they could find those they searched for in the sea of excited faces.

Jim did not wait a minute longer either, moving through the expectant masses back to Ann Street on a mission that clearly said there was somewhere he needed to be. The Roma Street Markets were abuzz with activity just up the hill, and that was where he headed.

Making his way across Roma Street through the traffic of Model T Ford 'Tin Lizzies', hansom cabs and waiting horse-drawn carts, Jim looked over to the line-up of harnessed horses where he knew his father would have parked the spring cart with his long-missed horse, Cobber...that is if they were even here. Not noticing his horse obscured by scores of parked carts, he considered briefly that his father may have acquired another horse or, still yet, another buggy.

He was sweating with anticipation in the bright October morning, cooled slightly by the gentle breeze behind him as he came ever nearer to the stall where his father sold his chickens and bananas. There were those in the crowd of faces he recognised and stopped briefly to greet, one being John Livingstone, his father's business partner.

One hundred yards away, the harnessed chestnut with a blaze down his gentle face, contentedly dozing with one foot lazily at rest, suddenly twitched his ears involuntarily as something in his senses responded to a scent on the wind, a scent he had missed for the longest time. Snorting softly, Cobber turned his head, his ears alerted to a voice he waited for and his quivering nostrils to that aroma lingering above all others.

Approaching the stall he looked for, Jim made his way closer to his father's familiar frame leaning over bunches of bananas, sorting them into orders for his customers.

You might want a hand with that, hey? were the handful of words that stopped the 58-year-old who dared to believe he had just heard his son's voice.

George Rainey's face strained with emotion at the sight of his boy come home, his legs suddenly threatening to give way under his wiry frame. Managing to overcome his choking throat enough to greet his son hoarsely, George temporarily abandoned any further attempts at even remotely trying to speak as he held his son in a tight grip.

Every day he had been away was another day out of their lives they would never get back, but this day was finally here...their *boy* was back, unlike the 60,000 lives whose families would forever ache for them.

Jim's throat was tight with emotion, but his strangled voice managed just a few hoarse words; it was as tough a moment as he'd expected. With suitable timing, John Livingstone arrived, insisting the two head home while he saw to any waiting tasks himself. Then, together, father and son walked to the spring cart, where Jim was elated to greet his dependable chestnut gelding, the colt he had helped break in ten years earlier.

Jim was somehow unsurprised that Cobber seemed already aware of his arrival; the wind, after all, had been behind him while passing the parked spring carts. Murmuring those old, unifying words that came so readily between a man and his horse, he slipped an arm under Cobber's neck, reaching up to the back of his ears as the faithful horse nudged his head against his damp shirt in acknowledgement.

Jim's image was that of the same young man who had ridden him across creeks and along dirt tracks for so long, then suddenly vanished; the last vision of him dressed in the same clothes.

George scaled the cart, its wooden-spoked wheels standing to the height of the cart itself, with its heavily varnished low timber sides and wooden floor jolting under the sudden movement. Jim offloaded his kit bag from his shoulder into the back before swinging up effortlessly to join his dad on the bench seat. A smile passed between them as George contentedly took in the matured, manly features of his son before a gentle flick of the reins prompted Cobber to lead them out of the markets and onto the northern road bound for home.

As they neared Bowen Park's popular gardens, Jim absorbed how many new businesses, houses and hotels had rapidly increased the size of the growing city, the state's 60-year-old capital. Becoming a nation under the Federation was supposed to elevate Australia, relieving her of her reputation as a 'colony' once and for all. It was now clearly obvious that that notion alone was never enough…the new nation of Australia was born, and over 60,000 souls lay in silent testimony to its cost.

Out of the sheer enjoyment of driving home led by his horse, Jim took the reins from his father, noticing there seemed to be a low haze out on the western horizon as they passed the increased numbers of timber 'Queenslander' cottages, the style uniquely adapted for the Queensland climate. Pedestrians and patrons everywhere were going about their daily business, some in Model Ts, others in the more numerous motorised tram cars similar to those Jim had seen in Glasgow, London, France and South Africa. Scores of onlookers waved to him with cheery greetings of *Welcome home, Digger!* as they passed.

Ever closer to home, his father had been updating him on whatever news he could share with his newly returned boy, now a grown man. Emmel Bray had been up this way from Lismore breaking in horses a couple of months ago, a good excuse also to call on Ev. They would later marry and move to Lismore. Ev was two years younger than Jim, making her 18, now, the same age he was when he left for the war and the same age as Ciss when she married Steve.

Steve Johnson had finally arrived back home with his shattered shoulder in February, eight months prior, and Ciss was now pregnant, much to 'Uncle Jim's' sheer delight. The four boys, Harry (who was still the worst for wear), Bill, Ted and Ernie, had all visited the family since their earlier arrival home, sharing their mutual concern that the *Main* had not arrived. George had taken Ernie to show him their names, his and Jim's, on the newly established Roll of Honour at the school, something he would take Jim to see in due course.

Jim's brother, Bert, now taught at their old Chermside State School, including swimming lessons conveniently provided in their dam. Bert's priority in water safety had swiftly manifested itself when Francie nearly drowned in the dam's murky depths, Bert narrowly averting tragedy by pulling her out by her hair.

Gradually, the Chermside Army Camp came into view. The camp was bordered by their back paddock, where Jim had once stood at the boundary's treeline watching the new enlistments marching and training, wishing his years away to be old enough to join them.

There was nowhere near the same activity as there had been before Jim had left for war, although there were masses of Army stores and an ammunition dump taking shape.

In a moment, he would see their new house, which had been built while he was away. And finally, there it was - the Queenslander cottage. It wasn't the vision he had taken with him of the pioneer shingle hut, but still, it was the beacon that had brought him home.

Unbeknown to either of them at that moment, Francie had excitedly spotted them from the back laundry behind the house and stood speechlessly watching them, mesmerised in both joy and disbelief to see her brother alongside their dad. Jim answered Francie's gaze from 100 yards away with smiling eyes and a wave towards his little sister as she ran headlong down the track to greet them, calling out excitedly to her mother, sisters and Bert.

Handing George the reins, Jim jumped down from the buggy to greet his beaming little sister, who, after two long years, was suddenly the shape of a young woman. Francie still prided in her long blonde hair, but her child-like face encapsulated in his memory now made way for a more womanly composure with slightly more definitive contours to her brow and cheekbones...*and* elsewhere!

The others caught up as she hugged him tightly in her joy. He had come close to not coming home when one of the troops had copped some shrapnel only a few feet from him, killing him instantly. And so it began - the *creed of silence*. In true Digger style, Jim assured her he had never been at any risk, so she did not need to worry any more.

Adelaide, Jim's mother, arrived and stood quietly as he looked into her tired face, disbelieving that he could be standing here in front of her after all this time. She simply could not speak.

Deanie, Jim's older half-sister, Bert and Ev were all grown up, although Bert was now emitting a definite air of authority. Laughing together, the two brothers clasped each other in a greeting of brotherly hugs and good humour, immediately followed by the two overjoyed sisters, each taking their turn welcoming Jim home with hugs, tears and kisses.

How everyone seemed to have grown in the time since he had gone, yet one of the changes Jim noticed the most was the weariness etched into the creases of his parents' faces. To be expected, they, too, were absorbing significant changes about him. That boyish softness was gone, replaced with his square jaw sharply set. This accentuated Jim's resemblance to George's father, a sight George found simply staggering.

It was late October, and the Spring storms that had been rolling in from the Darling Downs continued for the third day in a row. As the closely gathered family made their way up the track alongside the cart, Jim could see the anvil-shaped storm cell building out to the West, a sure sign they would soon hear the first rumbles of thunder. The long, raucous calls of the Black Cockatoos filled the air in warning as the flock flew past to settle in a nearby stand of Blue Gums by the creek. Their unmistakable calls began filling that void within him, suddenly surprising him by its vastness.

The first distant rumbles of thunder drifted noticeably on the afternoon air from out in the distance as the family reunion reached the front steps. This was where Adelaide left them briefly to organise lunch. As continuing thunder came to them, George prompted the girls to attend to any unfinished outside tasks ahead of the storm while he unloaded the feed from the markets, and Bert attended to Cobber, unhitching him from the cart.

Still smiling, Jim walked through the rooms of the new family home, exploring the layout, taking in the fresh pale green paint and cabinetry containing the home's finery, until his eyes settled on the pair of iridescent blue Egyptian vases from Suez. Jim could not help his astonishment; they were as striking now as when he had first seen them *and* had arrived intact. Everything was familiar around him, only in a different, displaced way, almost like he was a visitor.

Moving along the hallway to the back of the house, he passed the four bedrooms, the girls' on the right, with his parent's more roomy bedroom on the left adjacent to Bert's. As comfortable and reassuring as home was, Jim was resigned to sleeping out on the front verandah. He had slept on the open deck of the *Main* and most other troopships he had sailed on, an improvement from the earthen bivouacs in trench walls, so the front verandah looked just fine.

The hallway led through the dining room in the middle of the house to a sitting area where his mother's piano adorned the corner. Every room had elegant lace curtains replacing the torn linen of the original shingle cottage's timber push-out windows, their wooden props now giving way for these modern adjustable hoppers. As he moved through the cottage, No. 12 in the Queensland Housing Scheme, Jim admired the fashionable silky oak windows, adjustable to two heights, that showcased their subtly distorted, hand-made glass panes, each one rippling slightly as he passed. Not only were they stylish, but they drew the breeze just as their design intended.

Arriving at the semi-detached kitchen with its wood stove banked safely in an alcove on a protective sheet of tin, he found his mother energetically bustling, preparing a lunch of corned beef, pickles and damper, spread with her freshly home-made butter. There would be time to prepare a celebratory homecoming dinner for him, but for now, she wanted to hear her son's voice in every reach of the house. She had waited so long for this moment.

Questions chirped from all directions as the young women returned from their rushed chores to congregate around him in the kitchen like bees to a honey pot; *What was it like to see Australia again? Why was the ship so late? Do you have a girlfriend? So* many questions.

Contentedly talking his captivated family through the many happier times of the past two years, he portrayed the mates he had shared so much with and the adventurous sights he had seen on leave, all the while aware of the approaching storm. By now, George and Bert had arrived at the kitchen table to join the conversation, enjoying Jim's stories and the exotic news they had waited to hear. They simply talked and talked from anything to almost everything.

Finally, the fast-approaching storm had reached them. Blinding forks of lightning cracked overhead in successive bone-shuddering explosions that he felt rise through his feet, an ominous fury bearing the unsettling similarity to the Front Line barrages. How could his beaming family sitting around the hoop pine table with him possibly imagine what he was feeling right now?

But he was better than he might have been…certainly better than many others who would be forever broken in mind and spirit. Rehabilitation through the A.C.S. had re-set his thinking towards rebuilding his life in the promise of a new future.

In time, the good would outweigh the bad of these past two years, and the anguish within him would gradually become more manageable the more he grew into it…or drank to reduce it. This pain and the nights of fitful sleep would not be his to bear alone, though, as leagues of the returned would verify. Many, like Jim, would resort to drinking in the hopes of escaping both the merciless demons that haunted them and their own impatience with those who could not grasp these unspoken horrors. This was only ever going to be a recipe for more pain to come, but there was no one to turn to for empathy, so the Diggers' creed of silence prevailed instead.

Surrounded by the spirit of reunion and family love, the night closed in around the family gathered at the kitchen table in the yellow glow of the kerosene lamps. Only now did Jim realise just how intensely he had missed that warm, mineral aroma of these homely lights, now as the storm's anger rumbled unthreateningly into the distance. Like a thousand others, tonight would see them catching up on valuable lost time as a family, talking like they had never talked before, long into the early morning hours.

Life for Jim and the returned veterans was about to reinvent itself as a new beginning awaited them. They would be taken through the catastrophe of the Great Depression years when the world itself had barely healed from the war's horrendous scars. Unimaginably worse still, a *second* World War would erupt on the heels of Germany's reneging on the Peace Treaty reparations for all damages of World War 1, both wars initiated by Germany.

The veterans would raise their own children and tell their grandchildren amusing stories; some would even re-enlist in World War 2, but remain forever mute to the horrors they experienced when they were just adventurous young boys. Similarly, those alongside Robert Wilkie in the Graves Detachment, re-interring the fallen in their last honourable duty to their mates, remained as silent as the graves they dug. They did not want sympathy or pity, only the unspoken understanding between mates who had been there.

Time would give many the luxury of looking upon the generations that followed as the years unfolded into the future they had fought to protect, a future built from the destroyed aftermath of World War 1 and the Army's Australian Corps Schools that reshaped their shattered boyhood dreams. Sadly, within 20 years of their safe return, 50 per cent of these veterans would succumb to injuries, illnesses that plagued them, or to the vicious, interminable demons that ate their desperate souls from within.

Whatever the future held for them, in the names of all those who never came home and those suffering from the overwhelming torment of war's brutalities beyond all endurance, let it be said in Jim's own timeless words:

It should never happen again.

*　*　*

Produce Markets, Roma Street, Brisbane. Photograph courtesy of Queensland Places.

Rainey's 12-acre farm is believed to be on the hill in the background. Photograph courtesy of the Chermside & Districts Historical Society.

9/41ST BATTALION

9th Reinforcements 41st Battalion. Photograph courtesy of the Queenslander Pictorial and the State Library of Queensland.

Jim Rainey is seated in the front row on the far left; Harry Larsen is seated in the front row on the far right; Bill Mitchell is 6th from the left in the 3rd row; Ted Marsh is on the far right of the 2nd back row, and Ernest Murr is 6th from the right in the 5th row.

Motto: Death Before Dishonour

AFTERWORD

IT WAS ENGRAINED IN THE four of us as kids that we were not to push our grandfather, James Henry Rainey Snr, with questions about the war. He would neither talk about it nor could he be expected to give a truthful answer if we chanced to be so bold.

Instead, our mother hinted at the stories she had heard, hushed stories that he had witnessed his own men escaping their bombed, burning tanks only to be consumed by the flames. Other stories told of his battalion fighting alongside the American troops during an assault where he fought at the Somme in France, and above all else, he was a sniper, a revered level of shooter.

A moment of reflection brought an unexpected shift in our grandfather's silence, as his mortality allowed a few subtle reprieves. And so it was that at lunch with my grandparents during the school holidays in the 1970s, he broke his silence with the then 10-year-old me. It could (or should) have been any of my three older brothers, particularly the youngest of them, who dreamt of following in our grandfather's footsteps, but it was me.

With his thoughts filled with distant memories, Jim proceeded to tell me he was saluted on parade by the king before the 9th Reinforcements left for France, a proud moment that was quite obviously a highlight in his life. The joy filling me was soon extinguished by his tragic account of the 41st Battalion's voyage in convoy from Suez, where their sistership was sunk by a torpedo directed squarely at them. By the time they had reached Le Havre, only three had survived the convoy of 11.

Appreciating the direction of this privileged conversation, I did not interrupt as he continued his recollections. They had to wear gas masks in battle as the poisonous clouds were thick around them, then the painfully vivid memory caused him to glance away.

His captivating stories told of him being a sniper and that he'd had a French girlfriend who had wanted him to pierce her ears, only to run off after he had only pierced one. He had also been smitten with another girl, Susie, as her fond memory brought a distant expression to his ageing grey eyes. He finished the conversation with this final word on the whole subject of war:

It should never happen again.

One evening soon after, Mum and our grandmother showed me some of Jim's World War 1 memorabilia, including a photo of him with his rifle and bayonet at Fovant, England. It is worth mentioning here that our grandfather remained out in the lounge. And that was the extent of it...the rest was for me to find out, but I did.

When Jim's youngest sister, Francie, heard I had sourced his service records in 1991, she graciously sent me his World War 1 possessions that the Rainey family had kept. The delicate brown paper package contained numerous aged greeting cards he had sent home along with some his family had sent him, including one in his mother's handwriting depicting Armistice Day in Brisbane. I have rarely known a more poignant moment.

His address book showed the pencilled notes he had written during the 9th Reinforcement's voyage from Suez to Le Havre, where ship after ship in convoy was sunk by U-boats, including their ill-fated sister ship, but that they had ultimately sunk one U-boat, themselves.

There was also his rifle practice scorebook, where he had noted achieving Marksman First Class, and a photo of him with four other young men in uniform; their names on the back read H. (Harry) Larsen, E. (Ted) Marsh, E.A. (Ernest) Murr and W. (Bill) Mitchell. Lastly, his coveted Crossed Rifles Badge. Every item was in perfect condition.

The precious memorabilia I was privileged to see as a child also came to me after my mother died. These extraordinary possessions of a time when the world was devastated by war enabled Jim to finally tell his story posthumously.

There were no military medals, though, he had seen to that. One Anzac Day, the torment had become too great, and he had thrown them into Humpybong Creek after leaving the Redcliffe R.S.L.

My quest for answers to a lifetime of questions weaves the history of Jim's rare mementos into his unit's official extracts recorded in 1918, telling the story of a young boy hurled into a world at war, to return as a humble and troubled man, prickly at the best of times, who sought no recognition or thanks, only peace; a difficult peace doused with alcohol like so many of his returned mates.

When Jim died in 1988, two months short of his 89th birthday, his failing body was bedridden, imprisoning him against his alert mind and will. My last vision of him was in a wheelchair, attending church in the nursing home caring for him when our aunty, a nurse herself, could no longer provide sufficient care. Church was the last place I expected to see him as he had spent his life distancing himself from its piety amid outbursts of *Jesusbloodychrist!* whenever the mood took him.

Endless hours of research now reveal the footsteps of this earthy, cranky grandfather's tumultuous life in war.

This war was heralded by a new era when revolutionary planes regaled the skies and motor cars and lorries were here to stay, let alone gargantuan steel ships that took our troops away to etch their courage and sacrifice into the parables of history in those far-off battle zones.

Through the years spent attending Anzac Day commemorations, including three Anzac Day Dawn Services in the shadows along the Kokoda Track, Papua New Guinea, I have felt our grandfather close; both him and our great grandfather Private William Hipathite (6033), who died of wounds at Messines in Belgium.

Now, after many dedicated months of delving into Jim's everyday life during those war-torn years and in the Army's rehabilitation programs following Armistice, his presence continues to inspire me.

But today, if there was any question the ten-year-old girl in me could ask our grandfather, it would not be about the moment he saw his family on arriving home or his first sight of Western Australia's shoreline after nearly two years, as tantalising as that is for me. No, it would be something of far more consequence:

Have we, the generations that followed, done the Diggers' legacy justice?

* * *

ILLUSTRATION REFERENCE NUMBERS

The illustrated pages throughout this book are deliberately numbered to provide more information where possible.

1. Cover photograph – Private J.H. Rainey (3653) official World War 1 portrait. Photograph courtesy of family collection.
2. Dedication: July 1917. Newly enlisted, Private James Henry Rainey 3653. (Note the absence of A.I.F. badges.) Photograph courtesy of the Queenslander Pictorial and the State Library of Queensland.
3. Pg 1: Troopship *R.M.S. Ormonde* in dazzle camouflage 1918. Photograph courtesy of the State Library of Victoria.
4. Pg 12: 41st Battalion marching through Brisbane, 1916. Photograph courtesy of the Imperial War Museum.
5. Pg 12: Australia Camp, Suez. AWM P00369.012.
6. Pg 13: An Australian battalion marching out past the tent lines of a camp in Egypt to the training ground. AWM C03037.
7. Pg 13: Australian soldiers and locals at The Sphinx and Pyramids. AWM P05382.001
8. Pg 14: S.S. Ellenga 1918. AWM P02400.011.
9. Pg 14: Kantara Camp, Suez Canal from H.M.A.S. Australia. AWM J03224
10. Pg 15: Australian troopships leaving Port Said Harbour. Photograph courtesy of the National Australian Archives M1145 3B43.

11. Pg 23: Some of Jim's notes during the convoy between Suez and Le Havre. From personal collection.
12. Pg 24: An unidentified British steamer sinks after being torpedoed by an enemy submarine. AWM C00598.
13. Pg 24: No. 2 Australian General Hospital, Le Havre. Photograph courtesy of the Imperial War Memorial.
14. Pg 25: Jim's Crossed Rifle Badge from Fovant, 1918. From personal collection.
15. Pg 33: 28 August 1918. The 'mad minute'. Practices 16 and 17 of Jim's General Musketry Course. Photograph courtesy of Bryan James.
16. Pg 37: Fovant, 1918. Marksman page Jim's scorebook. Photograph courtesy of B. James
17. Pg 38: Pte James (Jim) Henry Rainey 3653. Fovant, August 1918. Photograph courtesy of Raymond Pepper and Chermside Historical Society.
18. Pg 39: L to R sitting. J.H. (Jim) Rainey, W. (Bill) Mitchell. L to R standing. H. (Harry) Larsen, E. (Ted) Marsh, E.A. (Ernest) Murr. Fovant, 1918. Photograph from personal collection.
19. Pg 40: 1918 Codford No. 7 Training Camp Fovant. AWM C01288.
20. Pg 40: 1917 Rifle practice, Fovant. Photograph courtesy of the State Library of Victoria (H85.55/160/65).
21. Pg 41: 13 August 1918. 41st Battalion Guard of Honour being inspected by King George V at the opening of Australia House. AWM D00003.
22. Pg 41: Colour patches chart of the 3rd Division. Courtesy of the Western Front Association.
23. Pg 43: Colonel Alexander Robert Heron DSO CMG of 41st Battalion. AWM H00043.
24. Pg 55: Codford Training Camp Bombing Range. AWM P01688.015.009

ILLUSTRATION REFERENCE NUMBERS - 271

25. Pg 55: 29 September 1918. Australian Sergeants seek instruction prior to the American and Australian offensive against the Hindenburg Line. AWM E03392.
26. Pg 56: 30 September 1918. Australian reinforcements marching along the Villeret-Hargicourt Road, on their way to the front line near Bellicourt, passing an Australian Battery of 18-pounders operating in that sector. AWM E03513.
27. Pg 56: 1 October 1918. Australian Infantry passing along a sap towards Guillemont Farm, near Ronssoy during the struggle for this section of the Hindenburg Defence System. AWM E03418.
28. Pg 57: Harry Larsen 3589, Fovant 1918. From personal collection.
29. Pg 59: Bodies of 27th American Dvn troops laid out for burial after heavy losses at the Hindenburg Line 29 September 1918. AWM E04942C.
30. Pg 65: Battle lines for the 41st, 43rd and 44th 29 September 1918. AWM RCDIG1004546.
31. Pg 66: Positions of the 41st Battalion's A, B, C and D Companies during the Battle of the Hindenburg Line. Jim was in B Company. The 27th American Division made it to the green line but neglected to mop up, causing severe losses to the Americans. AWM RCDIG1004547.
32. Pg 72: Illustration drawn by Lieut. Smith at 6:30 am on 1 October 1918, during the battle of the Hindenburg Line. AWM Appendix 582 of RCDIG1004547Pg 70: 29 September 1918. Allied tanks and infantry troops preparing to go into action near Bellicourt, France. Photograph Q9364 courtesy of the Imperial War Museum. AWM H12514.
33. Pg 76: 29 September 1918. Allied tanks and infantry troops preparing to go into action near Bellicourt, France. Photograph Q9364 courtesy of the Imperial War Museum. AWM H12514.
34. Pg 76: A captured German concrete dugout in the Hindenburg defences near Bony. AWM E03591.
35. Pg 77: Allied soldiers at the entrance to the St Quentin Canal near St Quentin. AWM H15944.

36. Pg 77: Australian Graves Registration Detachment, Australian section of the Imperial War Graves Unit loading bodies from a mass grave at to be put in single graves. AWM A00948.
37. Pg 79: 29 September 1918 Australian engineers repairing the sabotaged Corduroy Track to Bellicourt. AWM E03630.
38. Pg 88: Templeux le Guerard 3 October 1918. AWM E03788.
39. Pg 88: Light rail used to transport troops to and from the Front, France 1918. Its convenient lightweight fabrication provided the ability for rapid assembly and deconstruction. AWM E02768.
40. Pg 89: 2 October 1918. German prisoners at the clearing station, Abbeville. Photograph courtesy of the Imperial War Museum. IWM Q9353.
41. Pg 90: A Peronne street sign reading 'Roo de Kanga', characteristic of the Australian digger's humour. AWM E03412.
42. Pg 91: Warlus – Rue d'Airaines. Photograph courtesy of Info Bretagne.
43. Pg 91: Abbeville – Photograph courtesy of Info Bretagne.
44. Pg 93: 11 November 1918. A crowd of civilians and Australian soldiers gather in the Vignacourt Town Square on Armistice Day. Officially the troops weren't informed of the armistice until three days later. AWM P10550.089.
45. Pg 103: Front of the card Jim's mother, Adelaide, sent him following Armistice Day, 1918. From personal collection
46. Pg 104: Jim's mother's Christmas card to Jim dated 25 November, 1918, mentioning the Armistice Day celebrations in Brisbane. From personal family collection.
47. Pg 104: Jim's embroidered card to his ten-year-old little sister, Francie. From personal family collection.
48. Pg 105: Training continued following Armistice Day, November, 1918. Australians undergoing bayonet training at the Australian Corps School to remain prepared for war. Note the men are wearing gas masks. AWM E01673.
49. Pg 105: The start of a 440 yards foot race in France. AWM H03965.

50. Pg 107: Jim's 41st Battalion Christmas card to his parents. From personal family collection.
51. Pg 118: Chateau de St Maxent where the 41st Battalion enjoyed their Christmas lunch, 1918, at 12:00 midday. Photograph courtesy of Infobretagne.
52. Pg 118: British Army soldiers inspecting some of the streets in the ruined village of Bellicourt. AWM H15943.
53. Pg 119: Ted Marsh 3644, Fovant 1918. From personal collection.
54. Pg 121: A sculpture of a kangaroo and joey made from snow. From the collection of 1070 Sergeant Sydney Vincent Barratt, 43rd AWM P10700.001.
55. Pg 129: Unidentified students and German prisoners at work in the Carpenters Shop at the Australian Corps Technical School. AWM E05024.
56. Pg 129: A group of unidentified students at work in their Motor Mechanics Shop at the Australian Corps Technical School. The students had seven types of lorries and cars from which they learned and compared the mechanism of internal combustion engines. The instructors were qualified mechanics and tradesmen in the A.I.F., and while the blackboard (far right) was used for lectures, most of the instruction was practical. AWM E05036.
57. Pg 130: A group of unidentified students in the Plumbers and Tinsmiths Shop at the Australian Corps Technical School. AWM E05037.
58. Pg 130: A group of unidentified soldiers in the Electrical Generating Room at the Australian Corps Technical School. This plant provided two voltages of 220 and 110 and in case of interruption, it could transform the local supply from 10,000 to 220 volts. AWM E05015.
59. Pg 131: Unidentified students in the Engineers Machine Shop at the Jeumont Australian Corps Technical School. AWM E05028.
60. Pg 139: A group of unidentified students at work in the Fitters Workshop at the Australian Corps Technical School. On the right is a stationery engine under repair. AWM E05032.

61. Pg 139: Unidentified students and German prisoners in the Wood-Working Machine Shop at the Australian Corps Technical School. On the far right, some of the students are operating a pendulum circular saw. The German prisoners were engaged in unskilled labour in the workshop. AWM E05022.
62. Pg 140: A group of unidentified students and German prisoners in the Blacksmiths Shop at the Australian Corps School. The tools used were all made by the students from pieces of salvaged scrap iron. AWM E05033.
63. Pg 140: Unidentified students in the Joiners Shop at the Australian Corps Technical School. AWM E05075.
64. Pg 141: Ernest A. Murr 3656, Fovant 1918. From personal collection.
65. Pg 143: The soldier's kit. Photograph courtesy of Encyclopaedia 1914-1918 Online.
66. Pg 156: Informal group portrait of members of 41st Battalion Camera Club. Jim Rainey is on the far left. Ted Marsh is believed to be seated in front of Jim and Bill Mitchell is believed to be on the far right. AWM P01861.005.
67. Pg 156: 29 September 1918. An interior view of the damaged Medical Dressing Station used by the Australians during operations in the Hindenburg Line near Bellicourt. AWM E05244.
68. Pg 157: Liberty Trucks of the 1st Australian Motor Transport Company, Peronne. The men of the Australian Corps School learnt to drive in Liberty Trucks as part of their rehabilitation. AWM P00520.005.
69. Pg 157: Le Crotoy – the Statue of Joan of Arc and Hotel de la Marine in the background. From personal collection.
70. Pg 159: 3rd Division Demobolisation Quota 39 marching into A.B.D. Le Havre. April, 1919. AWM C04797.
71. Pg 165: April 1919 A group portrait of 3rd Aust Dvn officers and men of Quota 39 at Gamaches railway station before embarking for the Demobilisation Base. AWM E05161.

ILLUSTRATION REFERENCE NUMBERS - 275

72. Pg 165: April 1919. A group of 3rd Dvn officers and men of Quota 39 at Gamaches Railway Station before embarking for the Demobilisation Base. AWM E05159.
73. Pg 166: Australian Base Depot (A.B.D.) at Rouelles near Le Havre. AWM A02044.
74. Pg 166: 1918. S.S. Lorina. The Lorina served as a troopship during WW1 and WW2. On 29 May 1940, she was divebombed and sunk during the Dunkirk evacuations. Photograph courtesy of unknown donor.
75. Pg 167: Australians drawing up a gangway for disembarkation. AWM C02574.
76. Pg 173: Jim's Demobilisation Card. Note Unit as Australian Corps Central School (41st Btn) From personal collection.
77. Pg 174: 1919. Sutton Veny, England. Australian soldiers at the front of the Y.M.C.A. Headquarters at Greenhill House. AWM H01729.
78. Pg 174: The famous chalk badges of Fovant. Note the Australian Rising Sun insignia on the right. AWM P05845.046.
79. Pg 175: A typical 1914-1918 hut. Note the Australian humour... 'Ye olde coal hole' and 'Down pan'. Photograph courtesy of Australian War Memorial.
80. Pg 185: No. 3 Codford midday meal being brought in from the cook house. AWM P0002.006.
81. Pg 185: Australian soldiers playing Two-Up at Hurdcott. Note the chalk map of Australia on the hillside. AWM P11848.002.
82. Pg 186: 1914-1918 Fovant Military Station. Photograph courtesy of Rupert Williamson - Fovant History Interest Group, and Peter Harding.
83. Pg 186: Glasgow Central Station where Jim and his mates were arrested for being A.W.L. Photograph courtesy of Network Rail, UK.
84. Pg 187: 19 July 1919. Peace Day Celebration Parade through Admiralty Arch. Photograph courtesy of the Imperial War Museum.

85. Pg 188: William (Bill) Mitchell 3643, Fovant 1918. From personal collection.
86. Pg 189: 1919. Exeter, England. Australian troops travelling by train to Devonport. AWM H01851.
87. Pg 197: *S.S. Bremen* (left) and *S.S. Main* (right) on fire during the Hoboken Pier, New Jersey, disaster 30 June 1900. Photograph courtesy of the Hoboken Historical Museum.
88. Pg 197: Damage to *S.S. Main* from the fire disaster at Hoboken Pier, New Jersey, 30 June 1900. Photograph courtesy of the Hoboken Historical Museum.
89. Pg 198: Devonport, England, 1919. Australian troops leaving the train prior to embarking on *H.M.A.T. Takada* for their journey home. AWM H01840.
90. Pg 198 Devonport, England, 1919. Australian troops embarking on *H.M.A.T. Takada* for their journey home. AWM H01809.
91. Pg 199: Freetown, Sierra Leone. Photograph courtesy of Lisk-Carew Brothers.
92. Pg 206: April 1919. Australian soldiers relaxing onboard *S.S. Shropshire* on their way home to Australia. Donor W.J. Deane. AWM H04170.
93. Pg 206: 1919. Troops returning to Australia onboard the *S.S. Orca* playing Two-Up on deck. Donor Mr J. Lee. AWM J02913.
94. Pg 207: February 1919. Troops lined up on the deck of the *H.M.A.T Derbyshire* on Thermometer Parade, a measure to prevent the spread of the Influenza Epidemic. AWM P01425.015. Donor J.A. Bate.
95. Pg 207: Church Parade onboard Troopship *Argyllshire (A8)*. AWM H02398. Donor Mrs Mercer.
96. Pg 208: Lectures and drills on deck as seen from the main mast of *S.S. Euripides*. Photograph courtesy of the Royal Australian Navy.
97. Pg 209: Cape Town Pier, 1919. Photograph courtesy of Cape Town History.

ILLUSTRATION REFERENCE NUMBERS   −   277

98. Pg 222: Troopships at anchor in Cape Town Harbour. Photograph courtesy of Cape Town History.
99. Pg 222: *H.M.A.T. Main*, Cape Town, 22 August 1919. Photograph courtesy of unknown donor.
100. Pg 223: Durban, 1919. Informal portrait of Miss Ethel Campbell, known as the Angel of Durban. AWM P08129.002.
101. Pg 224: 1919. Miss Ethel Campbell, known as the 'Angel of Durban' distributes newspapers to Australian troops at Durban Port. AWM P08129.005.
102. Pg 224: 1919. The Criterion Cinema seen in the picture was on the corner of Field Street (now Joe Slovo Street) and the Embankment. It was built as a music hall designed by architect Stucke and Harrison, and opened on 20 May 1912. Illustration courtesy of 432 Postcards. (Monissa.com).
103. Pg 225: April, 1919. Members of the 1st Wireless Signal Squadron catching their first glimpse of Australia on the return trip home. AWM P00562.158.
104. Pg 234: 21 July 1916. Heavy seas experienced aboard the *H.M.A.T Bulla* during her crossing of the Indian Ocean. Photograph taken by Private Arthur Harris, courtesy of Virtual War Memorial.
105. Pg 234: September 1919. Crowds greet *H.M.A.T. Main* docked in Fremantle. Photograph LH004708 courtesy of Fremantle City Library History Centre and State Library of Western Australia.
106. Pg 235: October 1919. Australian soldiers view Australia at last from the deck of the *Barambah*. AWM H16799.
107. Pg 235: Onboard a 'family ship' similar to the *H.M.A.T. Main*, the *H.M.A.T Borda* was bound for Australia in December 1919. More than 10,000 Australian soldiers had married in Britain, and many returned accompanied by wives and young children although facilities onboard were considered lacking. AWM D00935.
108. Pg 237: Sydney women awaiting the return of loved ones from the war. AWM H11576.

109. Pg 249: 28 September 1919. Returning soldiers welcomed outside the Town Hall, Fremantle. Photograph LH002058 courtesy of the Fremantle City Library History Centre.
110. Pg 249: 15 October 1919. *H.M.A.T. Main* flying the Armistice Flag, Sydney, Australia. Note the gangway dropped alongside for the routine boarding of officials. Photograph courtesy of unknown donor.
111. Pg 250: October 1919. Cheer-Up Hut welcome for the returning Diggers, Adelaide, Australia. From personal collection.
112. Pg 250: Soldiers at a Sydney train station, possibly Liverpool. AWM H03422.
113. Pg 251: A returning soldier is greeted by his mother. AWM H11575.
114. Pg 261: Produce Markets, Roma Street, Brisbane. Photograph courtesy of Queensland Places.
115. Pg 261: Staibs' farm with what is believed to be the Rainey's hilltop 12 acre farm on the hill in the background. The Rainey's boundary bordered the Chermside Army Camp until eventually becoming part of the Prince Charles Hospital grounds. Raineys Hilltop Park Estate was established in 1925 when the farm was subdivided. The family residence then fronted the newly gazetted Hilltop Avenue. Photograph courtesy of the Chermside & Districts Historical Society.
116. Pg 263: 9th Reinforcements 41st Jim Rainey is seated in the front row on the far left; Harry Larsen is seated in the front row on the far right; Bill Mitchell is 6th from the left in the 3rd row; Ted Marsh is on the far right of the 2nd back row, and Ernest Murr is 9th from the left in the 3rd back row. Photograph courtesy of the Queenslander Pictorial and the State Library of Queensland.
117. Pg 299: James (Jim) Henry Rainey in 'civvies'. Circa 1919. Photograph courtesy of Chermside Historical Society.

ACKNOWLEDGEMENTS

I acknowledge and thank the Turrbul people of the Barrabim Clan (Chermside) and Bundjalung Nation people (Lismore), traditional Custodians of lands portrayed in this book, and pay my respects to their Elders past and present.

I extend that respect to Aboriginal and Torres Strait Islander peoples and their ancestors who gallantly enlisted in World War 1.

I particularly wish to thank;

My husband, Brian, and son, Rob, for their belief in me and sharing my ever-growing enthusiasm.

My Uncle, James Henry Rainey Jnr, who is not only the living image of his father and ex-serviceman (R.A.A.F.) but has shared a keen interest in this evolving expedition into his father's history.

All my three brothers, Cliff, Paul and Russell (ex-serviceman of the Australian Army), who have my utmost love and admiration.

The only other Rainey granddaughter in Jim's family, Michelle Bevan (nee Rainey), who was destined to share this journey with me as my editor.

Our nephew, Bryan James (ex-serviceman of the R.A.N.), for sending me the photos of Jim's rifle practice scorebook.

To Raymond Pepper for sending me our grandfather's photo taken at Fovant.

The extended families of J. H. Rainey Snr, E. Bray, S. Johnson and F. Spry (nee Rainey). I also extend this same gratitude and deepest appreciation to the families of H. Larsen, E. A. Murr, E. Marsh, W.G.A. Mitchell, C. G. Arthur, E. Barnett, T. Edwards, E. Walker, W. Clayton and S. van Rensburgh; I have endeavoured to honour their memories as if each were a member of my own family.

Patrick Lindsay, author and mentor, for his masterful support and recommendations - you *are* inspiration.

John Mapps for his valuable editorial support and guidance.

Stewart Alger of the Fremantle City Library History Centre for his genuine interest and the quality of the Fremantle photographs he provided for this book.

The Chermside District Historical Society for their support and providing me with Jim Rainey's Fovant and 'civvies' photos, the latter being one I had never seen.

The Australian War Memorial, National Archives Australia, Virtual War Memorial, The Australian Army History Unit - Canberra, Dept. of Veteran Affairs, Anzac Portal, Australian Archives – Canberra, Discovering Anzacs, Following the 22nd, Australian Light Horse Association, National Library of Australia, State Library of New South Wales, State Library of Victoria, State Library of Western Australia,

Australian Aboriginal Culture, The A.I.F. Project - Australian Defence Force Academy (A.D.F.A.), Vintage Camera Lab, History Daily, Western Front Association, Forces War Records, Australian National Maritime Museum, Royal Australian Navy History, Guildford Anzacs, Anzac Day Commemoration Committee, the Frank Blake diaries, the Verdi Schwinghammer diary, Burstall's Narrative, Geoffrey Rose Memoirs, Arthur John Moore diary and M.C. Evans diary, the Queensland Times, Trove, The Shepparton News, Australian University-School of Literature Languages and Linguistics, Veterans South Australia, Digger History, Fovant History, Wiltshire at War, J Walking In, Aussie Towns, Long Long Trail, National Archives UK, Africa Centre, BlackPast, South Africa History, Cape Town History, InfoBretagne, Map-France, Google Maps, World War 1 Cemeteries, Freemantle Stuff, Freemantle Ports, Liquid History, Port Adelaide Historical Society, Zoos South Australia, Queensland Places, Swarthmore College Peace Collection, Queensland Places, Roma Street Parkland Precinct E-brochure, The Queenslander Newspaper 1914-1918, The Camera House (Bundaberg), Bonhams, Amazon Media Collection, SSMaritime, Wartime Memories Project, World News, Hoboken Historical Museum Online Collection, Anzac Biographies, Military Wikia, Arts and Culture, War Relics Forum, Library - University of Queensland, Ships Nostalgia and Skyscraper City.

GLOSSARY

A.I.F. – Australian Imperial Force

A.L.H. – Australian Light Horse

A.N.Z.A.C. – Australian and New Zealand Army Corps

A.C.S. – Australian Corps School

A.S.C. – Army Service Corps

Batman – A soldier who is an officer's personal servant.

Battery – An artillery battery consisted of four 9-pounder guns and two 24-pounder Howitzers with 25-30 personnel per gun.

Big Bertha – 16.5 inch Howitzer of the German heavy artillery.

Bosche - Germans

Buckshee - free; no charge

Cadre – groups of men assigned to specific duties.

Cenotaph – Memorial to fallen servicemen and women.

Civvies – Civilian clothes.

C.O. – Commanding Officer

Cookers – Cooks and their equipment.

Crack shot – An accurate shooter, sharpshooter, marksman, sniper.

Dazzle camouflage – An array of coloured patterns painted on a vessel to distort the enemy's calculation of its speed and distance. Also known as 'razzle dazzle'.

D.N.T.O. – Divisional Naval Transport Officer

Detail – A specific number of shots required for a section of a shooting event.

D.I.G.A. – Battalion Head Quarters on the Front Line.

Entrain – Boarding a train.

Group – points of impact on paper targets resulting from a series of shots, indicating their pattern.

Housewife – Soldiers sewing kit consisting of two needles, grey yarn, cotton and linen threads for emergency mending.

Key-holed – the pattern caused by two shots cutting into each other on a paper target

Limber – Horse-drawn artillery used before motorised methods were introduced.

Marching In – Arriving at the post for being Taken On Strength.

Marching Out – Departing from the post after being Taken Off Strength.

Marching Out State – An inspection provided to Headquarters verifying troops in position and ready to march.

Mopping Up – Clearing out the trenches to remove or neutralise all enemy engagement.

O.C. – Officer in Charge

Other Ranks – Soldiers, N.C.O.s and W.O.s, including recruits, privates, lance corporals, corporals, sergeants, staff sergeants, warrant officers Class 2.

Possible – A perfect shooting score of 100%.

Prone – A shooting technique performed in the lying position.

Push – Forward engagement with the enemy to advance and gain territory.

Provos - Australian Army Provost Corps (Military Police)

Reos – Reinforcements.

Sapper – A soldier in the tunnelling regiment.

Scamperer – A runner relaying messages either during an engagement or between departments.

Semaphore – Communication signals by lights or flags. The earlier technique displayed pivoting arms on a post.

Sitrep – Situation Report provided of the current situation.

Taken On Strength – Received into Unit.

Taken Off Strength – Released from Unit.

The Brass – A.I.F. hierarchy. The term relates to the brass depicting higher rank and status.

Vanguard – leading unit in formation.

REFERENCES

Aboriginal Culture
Ndjuling People, Lismore: https://lismore.nsw.gov.au/our-first-peoples
Turrbul Tribe of the Barrambil Clan, Chermside: http://www.chermsidedistrict.org.au/01_cms/details.asp?ID=38
Indigenous Diggers: https://www.u3abrisbane.org.au/documents/ws/Serving_Country-Aboriginal_and_Torres_Strait_Islander_diggers_2017.pdf
Eddie Walker (3754B): https://www.slq.qld.gov.au/blog/edward-walker-3754b
Wilfred Clayton((2008): https://www.slq.qld.gov.au/blog/wilfred-clayton-2008

41st Battalion
41st Infantry Battalion Association Inc: http://www.41bnassoc.com.au/Unit-History.php
41st Battalion inspected by King George V: https://www.awm.gov.au/collection/C387667
Australian Archives, Canberra: https://recordsearch.naa.gov.au/SearchNRetrieve/Interface/SearchScreens/BasicSearch.asp
Bells Paddock, Enoggera; Chermside Army Camp: https://artsandculture.google.com/exhibit/first-world-war/uQIymEcVLn4hJA
Charles Henry Merlehan: http://www.reinforcements.com.au/wp-content/uploads/CHARLES-HENRY-MERLEHAN.pdf
Lieutenant John Grant SMITH: https://s3-ap-southeast-2.amazonaws.com/awm-media/collection/RCDIG1068563/document/5507948.PDF
The AIF Project 41st Battalion 9th Reinforcements: https://aif.adfa.edu.au/showUnit?unitCode=INF41REIN9

Anzac Archives
Anzac Archive website, Lest We Forget: http://anzac.emmaus.qld.edu.au/

Anzac Portal
Website: https://anzacportal.dva.gov.au/

1st Detachment on 1 November, 1914: https://anzacportal.dva.gov.au/resources/media/image/naa-810791

Amiens-Hindenburg Line: https://anzacportal.dva.gov.au/resources/media/file/1918-amiens-hindenburg-line

Equipment: https://encyclopedia.1914-1918-online.net/article/soldiers_equipment

International Encyclopaedia of the First World War, 1914-1918 (Sea and Transport Supply) Online website: https://encyclopedia.1914-1918-online.net/article/sea_transport_and_supply

Repatriation: https://anzacportal.dva.gov.au/wars-and-missions/ww1/politics/repatriation

Roles of Australian Women in World War 1: https://anzacportal.dva.gov.au/wars-and-missions/ww1/personnel/australian-women

Royal Australian Navy:
https://anzacportal.dva.gov.au/wars-and-missions/ww1/military-organisation/royal-australian-navy#5
https://www.navy.gov.au/history/feature-histories/1st-royal-australian-naval-bridging-train

Australian Light Horse

Australian Light Horse Association: http://www.lighthorse.org.au/mounted-troops/

Australian War Memorial

3rd Division War Diaries: https://www.awm.gov.au/collection/C1347326?image=3

Archives – Listing of Official Records Series: https://www.awm.gov.au/collection/accessing-records-at-the-memorial/findingaids/chronological-guide/ors

Australian Army History Unit: https://www.awm.gov.au/collection/U51481

Australian War Graves Detachment: https://s3-ap-southeast-2.amazonaws.com/awm-media/collection/AWM2018.8.765/bundled/AWM2018.8.765.pdf

Official Records Series: https://www.awm.gov.au/collection/accessing-records-at-the-memorial/findingaids/chronological-guide/ors

Official War Records (Chronological Order): https://www.awm.gov.au/collection/accessing-records-at-the-memorial/findingaids/chronological-guide/ww1

Recruitment and Casualties: https://s3-ap-southeast-2.amazonaws.com/awm-media/collection/RCDIG1069563/document/5519060.PDF

Suez (Disembarkation of IRL Ormonde & Embarkation of HMAT T15 Ellenga): https://s3-ap-southeast-2.amazonaws.com/awm-media/collection/RCDIG1015826/bundled/RCDIG1015826.pdf

Australian Imperial Force Official War Diaries

41st Battalion: https://www.awm.gov.au/collection/C1338975
September 1918 Part 1: https://s3-ap-southeast-2.amazonaws.com/awm-media/collection/RCDIG1004546/bundled/RCDIG1004546.pdf
September 1918 Part 2: https://s3-ap-southeast-2.amazonaws.com/awm-media/collection/RCDIG1004547/bundled/RCDIG1004547.pdf
October 1918: https://s3-ap-southeast-2.amazonaws.com/awm-media/collection/RCDIG1004548/bundled/RCDIG1004548.pdf
November 1918: https://s3-ap-southeast-2.amazonaws.com/awm-media/collection/RCDIG1004549/bundled/RCDIG1004549.pdf
December 1918: https://s3-ap-southeast-2.amazonaws.com/awm-media/collection/RCDIG1017643/bundled/RCDIG1017643.pdf
January 1919: https://s3-ap-southeast-2.amazonaws.com/awm-media/collection/RCDIG1004550/bundled/RCDIG1004550.pdf
February 1919: https://s3-ap-southeast-2.amazonaws.com/awm-media/collection/RCDIG1017881/bundled/RCDIG1017881.pdf
March 1919: https://s3-ap-southeast-2.amazonaws.com/awm-media/collection/RCDIG1004937/bundled/RCDIG1004937.pdf
April 1919: https://s3-ap-southeast-2.amazonaws.com/awm-media/collection/RCDIG1004939/bundled/RCDIG1004939.pdf
May 1919: https://s3-ap-southeast-2.amazonaws.com/awm-media/collection/RCDIG1005041/bundled/RCDIG1005041.pdf

Australian Corps Schools

Australian Corps School tactical training: https://www.iwm.org.uk/collections/item/object/1060022669
List of School Unit diaries - AWM4 Subclass 32/2: https://www.awm.gov.au/collection/C1339458
List of Students: https://www.awm.gov.au/advanced-search/people?people_preferred_name=&people_service_number=&people_unit=School&roll=First+World+War+Nominal+Roll&ppp=100&page=1
January 1919: https://www.awm.gov.au/collection/C1341800
February 1919: https://www.awm.gov.au/collection/C1341801
March 1919: https://www.awm.gov.au/collection/C1341802
April/May 1919: https://www.awm.gov.au/collection/C1355637
Trove: https://trove.nla.gov.au/newspaper/article/15775356
Trove: https://nla.gov.au/nla.obj-7505083/view?sectionId=nla.obj-76403045&partId=nla.obj-7508636#page/n12/mode/1up
Jeumont, Australian Technical Corps School:
October-December 1918: https://www.awm.gov.au/collection/C1350033

December 1918-June 1919: https://s3-ap-southeast-2.amazonaws.com/awm-media/collection/RCDIG1011456/bundled/RCDIG1011456.pdf

Charles E.W. Bean:
The Official War History of the 41st Battalion 1914-1918 (1st edition, 1942) written by C.E.W. Bean: https://www.awm.gov.au/collection/C1417018
Hindenburg Line: https://s3-ap-southeast-2.amazonaws.com/awm-media/collection/RCDIG1069560/document/5519057.PDF
The Hindenburg Outpost: https://s3-ap-southeast-2.amazonaws.com/awm-media/collection/RCDIG1069561/document/5519058.PDF
The Old Force Passes: https://s3-ap-southeast-2.amazonaws.com/awm-media/collection/RCDIG1069562/document/5519059.PDF
The War Ends: https://s3-ap-southeast-2.amazonaws.com/awm-media/collection/RCDIG1069561/document/5519058.PDF
Mont St Quentin: https://s3-ap-southeast-2.amazonaws.com/awm-media/collection/RCDIG1069558/document/5519055.PDF

Embarkation - May 1919
Draft 98 23/5/1919: https://s3-ap-southeast-2.amazonaws.com/awm-media/collection/RCDIG1016859/bundled/RCDIG1016859.pdf
Embarkation ex Le Havre: https://s3-ap-southeast-2.amazonaws.com/awm-media/collection/RCDIG1003398/bundled/RCDIG1003398.pdf

Repatriation & Demobilisation A.I.F.
October 1918 – February 1920: https://www.awm.gov.au/collection/C1339454
Base & Depots (Item 33/11/1) No. 3 Australian Base Reception Camp February-June 1919: https://s3-ap-southeast-2.amazonaws.com/awm-media/collection/RCDIG1011658/bundled/RCDIG1011658.pdf
Bases and Depots (No. 5 Group) June 1919: https://s3-ap-southeast-2.amazonaws.com/awm-media/collection/RCDIG1011173/bundled/RCDIG1011173.pdf

June 1919:
Repatriation & Demobilisation AIF Part 1 : https://www.awm.gov.au/collection/C1341965
Repatriation & Demobilisation AIF Part 2: https://www.awm.gov.au/collection/C1341966
Repatriation & Demobilisation AIF Part 3: https://www.awm.gov.au/collection/C1341967
Repatriation & Demobilisation AIF Part 4: https://www.awm.gov.au/collection/C1341968
Repatriation & Demobilisation AIF Part 5: https://www.awm.gov.au/collection/C1341969

Repatriation & Demobilisation AIF Part 6: https://www.awm.gov.au/collection/C1355657

Repatriation & Demobilisation AIF Part 7: https://www.awm.gov.au/collection/C1341970

Repatriation & Demobilisation AIF Part 8: https://www.awm.gov.au/collection/C1341971

Repatriation & Demobilisation AIF Part 9: https://www.awm.gov.au/collection/C1341972

Repatriation & Demobilisation AIF Part 10:https://www.awm.gov.au/collection/C1355656

July 1919

Repatriation & Demobilisation AIF Parts 2, 3 & 4: https://s3-ap-southeast-2.amazonaws.com/awm-media/collection/RCDIG1003378/bundled/RCDIG1003378.pdf

A.I.F. Repatriation & Demobilisation 1918-1919: https://www.awm.gov.au/collection/C1339454

Repatriation & Demobilisation AIF Part 9m July 1919: https://s3-ap-southeast-2.amazonaws.com/awm-media/collection/RCDIG1002999/bundled/RCDIG1002999.pdf

Repatriation & Demobilisation AIF Part 8 July 1919: https://s3-ap-southeast-2.amazonaws.com/awm-media/collection/RCDIG1002998/bundled/RCDIG1002998.pdf

Repatriation & Demobilisation AIF Part 7 July 1919: https://s3-ap-southeast-2.amazonaws.com/awm-media/collection/RCDIG1002997/bundled/RCDIG1002997.pdf

Department of Repatriation & Demobilisation AIF Part 6 July 1919: https://s3-ap-southeast-2.amazonaws.com/awm-media/collection/RCDIG1002996/bundled/RCDIG1002996.pdf

Repatriation & Demobilisation AIF Part 5 July 1919: https://s3-ap-southeast-2.amazonaws.com/awm-media/collection/RCDIG1002995/bundled/RCDIG1002995.pdf

Repatriation & Demobilisation AIF Part 4 July 1919: https://s3-ap-southeast-2.amazonaws.com/awm-media/collection/RCDIG1002994/bundled/RCDIG1002994.pdf

Repatriation & Demobilisation AIF Part 3 July 1919: https://s3-ap-southeast-2.amazonaws.com/awm-media/collection/RCDIG1002993/bundled/RCDIG1002993.pdf

Repatriation & Demobilisation AIF Part 2 July 1919: https://s3-ap-southeast-2.amazonaws.com/awm-media/collection/RCDIG1002992/bundled/RCDIG1002992.pdf

Repatriation & Demobilisation AIF Part 1 July 1919: https://s3-ap-southeast-2.amazonaws.com/awm-media/collection/RCDIG1002985/bundled/RCDIG1002985.pdf

Cities and Localities
Adelaide:
Adelaide Zoo: https://www.zoossa.com.au/about-us/history/
History of Adelaide: http://www.liquidhistory.com.au/Flu.html
Port Adelaide Historical Society: https://portadelaide.org/semaphore/

Brisbane
Central Station: https://www.skyscrapercity.com/threads/brisbanes-central-station-%E2%80%93-past-and-present.1640906/

Roma Street
Roma Street: https://www.thomblake.com.au/downloads/HistoryEBrochure.pdf
Roma Street Markets: https://queenslandplaces.com.au/sites/queensland-places.com.au/files/exhibits/books/PS429.jpg
Roma Street Parkland Precinct E-brochure (History of Roma Street): https://www.thomblake.com.au/downloads/HistoryEBrochure.pdf

Cairo
Currency: https://en.wikipedia.org/wiki/Egyptian_pound
Mena Camp: https://veteranssa.sa.gov.au/story/great-war-training-camps-in-egypt/ and
http://www.diggerhistory.info/pages-conflicts-periods/ww1/mena-camp.htm
and
https://anzac-22nd-battalion.com/training-camps-egypt/

Cape Town
Advertisement Listing Newspaper: https://s3-ap-southeast-2.amazonaws.com/awm-media/collection/PUBS002/002/005/002/003/bundled/PUBS002_002_005_002_003.pdf
Cape Town History: http://Cape Townhistory.com/?page_id=152
Cape Town Municipal Theatre: https://s3-ap-southeast-2.amazonaws.com/awm-media/collection/PUBS002/002/005/002/003/bundled/PUBS002_002_005_002_003.pdf
Cape Town Photos: https://www.flickr.com/photos/hilton-t/7414134990/in/photostream/
Cape Town SAR&H Magazine: https://railways.haarhoff.co.za/issue/213/page/0
History of Cape Town
https://www.sahistory.org.za/article/cape-town-segregated-city
History of Cape Town Harbour: https://i.pinimg.com/originals/2b/1f/6e/2b1f6ed100321b3d8bbebd3ede3b448b.jpg
History of Rhodes Memorial
https://www.sahistory.org.za/place/rhodes-memorial-vredehoek-table-mountain

Soldiers on leave in Durban and Cape Town: https://www.nationalarchives.gov.uk/education/resources/letters-first-world-war-1916-18/troop-ship-the-ship-was-actually-lousy/

Chermside

Chermside and District Historical Society website: http://www.chermsidedistrict.org.au/default.asp

Chermside District Historical Society: http://www.chermsidedistrict.org.au/default.asp

Chermside State School Cadets and Junior Red Cross: http://www.chermsidedistrict.org.au/01_cms/details.asp?ID=295

Rainey's residence: http://www.chermsidedistrict.org.au/01_cms/details.asp?ID=38

Durban

Durban Postcards: https://432postcards.monissa.com/criterion-theatre-esplanade-durban-south-africa/

Ethel Campbell (The Angel of Durban): https://discoveringanzacs.naa.gov.au/browse/groupstories/5029

History of Durban: https://www.sahistory.org.za/article/durban-timeline-1497-1990

'Khaki and Blue...We Welcome You' Brochure: https://ibccdigitalarchive.lincoln.ac.uk/omeka/files/original/1246/16384/MNealeETH1395951-150731-048.1.pdf

Mitchell Park Zoo: https://www.sahistory.org.za/archive/interview-swami-gounden-vino-reddy-29-may-2002

Scarrows of Cumberland – History of Port Natal (Durban) http://www.cumberlandscarrow.com/portnatal.htm

Fovant

Fovant Military Railway: http://www.fovanthistory.org/railway.html

Wiltshire at War: http://www.wiltshireatwar.org.uk/story/we-were-here-remember-us-the-story-of-fovant-camp/

Chalk Badges: https://jwalkingin.com/2019/10/09/fovant-badges/

Freetown

Freetown, Sierra Leone (West Africa): https://www.blackpast.org/global-african-history/places-global-african-history/freetown-sierra-leone-1792/

Freetown Port: https://eprints.soas.ac.uk/26223/1/10731720.pdf

West Africa and WW1: https://media.nationalarchives.gov.uk/index.php/west-africa-first-world-war/

West Africa and Spanish Flu: https://africacenter.org/spotlight/lessons-1918-1919-spanish-flu-africa/

Fremantle

Fremantle Stuff – The Great War: https://fremantlestuff.info/fhs/fs/9/Morrison.html

Gage Roads (Fremantle Harbour): https://www.fremantleports.com.au/docs/default-source/shipping-docs/port-information-guide-2018.pdf

Fremantle Harbour (Gage Roads): https://www.fremantleports.com.au/docs/default-source/shipping-docs/port-information-guide-2018.pdf

Glasgow

Dumbarton: https://www.west-dunbarton.gov.uk/libraries/archives-family-history/archive-photograph-of-the-month/archive-photos-2005/townend-road-dumbarton-1964/

Dumbarton Railway Station: https://www.west-dunbarton.gov.uk/media/4317451/19-05-09_volume1-finalcmp.pdf

Visit Scotland: https://www.visitscotland.com/blog/attractions/iconic-scottish-bridges/

Gresford, N.S.W.

Gresford: https://www.aussietowns.com.au/town/gresford-nsw

Le Havre:

1914-1918 Map of Le Havre/Rouelles/Mont Villiers region: https://www.long-longtrail.co.uk/wp-content/uploads/2018/03/Lehavre-1914camps2.jpg

Messines

Messine Ridge explosion: https://vwma.org.au/explore/campaigns/7

Queensland

History of Queensland: https://espace.library.uq.edu.au/data/UQ_216975/AU4021_Foxs_History_Queensland_2d.pdf?Expires=1623417680&Key-Pair-Id=APKAJKNBJ4MJBJNC6NLQ&Signature=avNBZGWLK7dpbJyTKnheKF-yGeSNf0sLbsHadCS4WKz6sZmde0O3-nmpOoSQr5vsbmc9KQHUu37~WCbWWJ6HpY~BCgWiRge7w8Sz~ujQsHw2aG3km64nfLaUDKpNDeOQ6SEa1hcHU8Mbi7m1rkbt2-wPd5ccsljil8vidOgOxOXYjS7RCOxFWe-KcUNCyaqtpvfo-~lkxZeLL~X3~~CKpHKgJM0G2wDB3yBW2kbXumUsJnqxyfnPYsuQAxGit4BEayfPXGx8708v7jS3vgMKxH18HybDyNRTjmSJvLEmISehOTSVax1rZq26li-txHUbnkGLT89A1CQr-icWV3bKQA__

St Maxent

Chateau and Churches history: http://www.infobretagne.com/maxent.htm

Sutton Veny

No. 2 Group A.I.F. Sutton Veny: https://s3-ap-southeast-2.amazonaws.com/awm-media/collection/RCDIG1010428/bundled/RCDIG1010428.pdf

The Somme

Templeux le Guerard: https://www.map-france.com/Templeux-le-Guerard-80240/photos-Templeux-le-Guerard.html

Surrounding areas of Templeux le Guerard: https://www.google.com/maps/place/80240+Templeux-le-Gu%C3%A9rard/@49.9591793,3.1460748,3a,75y,77.01h,90t/data=!3m7!1e1!3m5!1sdXie_I2o4sldJH1_J24pNQ!2e0!6shttps:%2F%2Fstreetviewpixels-pa.googleapis.com%2Fv1%2Fthumb-nail%3Fpanoid%3DdXie_I2o4sldJH1_J24pNQ%26cb_client%3Dsearch.gws-prod.gps%26w%3D211%26h%3D120%26yaw%3D77.01062%26pitch%3D0%26thumbfov%3D100!7i13312!8i6656!4m5!3m4!1s0x47e81d429eb382e7:0x40af13e8161f640!8m2!3d49.9622699!4d3.147457?hl=en

Templeux le Guerard: https://www.ww1cemeteries.com/templeux-le-guerard-communal-cemetery-extension.html

Templeux le Guerard to Gamaches (map): https://www.google.com/maps/@49.8846175,2.3427906,10.2z

Colour Patches:

Army Museum of Tasmania: http://armymuseumtasmania.org.au/wp-content/uploads/2015/10/No-26-AIF-Unit-Colour-Patches.pdf

Western Front Association: https://www.westernfrontassociation.com/world-war-i-articles/colour-patches-in-the-australian-forces/

Desertion

Executed - Albert Edward Parker: https://www.ww1cemeteries.com/warlus-communal-cemetery.html

Diaries:

1914-1919 Diary Transcripts: https://transcripts.sl.nsw.gov.au/section/world-war-1-diaries

Burstall's Demobilisation Report: https://transcripts.sl.nsw.gov.au/page/burstals-narrative-demobilisation-events-1919-john-acheson-burstal-page-1

Transcripted diaries: http://transcripts.sl.nsw.gov.au/

Transcriptions: https://transcripts.sl.nsw.gov.au/user

Frank Blake 1917-1919: https://transcripts.sl.nsw.gov.au/page/blake-diary-1917-1919-frank-blake-page-28

Geoffrey Rose May–August, 1918: https://transcripts.sl.nsw.gov.au/page/item-02-geoffrey-rose-memoir-based-war-diaries-and-letters-28-may-1918-18-august-1918-page-359

John Acheson Burstal Codford Diary: https://transcripts.sl.nsw.gov.au/page/burstals-narrative-demobilisation-events-1919-john-acheson-burstal-page-1

Verdi George Schwinghammer (5/42nd Battalion) diary 6 May, 1916 – 26 September 1919. State Library of New South Wales - Mitchell Library: http://acms.sl.nsw.gov.au/_transcript/2012/D16592/a5657.htm

Discovering Anzacs

Discovering Anzacs website: https://discoveringanzacs.naa.gov.au/

Following the 22nd

Following the 22nd website: https://anzac-22nd-battalion.com/
Hospitals: https://anzac-22nd-battalion.com/hospitals-france/

Glossary

Glossary: https://www.awm.gov.au/learn/glossary
Govt Dept of Veterans Affairs
Anzac Portal website: https://anzacportal.dva.gov.au/
Anzac Portal: Amiens-Hindenburg Line: https://anzacportal.dva.gov.au/resources/media/file/1918-amiens-hindenburg-line

Gutenberg:

Files and archives: https://www.gutenberg.org/files/50066/50066-8.txt
The Project Gutenberg eBook of War Services of the 62nd West Riding Divisional Artillery, by A.T. Anderson.

This eBook is for the use of anyone anywhere at no cost and with almost no restrictions whatsoever. You may copy it, give it away or re-use it under the terms of the Project Gutenberg License included with this eBook or online at www.gutenberg.org/license

Title: War Services of the 62nd West Riding Divisional Artillery
Author: A.T. Anderson
Release Date: September 27, 2015 [eBook #50066]

Military Classifications for Draftees

Swarthmore College Peace Collection: https://www.swarthmore.edu/library/peace/conscientiousobjection/MilitaryClassifications

State Library of Victoria:

http://digital.slv.vic.gov.au/view/action/nmets.do?DOCCHOICE=97660.xml&dvs=1613038073097~161&locale=en_GB&search_terms=&adjacency=&VIEWER_URL=/view/action/nmets.do?&DELIVERY_RULE_ID=4&divType=&usePid1=true&usePid2=true
and
https://www.slv.vic.gov.au/search-discover/explore-collections-theme/war/world-war-one/world-war-one-unit-histories

Miscellaneous

Abbreviations and Acronyms: https://www.allacronyms.com/
Bearing and Picket (B&P): https://www.warrelics.eu/forum/docs-paper-items-photos-propaganda/artillery-bearing-picket-hill-112-memorial-110757/
Cyclone – Innisfail: https://hardenup.org/be-aware/weather-events/events/1910-1919/cyclone-march-1918-1918-03-10.aspx

Drills: https://www.abileneisd.org/abilene-high/wp-content/uploads/sites/23/2019/05/01-Army-Drill-and-Ceremonies-Chap-9-End.pdf
Education: https://www.awm.gov.au/visit/exhibitions/1918/victory/returnhome
Kit Bag: https://www.somme100film.com/wp-content/uploads/2016/09/Fact-File-A-WW1-Kit-Bag.pdf
Meal dixies: https://www.iwm.org.uk/history/the-food-that-fuelled-the-front
Weather: https://www.meteoblue.com/en/weather/historyclimate/climatemodelled/great-australian-bight-marine-national-park_australia_8155998
and
https://www.timeanddate.com/weather/@8155998/historic?month=3&year=2020
Slang and Peculiar Terms used in the A.I.F.: https://slll.cass.anu.edu.au/centres/andc/annotated-glossary/a
Vintage Camera Lab - Kodak Eastman No. 3A Folding Camera: https://vintage-cameralab.com/kodak-no3a-autographic/

Museums
Museums Victoria Collections: https://collections.museumsvictoria.com.au/items/731772

National Archives
National Archives of Australia: https://recordsearch.naa.gov.au/SearchNRetrieve/Interface/SearchScreens/BasicSearch.asp

Navy
Royal Australian Navy: https://www.navy.gov.au/history/feature-histories/1914-1918-wwi
Royal Australian Navy: https://www.navy.gov.au/history/feature-histories/australian-sea-transport-1914
Australian Naval Museum: https://issuu.com/anmmuseum/docs/sea_transport_of_the_aif
Anzac Day Commemoration Committee: https://anzacday.org.au/australian-ww1-hospitals
Guildford Anzacs: https://www.guildfordanzacs.org.au/
Map of Australia: The Soldiers https://map-of-australia.com/the-soldiers/

Newspaper Articles
Anzac Day, 1919: https://trove.nla.gov.au/newspaper/article/239595027
Atherton Cyclone: https://trove.nla.gov.au/newspaper/article/27471900?browse=ndp%3Abrowse%2Ftitle%2FW%2Ftitle%2F30%2F1918%2F03%2F13%2Fpage%2F2808472%2Farticle%2F27471900
Australian Corps School: https://trove.nla.gov.au/newspaper/article/15775356

The Anzac Bulletin 23 May 1919: https://nla.gov.au/nla.obj-60982664/view?sectionId=nla.obj-68667319&partId=nla.obj-60984308#page/n11/mode/1up
The Queensland Times: https://www.qt.com.au/news/ships-carry-aussie-troops-battlefields-wwi/2423165/
The Shepparton News - Tales from the Trenches: https://sheppartonrsl.com/wp-content/uploads/2020/03/Rememberance-Day-SN-Feature-WEB.pdf
The Queenslander Newspaper 1914-1918:

Peace Day

19 July 1919 Western Front Association: https://www.westernfrontassociation.com/world-war-i-articles/19th-july-1919-peace-day-in-britain/
Forces War Records: https://www.forces-war-records.co.uk/blog/2013/07/19/on-this-day-19th-july-1919-peace-day-when-the-boys-came-home
Exploring London: https://exploring-london.com/2014/11/17/a-moment-in-londons-history-peace-day-parade-1919/

Photographs

https://www.awm.gov.au/advanced-search?collection=true&facet_type=Photograph&facet_related_conflict_sort=8%3AFirst%20World%20War%2C%201914-1918&ppp=100
Anzac Spirits of South Australia: https://saanzacspirits.weebly.com/1918---1919.html
Chemnitz: https://anzac-22nd-battalion.com/ss-chemnitz/#jp-carousel-9809
https://anzac-22nd-battalion.com/ss-chemnitz/
Collection including Cape Town and on deck life: https://collections.slsa.sa.gov.au/resource/PRG+1717/5/1-93
Edith Cavell: https://nla.gov.au/nla.obj-60982664/view?sectionId=nla.obj-68667319&partId=nla.obj-60984308#page/n11/mode/1up
https://www.iwm.org.uk/history/who-was-edith-cavell
Rough seas photograph taken by Private Arthur Harris: http://rslvwm.s3.amazon-aws.com/I/images/4933/photo/zoom_HarrisAP_27B_08.jpg
No. 4 Squadron – Australian Flying Corps
https://www.awm.gov.au/collection/U51019
Origins of World War 1 – 42nd Battalion by Ted Harris
http://www.oocities.org/thefortysecondinww2/level1/line1/origins.htm

Pte J.H. Rainey

State Library of Queensland:
http://onesearch.slq.qld.gov.au/primo-explore/fulldisplay?docid=slq_digitool1150089&context=L&vid=SLQ&lang=en_US&search_scope=SLQ&adaptor=Local%20Search%20Engine&tab=slq&query=any,contains,%3D702692-19171208-s0026-0063

REFERENCES - 295

http://onesearch.slq.qld.gov.au/primo-explore/fulldisplay?docid=slq_digitool1150089&context=L&vid=SLQ&lang=en_US&search_scope=SLQ_PCI_EBSCO&adaptor=Local%20Search%20Engine&tab=all&query=any,contains,J.E.%20Rainey%201917&offset=0
Associated reinforcements displayed on this same page of the Queenslander Pictorial: https://digital.slq.qld.gov.au/delivery/action/collectionViewer.do?collectionId=271290244&operation=viewCollection&displayType=thumbnails&pageNum=30

Return Trip Home ex Devonport:
A Tale of Two Quotas: https://nla.gov.au/nla.obj-6854669/view?partId=nla.obj-32105027#page/n6/mode/1up

Shipwrecks
Port Said to Le Havre (May, 1918): https://en.wikipedia.org/wiki/List_of_shipwrecks_in_May_1918
SS Waratah off Capetown (July, 1909): https://historydaily.org/the-nautical-mystery-of-the-ss-waratah
Telegrams Australia: https://telegramsaustralia.com/Forms/Regulations/Telegram%20rates.html#Rate_1902
Travel Speed in Nautical Miles: http://ports.com/sea-route/port-of-aden,yemen/suez-port-el-suweis,egypt/

The Long, Long Trail
The Long, Long Trail website: https://www.longlongtrail.co.uk/battlefields/gazetteer-of-the-western-front/gazetteer-western-front-hargicourt/

Transports (Vehicles)
Military vehicle records: https://www.awm.gov.au/articles/encyclopedia/military-vehicle-records
Model T Fords - Museum of Applied Arts & Services: https://maas.museum/inside-the-collection/2015/07/30/henry-fords-model-t-impact-in-australia/
Motor lorries: https://s3-ap-southeast-2.amazonaws.com/awm-media/collection/RCDIG1014743/bundled/RCDIG1014743.pdf
Crossley 20/25: https://www.bonhams.com/auctions/22201/lot/1231/

The Troopship Main:
S.S. Main Listings: https://trove.nla.gov.au/search/category/newspapers?keyword=Troopship%20Main
Still in South Africa: https://trove.nla.gov.au/newspaper/article/58004616
Letter to the Editor: https://trove.nla.gov.au/newspaper/article/81347857

Married Men on *Main* (Mon 29 September 1919): https://trove.nla.gov.au/newspaper/article/81346847

Suicide on the *Main* (Mon 29 September 1919): https://trove.nla.gov.au/newspaper/article/81346745

Troopship *Main* Arrives, Freemantle: https://trove.nla.gov.au/newspaper/article/58008491

Disembarkation at Sydney (Tues 14 October 1919): https://trove.nla.gov.au/newspaper/article/15852227

Arrival of Troopship *Main* – Port Adelaide News (10 October 1919): https://trove.nla.gov.au/newspaper/article/213607245?searchTerm=Troopship%20Main

The Hoodoo Transport; Main's eventful voyage – The Sun, Sydney (19 October 1919): https://trove.nla.gov.au/newspaper/article/222290543?searchTerm=Troopship%20Main

Chapter of Incidents - Warwick Daily News (Wed 29 October 1919): https://trove.nla.gov.au/newspaper/article/175745982?afterLoad=showCorrections

Troopships Main/Bahia Castillo (Western Argus, Kalgoorlie) https://trove.nla.gov.au/newspaper/article/34212812/4202551

Troopship *Bahia Castillo* – Transfer by Overland Train (The Register, Adelaide): https://trove.nla.gov.au/newspaper/article/62394788/4555099

Souvenir of HMT Main and Quota 48: https://nla.gov.au/nla.obj-6873386/view?partId=nla.obj-6878216#page/n0/mode/1up

Troopship *HMT Main* - Pte Walter Banville (9/9Battalion): https://www.anzacbiographies.com/2018/10/28/banvill-23549-leading-aircraftman-norman-robert/

The *Main* fire disaster 1900: https://timesmachine.nytimes.com/timesmachine/1900/07/03/102603419.pdf

SS Main: http://www.theshipslist.com/ships/descriptions/ShipsM.shtml

The *Main* (World News 30 June, 1900): https://www.marpubs.com/30th-june-1900-major-fire-at-hoboken-piers/

Hoboken Historical Museum Online Collection: https://hoboken.pastperfectonline.com/archive/752096E1-571E-4854-B302-516644201882

Troopships:

Convoy System World War 1: https://oshs.roaneschools.com/apps/video/watch.jsp?v=164277

HMAT SS Ellenga: https://wartimememoriesproject.com/greatwar/ships/view.php?pid=2802

HMS St George: https://www.naval-history.net/OWShips-WW1-05-HMS_St_George.htm

Nominal Roll of Troopships and official records, First World War: https://www.awm.gov.au/sites/default/files/files/ww1-troopships.pdf

RMS Ormonde: http://ssmaritime.com/RMS-*Ormonde*.htm
Sea Transport of the AIF: https://issuu.com/anmmuseum/docs/sea_transport_of_the_aif
Troopships of World War 1: https://www.awm.gov.au/research/guide/ww1-troopships
Vessels: German U-Boats, Naval Trawlers etc
SMU-32: https://military.wikia.org/wiki/SM_U-32_(Germany)
May, 1918: https://en.wikipedia.org/wiki/May_1918
British Navy: https://www.harwichanddovercourt.co.uk/warships/minesweepers-2/

Victorian War Memorial
Sappers and Tunnelling: https://vwma.org.au/explore/units/217

ABOUT THE AUTHOR

RUTH JAMES IS A T.E.S.O.L. English teacher with an inherent passion for writing and history.

Inspired by her grandfather's letters and war memorabilia from World War 1, Ruth brings James (Jim) Henry Rainey's war story to life in the illustrated non-fiction book, *Returned With a Creed*, the first in her proposed *Legacy's Gate* series.

The heart-warming sequel, *Coming Home From France*, crosses three generations and is the genuine story of the humble, prickly veteran's legacy. *Coming Home From France* is due for release in 2023.

Eternally enchanted by the people and highlands of Papua New Guinea, Ruth is compelled by the ruggedness of the Kokoda Track and teaches English in the isolated schools dotted along its remote corridor. Her compassion for these endearing people and teachers brings her back to these unforgiving regions repeatedly, engaging with the resourcefulness of life in the Papuan highlands and its bloody history.

Ruth is originally from Redcliffe, Queensland, where she grew up in the 1960s to '80s before settling in Bundaberg where her family roots began in the late 1800s.

James (Jim) Henry Rainey in 'civvies'. Circa 1919. Photograph courtesy of Chermside Historical Society.

www.ingramcontent.com/pod-product-compliance
Lightning Source LLC
Chambersburg PA
CBHW051534010526
44107CB00064B/2728